Developing Software
to
Government Standards

William H. Roetzheim

Prentice Hall, Englewood Cliffs, New Jersey 07632

Library of Congress Cataloging-in-Publication Data

ROETZHEIM, WILLIAM H. (date)
   Developing software to government standards / William H.
Roetzheim.
     p.   cm.
   Includes bibliographical references and index.
   ISBN 0-13-829755-X
   1. Computer software—Development. 2. Computer software-
-Standards—United States. I. Title.
QA76.76.D47R641991
005.1—dc20
                            90-7494
                                CIP

Cover design: *Wanda Lubelska Design*
Manufacturing buyer: *Kelly Behr*

© 1991 by Prentice-Hall, Inc.
A Division of Simon & Schuster
Englewood Cliffs, New Jersey 07632

The publisher offers discounts on this book when ordered
in bulk quantities. For more information, write:

    Special Sales/College Marketing
    Prentice-Hall, Inc.
    College Technical and Reference Division
    Englewood Cliffs, New Jersey 07632

Teamplan, Magnum, HyperText Standards On-line, HTSO, and Integrity are trademarks of William
H. Roetzheim & Associates. Microsoft Windows is a trademark of Microsoft Corporation.

LIMITS OF LIABILITY AND DISCLAIMER OF WARRANTY:

Printed in the United States of America

10 9 8 7 6 5 4 3

For information about our audio products, write us at:
Newbridge Book Clubs, 3000 Cindel Drive, Delran, NJ 08370

ISBN   0-13-829755-X

PRENTICE-HALL INTERNATIONAL (UK) LIMITED, *London*
PRENTICE-HALL OF AUSTRALIA PTY. LIMITED, *Sydney*
PRENTICE-HALL CANADA INC., *Toronto*
PRENTICE-HALL HISPANOAMERICANA, S.A., *Mexico*
PRENTICE-HALL OF INDIA PRIVATE LIMITED, *New Delhi*
PRENTICE-HALL OF JAPAN, INC., *Tokyo*
SIMON & SCHUSTER ASIA PTE. LTD., *Singapore*
EDITORA PRENTICE-HALL DO BRASIL, LTDA., *Rio de Janeiro*

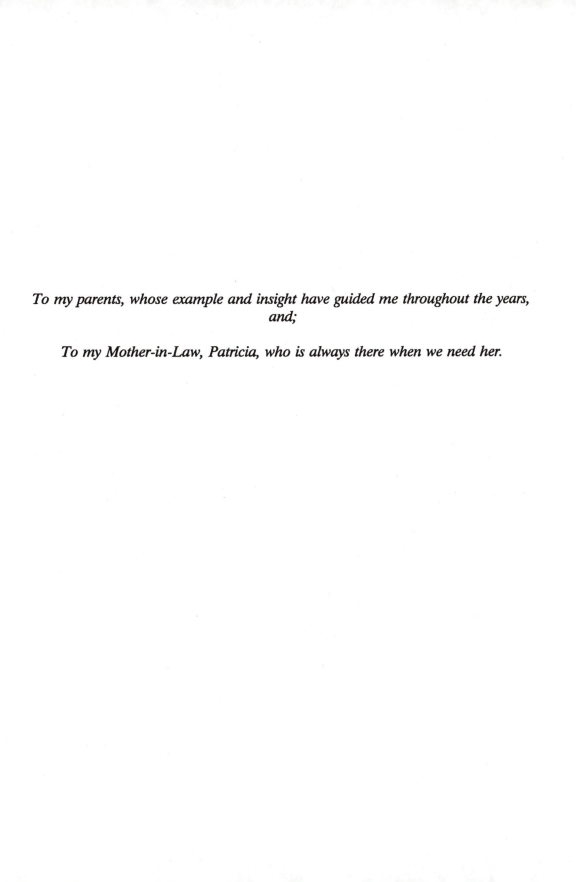

To my parents, whose example and insight have guided me throughout the years, and;

To my Mother-in-Law, Patricia, who is always there when we need her.

Contents

Preface

This text provides both an easy to understand introduction to Government standards and a valuable reference to be used during actual work on Government contracts. The text covers *all* software related standards and instructions that are required for Government work, including DOD-STD-2167A, DOD-STD-2168, MIL-STD-490A, and 38 others. Far from being a dry, formal treatment of the topic, the author emphasizes practical, cost saving hints which apply to large projects in general and Government work in particular. The author's extensive first-hand experience in this software development environment comes through in the numerous anecdotes, checklists, and behind-the-scenes insights common throughout the book. Whether you are currently working on Government projects, you want to add this valuable knowledge to your resume for future work, or you are simply interested in how extremely large projects are managed, this book is for you.

Acknowledgement

The author would like to thank the Computer Support Corporation for permission to use Arts and Letters^{tm}, which was used to create most figures and illustrations in this book.

1 You'll Love This Book

I was recently responsible for preparing a presentation describing the impact of various government standards on a software development project. After wading through several dozen standards, instructions, handbooks, etc., I suddenly had a brainstorm. Turning to my office mate, I exclaimed "Hey Mary! I just had a great idea for a book!" Pausing with her work, she gave me her undivided attention. "I'll write a book about all of these standards. I could call it *Developing Software to Government Standards.*" I looked at her expectantly. The clock on the wall ticked for what seemed like an eternity. "That," she finally said, "sounds like the most boring idea I have ever heard."

In spite of what Mary predicted, I *promise* I'll do my best to keep you from being bored. We are about to embark on an adventure, a journey through a maze of standards and guidelines. Enroute, you will learn a lot about how software engineering is done when informal methods just will not work. Rather than simply restating the standards, we will spend time understanding the logic behind the requirements. We will learn how to differentiate between rigid requirements and flexible guidelines. In the end, I believe that you will agree with me that developing software to government standards is not only possible, but can be done in a cost effective manner. Perhaps just as important, I believe that you will learn how to develop software to government standards and still have fun.

This book is designed to introduce you to the important government standards applicable to software development; familiarize you with the terminology and basic content of these standards; provide some guidance on applying these standards; and serve as a reference during your use of the standards. This is *not* a book on software development in general, and I will make no attempt to describe general principles of software engineering.

This chapter serves as an introduction to the topic. In Sec. 1.1, we describe the crisis oriented environment that gave birth to software engineering standards. Section 1.2 then demonstrates how these standards can give you a competitive advantage in the government software engineering arena. In Sec. 1.3 we provide some insight into what the government hopes to gain by imposing software engineering standards. In Secs. 1.4 through 1.7 we summarize the intended audience of this book and provide some guidance about potential ways to maximize the benefits gained from reading this book. Finally, Sec. 1.8 introduces the remainder of the text.

1.1 We Have a Crisis

At every major software conference I have attended in the past year, the phrase "software crisis" has come up at least once. What is meant by "software crisis"? Simply put, the software engineering community cannot develop software fast enough to meet the demand. Barry Boehm describes two problems that are a direct result of this inability to meet software demand. (1)

1. The software deficit acts as a brake on our ability to achieve productivity gains in other aspects of our economy which would be improved if new software was available.

2. The intense demand for software engineers results in a situation where *just about anybody can get a job to work off this software backlog, whether they are capable or not.* The end result is a crisis not just of software quantity, but of software quality as well.

Perhaps the people hit the hardest by the software crisis are the managers. Managers have been burned so many times in the past that they automatically assume the software will be late and over budget . . . they just don't know by how much. What do *you* do when your job depends on the software being delivered when you promise it, and

• programmer productivity can vary by a factor of 30?

- program quality in terms of bugs per thousand lines of code can vary by a factor of 100?

- a high percentage (some say as much as half) of all software development projects never produce anything useful at all?

- you ask the software developers when a late module will be delivered and are told that *they don't know*?

- software engineering is still considered an "art" by the majority of software engineers?

I'll tell you exactly what you do; you write standards. To give you an idea of how desperate managers are to achieve predictability in software development, there are currently over 1000 software related standards, guidelines, and codes of good practice in use by government and industry. The U.S. government uses something like 50 standards and related documents just to control the software engineering process. It is these 50 software engineering documents which form the basis of this book.

1.2 There Is a Light at the End Of The Tunnel

I've started the book by painting a pretty bleak picture. Not only do we have to worry about delivering low quality software that is late and over budget, but now we are going to be deluged with an avalanche of paperwork designed to "help" us!

Well, there *is* a light at the end of the tunnel. Let's start by talking about one of *my* favorite topics, making money. The U.S. Defense Department's mission critical computer software costs alone were $11.4 billion in 1985 and are projected to be $36 billion in 1995. (4) Adding in government work not related to the Defense Department may easily double these numbers. Complex standards provide the perfect competitive advantage to smart companies. Here is what these standards do for you:

- they offer a barrier to entry which scares off many competitors.

•   they allow, perhaps even encourage, a wide variety of expensive blunders and misconceptions. Most companies working in this area are forced to dramatically inflate their bids to compensate for these misconceptions. There is no justification for the often quoted belief that developing software to government standards *must* drastically inflate (some say double) the cost of the software. This is only true if the standards are applied in a manner which is not cost conscious. Using both common sense and automated tools, I believe that it is possible to develop software to government standards at a cost little higher than developing equivalent systems to accepted commercial practices. Although there will certainly be up-front costs associated with transitioning to the new standards, the long-term benefits in terms of improved quality and economic predictability make these up-front costs acceptable. Companies using the principles in this book to make the government software-engineering process cost effective will be able to underbid virtually all of their competitors.

Working *with* the software standards, as opposed to *against* them, you will also find that

1.   projects are completed in a predictable amount of time and for a predictable amount of money.

2.   projects are completed to the customer's satisfaction.

3.   software produced is maintainable and of high quality.

We will also see that intelligent application of standards combined with an automated development environment may actually allow your software engineers to do more engineering and *less* paperwork than they are currently producing.

We will come back to each of these areas in later parts of this text, but first let's talk some more about the purpose of standards.

1.3 Who Needs Standards, Anyway?

Are government standards appropriate for small, stand-alone programs developed by one or two programmers? Normally not. Are government standards appropriate for throw-away programs which will be used once or twice then discarded? Normally not. What characteristics of government software development projects result in a requirement for software engineering to rigid standards? The Defense System Management College (DMSC) identified some of the more important factors as follows: (3)

- the programs are typically quite large, often involving hundreds or thousands of software engineers,

- the applications are often highly specialized and technically complex,

- many contractors are typically involved,

- many related (interdependent) hardware and software systems are often under concurrent development,

- system requirements are often at [*and unfortunately, sometimes beyond – Author*] the state-of-the-art.

I would add the following factors to this list

- The consequences of software failure are often more severe in the government world than the consequences of software failure in the commercial world.

- When comparing commercial program managers to government program managers, the government managers are often:

    - less experienced in the principles of software engineering, leading to a desire for guidance in the form of standards

- • not as closely involved in the detailed technical decisions during software development, forcing requirements to be expressed in a more formal fashion using standards

- • more risk averse (often because of bad experiences in the past), leading to explicitly stated and quite detailed requirements.

- • Unlike many commercial organizations, government program managers typically rely on a large number (perhaps as many as 100) contractors and subcontractors to perform much of the actual development work. Standards are necessary to allow the government reviewers to quickly focus on the technical details of a document without wasting time learning a new format for each contractor.

In addition, government experience has shown that forcing contractors to perform software engineering to rigid standards has decreased the overall life cycle costs associated with computer software.

Standards accomplish their goals primarily by controlling variety. In this way, they hope to

1. conserve money, manpower, time, and other resources through reuse of existing documentation and knowledge

2. enhance the interchangeability, reliability, and maintainability of the system, including the software

3. improve the overall product quality across a wide variety of programs.

1.4 Intended Audience of this Book

As shown in Fig. 1.1, the intended audience for this book is quite diverse.

Contractors interested in working as the prime contractor or a subcontractor on government software development projects will find that this

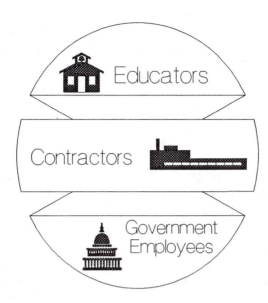

Figure 1.1 Intended audience.

book answers all the questions. Companies already working in this area will find the book especially valuable as a source of ideas for cutting costs and improving quality. The book can also be provided to new software engineers as a low cost, convenient method of bridging the gap between the commercial/academic software development environment and the government software development arena.

Government employees will find the book a convenient guide for balancing their software standard related requirements with the desires of the contractors to produce software in a convenient, cost effective manner. Contractors can be encouraged to use specific sections of the book as guidance in performing software engineering.

Educators teaching graduate software engineering courses, especially those with a focus on large projects and/or government work, will find this book an appropriate textbook. If the students have an inadequate background in general principles of software engineering, this book can be supplemented with relevant journal articles. Individuals or departments responsible for professional development and training within corporations will also find this book valuable when teaching professional software engineers how to work using government standards.

It is my hope that this book will serve as a catalyst to allow all of the individuals currently or potentially involved in developing software for the government to work with a common set of guidelines and understandings.

1.5 Special Note to Contractors

I've worked as the Senior Project Manager on literally dozens of government software development projects. Over and over I watched talented, bright young software engineers transfer into my projects . . . and screw things up. I knew then, and I know now, that it simply isn't their fault. Very few software engineers learn *anything* in school or on commercial jobs about the many unique aspects of software development when working to government standards. Maybe I should have had some of my top people (who did understand the standards) train the new people, but there was simply never enough time. These new engineers have always had to learn things the hard way, but not anymore. For a truly nominal cost per employee you can provide each of your software engineers with a copy of this book. There is absolutely no lower cost method of training your employees, and the moral boost from the free "gift" is a substantial side benefit. Contact Prentice-Hall directly for corporate discounts available for large volume purchases.

After you read this text, I would also encourage you to read Appendix B carefully. This appendix describes a software program which is tailored to government projects, and incorporates important "groupware" concepts. Site licenses for the programs *Teamplan* and *HyperText Standards On-Line* are also available.

1.6 Special Note to Government Employees

This book provides specific guidance for many aspects of software development to government standards. On many projects, you may wish to reference specific sections of this book for management, tailoring, and evaluation guidance. I am encouraging Prentice-Hall to be liberal in granting government agencies permission to extract portions of this book, with appropriate credit, for use in Requests for Proposals (RFPs).

1.7 Special Note to Educators

As previously mentioned, I believe that this book would be appropriate for a graduate software engineering class stressing large projects in general and government work in particular. The students should have a basic software engineering background, including structured design methods, prior to the class. I believe that a graduate class covering this topic is quite appropriate given the fact that the majority of graduating software engineers will work on government contracts at some point in their career. I also believe that the class would be very well-received by local companies if the class was offered late in the day or in the evening, thus allowing employees to attend the class after work.

Assuming a 15 week semester, a schedule similar to the following would be appropriate:

Weeks 1-2:	Introductory material based on Chaps. 1, 2, and 4 of this book combined with general software engineering principles review, as necessary.
Weeks 3-4:	Federal procurement model, cost estimating on government projects, and managing government projects, based on Chaps. 3, 5, and 6.
Week 5:	Introduction to the software program *Government Standards Toolbox (GST)*. GST is described in Appendix B. Students should have the opportunity to have hands-on time with GST, and should use GST for examples during the remainder of the semester.

Week 6:	Overview of standards, review of MIL-STD-490, and other standards covered in Chap. 12, based on Chaps. 8 and 12.
Weeks 7-11:	In depth look at DOD-STD-2167A and associated data item deliverables (DIDs), based on chap. 9 and Chaps. 13 to 30.
Weeks 12-14:	Overview of the government review and quality assurance processes, based on Chaps. 10 and 11 and 31 to 37.
Week 15:	Special topics, based on Chap. 7.

If you adopt this book for a class and would be willing to share any of your instructional material (curriculum, homework assignments, laboratory assignments, tests, viewgraphs, etc.,) please contact me via Prentice-Hall. If you are considering adopting this book for a class, you may wish to contact me to determine what instructional materials are available to help you. There are also special educational arrangements available to help incorporate the computer program *Teamplan* into your classroom instruction.

1.8 Where Do We Start?

We will begin in Chap. 2 with an overview of the government software development process, including descriptions of the players in the game, the system life cycle, and government system hierarchies. We also show how you fit into this big picture. Chapter 3 discusses the federal procurement model and presents suggestions on writing better proposals. This chapter is especially useful if you will be involved in assisting with the preparation of technical proposals. If you are not currently working on government projects, or you would like to improve your software engineering productivity, you will be interested in Chap. 4. This chapter presents some hints for establishing an effective foundation for working on large projects in general, and government projects in particular.

Chapter 5 presents some methods of estimating (and reducing) costs for government software development work. Chapter 6 discusses the management of government software projects, primarily from the perspective of a contractor as opposed to the program sponsor. Chapter 7 covers special topics such as configuration management, software quality assurance, and technical performance measurement.

Chapters 8 through 12 introduce the key government standards, including:

- MIL-STD-490, Specification Practices

- DOD-STD-2167, Defense System Software Development

- DOD-STD-2168, Software Quality Evaluation

- MIL-STD-1521, Technical Reviews and Audits for Systems, Equipments, and Computer Software

Chapters 13 through 30 discuss each of the Data Item Descriptions (DIDs) used on government software development project. Chapters 31 through 37 discuss each of the reviews and audits conducted during government software development. These chapters should be treated as a reference, to be read when it is time to prepare the actual DID or prepare for a review.

Appendix A describes a computer program called *HyperText Standards On-Line* which is an on-line reference containing the full text of 41 key government software development standards and a complete set of text search and retrieval tools.

Appendix B describes a computer program called *Teamplan* which supports the entire software engineering process and is tailored to government standards.

Appendix C describes a software design approach, called Hierarchy plus Input-Process-Output Two (HIPO-II), which is especially well suited to government software development.

Finally, Appendix D contains a complete list of acronyms, Appendix E is a glossary of terms, and Appendix F is a list of references.

2 Understanding the Big Picture

After reading this chapter you will have a better understanding of the various participants in government projects, including their role in the system engineering process and their objectives. You will be familiar with the components of government system hierarchies. You will be comfortable with the government system life cycle, and will recognize where configuration management baselines fit into this life cycle. Finally, you will look at the entire system engineering process from the perspective of the software engineer, showing where software development fits into the big picture.

2.1 Gaining Perspective

The key document used when trying to understand government software development is called *Defense System Software Development*. As with most government standards and handbooks, this document is more often referred to by its designator, DOD-STD-2167A. The DOD stands for Department of Defense. STD stands for standard. 2167 is the number of this particular standard and the trailing "A" tells us that this is the second formal edition of the document. The previous edition was called DOD-STD-2167 and the next edition will be called DOD-STD-2167B.

We will also discuss MIL-STDs, or military standards. Military standards differ from DOD standards only in the fact that DOD standards are approved for use under the metric system. In addition to standards, we will talk about directives (e.g., DODD 4005.1), instructions (e.g., DODI 4120.20), and handbooks (e.g., DOD-HDBK-248).

Government software development standards in general, and DOD-STD-2167A in particular, are only required for *military* software which is *mission critical*. You might be tempted at this point to heave a sigh of relief and toss this book aside, saying: "Hey, no problem. I just won't work on those mission critical military projects!" Don't be too hasty. In general, you will find that:

- All projects for the military, not just mission critical projects, normally require that you use some form of DOD-STD-2167A. The few exceptions are typically small projects in the research and development area, and even those are slowly jumping on the DOD-STD-2167A bandwagon.

- Nonmilitary government software for which reliability is a significant concern is typically either done to DOD-STD-2167A or to an agency's tailored version of this standard. Examples of government agencies falling into this category include the Federal Aviation Administration (FAA) and the National Aeronautics and Space Administration (NASA).

- Most large defense contractors require the use of DOD-STD-2167A for *all* software development, including software developed using internal research and development (IR&D) funds. Subcontractors to these companies are also frequently required to perform all work to DOD-STD-2167A.

- A significant number of other federal agencies, foreign governments, and state governments have generated software development standards which closely parallel the requirements found in DOD-STD-2167A.

The U.S. Department of Defense is significantly further along in developing and implementing a set of rigid requirements for consistent, effective software engineering than any other organization or group. The natural tendency is to use this operational set of standards as a guideline for any new standards that are developed. The bottom line is, well over half of all software engineers will be required to develop software to DOD-STD-2167A at some point in their careers. It is my belief that this trend will accelerate and we will soon see a set of software development standards, similar to those found in DOD-STD-2167A and related documents, used for *all* large software development projects.

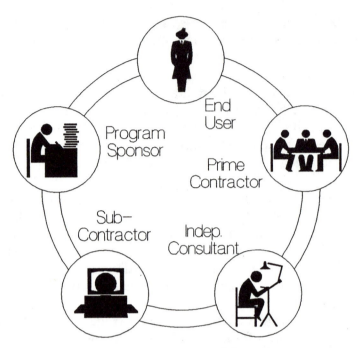

Figure 2.1 Key participants.

2.2 The Roles of the Players

It's helpful to have at least an overview perspective of who the key participants are on government software projects, and the roles each of those participants is expected to play during the system engineering process. As shown in Fig. 2.1 the key participants are:

1.   end users

2.   program sponsor(s)

3.   prime contractor(s)

4.   subcontractor(s)

5.   independent consultant(s).

Each of these five groups will be discussed individually in the following sub-sections.

2.2.1 End Users

End users are the group that will be required to use the software after it is completed. Examples include operational forces within the military, air traffic controllers, or claim administrators for the social security system. The majority of government software is developed based on requirements initially identified by the end users. End users identify a need which can be served by a new or improved system. These needs are written down in a memo (formally called an Operational Requirement or OR within the military) which is promulgated up the chain of command. This memo then forms the basis for an in-depth quantification of requirements by the government. During development of the new or improved system, end users are kept informed of progress by the program sponsor and are often asked to participate in trade-off decisions affecting the final product's functionality or user interface.

After the system is completed, end users are normally responsible for testing it in an operational environment. This operational testing, called Operational Test and Evaluation or OT&E (within the military) covers much more than simply looking for bugs or other flaws in the completed system. Operational test and evaluation is designed to assess the impact of the completed system on the operations of the end user's organization. This assessment includes factors such as

- interoperability with other systems and procedures

- human factors analysis under realistic usage

- reliability analysis under realistic usage

- requirements for modifications to the organization's procedures and policies (or tactics in the military) based on the new system.

In general, the end user focuses on *what* the system does, not *how* it does it. For most applications, the end user will define success in terms of:

1. the functions which the system performs for the user, either automatically or on command,

2. how pleasant the system is to use. Is the data input a reasonable burden on the user? Is the system easy to use? Is the software interface tedious after prolonged use? Is the software forgiving of mistakes?

3. Can the system be trusted? This applies to both the reliability of the software and the accuracy of the results.

4. Was the system completed in a reasonable amount of time? Can modifications be incorporated in a timely fashion?

The end users look to the government standardization process to help ensure that their goals are met. It is especially important to note that most end users do not really *care* about things like detailed data flow diagrams, program pseudocode, etc., except as necessary to achieve their real objectives outlined in the above four points.

2.2.2 Program Sponsors

Although the program sponsors manage the project and project funds, they generally rely on one or more prime contractors to do most or all of the actual technical work. Even the process of reviewing the technical documents delivered under the contract is often subcontracted out. In a contractual sense, the program sponsor represents the interests of the government in dealing with the prime contractor(s). In a technical sense, the program sponsor represents the interests of the end user.

The program sponsors are typically upwardly climbing managers in the agency involved. Very few people in this position can survive even one major blunder in their career. More than anything else, program sponsors *do not want to be scared by project failure*. Program sponsor objectives are typically:

1. avoiding major failure,

2. understanding exactly what the delivered system will do when delivered,

3. meeting all deadlines for demonstrations and deliveries,

4. protecting government interests against abuse by the prime contractor,

5. making a mark.

We will briefly address each of these objectives individually.

Avoiding major failure.   Program sponsors are typically more concerned with avoiding major failure than they are with achieving spectacular success. It is often said in this group that ten thousand spectacular successes don't make up for a single major failure.

Understanding the system. Program sponsors are required to present an almost endless series of verbal briefs to their bosses and to top level individuals representing the end users. These briefs must describe the system in terms that are important to end users (see Sec. 2.2.1). The program sponsor is normally not hurt by describing a system that is a little less capable than the end users would like, and then delivering what was promised. On the other hand, it may be a major failure if the program sponsor promises a system with one set of capabilities and is not able to deliver on the promise. Interestingly, this might be a failure even if the program sponsor promised much more than the end users wanted at the beginning, then was forced to deliver a system which met the end user's original requirements but fell short of the inflated expectations.

Meeting all deadlines. Last minute slips for demonstrations, reviews, and deliveries are extremely embarrassing to the program sponsor and may adversely impact other programs under concurrent development.

Protecting government interests. Some prime contractors promise the world when writing their proposal, then try to deliver a system with greatly reduced capabilities. Program sponsors attempt to evaluate all requested changes to the requirements to ensure that the end result is a system delivered to the government that is at least as good as that described in the contractor's proposal. It is the prime contractor's responsibility to convince the program sponsor that the net effect of proposed changes will be in the best interest of the government.

Making a mark. All program sponsors would like their project to do something which differentiates them in a positive way from other program sponsors. Examples include early development of a prototype for demonstrations to end users or preliminary delivery of a component of the system which will meet an immediate need of the end user.

As with the end user, the program sponsor is normally not concerned with specific implementation details except as they affect their areas.

2.2.3 Prime Contractors

Prime contractors are responsible for the actual work of developing the system. A prime contractor is defined as any contractor working directly for the program sponsor on the project. Large projects often have up to a dozen prime contractors working on various portions of the system. In general, prime contractors can (and do) hire subcontractors to assist them in performing their work. The prime contractor is then responsible for managing the subcontractors, including ensuring that all requirements imposed on the prime contractor by the program sponsor are met by the subcontractors as well.

Many prime contractors jump into a new project without giving adequate thought to their own goals during the project. After reflecting on the previously defined objectives of the end users and the program sponsors, the goals of the prime contractor should be apparent. They are to

1.   carefully monitor the proposal effort, the system design, and the system development to ensure that the products can be delivered at a profit

2.   keep the program sponsor happy by meeting their objectives

3.   resist the temptation to inflate expectations. Try to deliver a system which exceeds modest goals rather than a system which falls short of optimistic goals.

4.   Help the program sponsor understand the system in terms important to the end user. *Do not* emphasize internal details of the system except as necessary to describe their impact on the end user.

5.   Prioritize the work to be done and ensure that the highest priority work is done first (and best) so that any last minute slips or failures will impact on the least important functions.

2.2.4 Subcontractors

Prime contractors will typically use a significant number of sub-contractors to assist with portions of their work. One of the biggest advantages of subcontracted work is that it helps to stabilize the prime contractor's work force by meeting peak labor demands during the project. Prime contractors are especially interested in using small businesses as subcontractors because

1.   these smaller companies often have specialized technical knowledge, the acquisition of which would require an expensive learning curve for the prime contractor,

2.   small businesses typically have lower overhead and labor rates.

3.   the government looks with favor on prime contractors who subcontract to small businesses.

4.   small businesses are normally not capable of directly competing against the prime contractor on future related procurements, making them a safe partner.

Small business subcontractors typically focus either on one technical area or on one aspect of system engineering. For example, a technical subcontractor may specialize in radio antennas, or perhaps a certain type of radio antenna. A system engineering subcontractor might focus on configuration management, documentation, or quality assurance. Ideally, the subcontractor should be so strong in their particular field that the program sponsor has complete confidence in the subcontracted work because of the reputation of the subcontractor.

2.2.5 Independent Consultants

Independent consultants work very much like subcontractors, except that they normally work directly for the program sponsor. They may assist with independent verification and validation, technical review of delivered products, system engineering management, or trade studies.

2.3 Government System Hierarchies

Figure 2.2 summarizes how the military decomposes systems into organized hierarchies. At the system and segment level, we are dealing with entities which are normally a combination of software and hardware. A *system* is a collection of hardware, software, material, facilities, personnel, data, and services needed to perform a designated function with specified results. A *segment* is a grouping of elements that are closely related and often physi

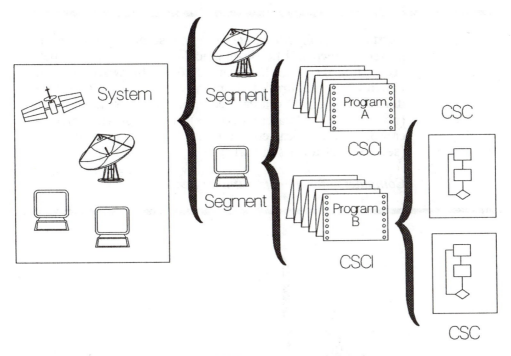

Figure 2.2 Military system hierarchy.

cally interfaced. For example, we might discuss the command and control system on-board a Navy ship. The command and control system consists of components that work together to accomplish a common mission, overlap each other or rely on each other for some data, but can be developed and tested independently. Within the command and control system, a dedicated computer and software program for command and control processing (the C^2P) might be one segment, the afloat correlation system (ACS) might be a second segment, the JTIDS/Link-16 terminal a third, and so on.

Each segment consists of some combination of hardware configuration items (HWCIs) and computer software configuration items (CSCIs). Each configuration item is normally responsible for a single top-level function and is normally developed by one prime contractor. The two types of configuration items are defined as follows:

1.   *Hardware configuration items* are system/segment components which will be developed or integrated and which are primarily of a hardware and/or firmware nature. Hardware configuration items are classified into prime items (complex, critical components), critical items (noncomplex, critical components), noncomplex items (noncomplex, noncritical components), and facilities or ships (see Fig. 2.3 for a summary).

2.   *Computer software configuration items.*

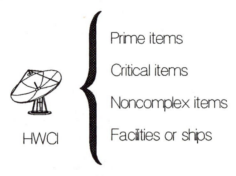

Prime items

Critical items

Noncomplex items

Facilities or ships

HWCI

Figure 2.3 Types of HWCIs.

Hardware configuration items consist of hardware components and software components. Hardware components can be further divided into subassemblies and parts.

Figure 2.4 illustrates the hierarchical decomposition of government systems. Software configuration items consist of computer software components (CSCs) and computer software units (CSUs). Computer software components consist of other computer software components and computer software units. Computer software units are discrete items and are not broken down any further in the hierarchy. As much as possible, configuration items should be selected in a fashion which will allow parallel development and testing (i.e. as few dependencies *between* configuration items as

possible). Section 2.6 gives additional guidance about decomposing software
requirements into configuration items.

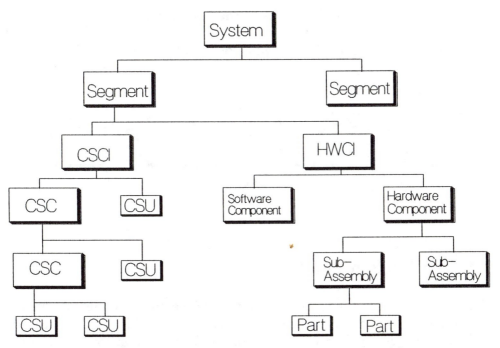

Figure 2.4 Government hierarchical decomposition.

Some of the factors used to decide how to partition software into
CSCIs are:

- functional complexity of the components

- estimated size and criticality of the components

- interface, data base, and integration complexity between
  components

- complexity of security requirements for components

- certification requirements of components

- probability of change during the development cycle

- operational criticality of the components

- development location(s) for the components

- schedule

Figure 2.5 Phases of System Procurement

2.4 The System Life Cycle

Figure 2.5 shows the four phases of system development and procurement. The cycle is started when a mission need is identified, which might be based on input from the operational military or government organization, one of the government research facilities, or occasionally, a private contractor. The mission need includes a definition of the required mission to be supported, the operational environment, constraints, and measures of effectiveness. The *concept exploration* phase is initiated with the approval of the program objective memorandum, and involves definition of system concepts for further development. Following successful completion of the concept exploration phase, the *demonstration and validation* phase is initiated, often with the assistance of private contractors. This phase includes preliminary design work, prototyping, and other activities necessary to determine if the project should proceed to full scale development. *Full scale development* involves the actual production of a product or program which can be evaluated in the field. Finally, successful completion of field level testing signals the start of *production and deployment* of the product or program.

2.5 The Importance of Baselines

DOD-STD-480A describes configuration management as consisting of activities to

- identify and document the functional and physical characteristics of a configuration item,

- control changes to those characteristics,

- record and report change processing and implementation status.

Section 7.1 of this book discusses configuration management in detail. At this point, it is only necessary to recognize that the current definition of *what* will be delivered to the government is known as the system's baseline. Most government programs will have three baselines:

1. the *functional baseline*

2. the *allocated baseline*

3. the *product baseline*

The *functional baseline* is established by the government at the Software Design Review, which normally corresponds to the end of the concept exploration phase. The functional baseline for a system consists of all system requirements, and is documented in the System/Segment Specification (Type A). This "A" specification then becomes the technical requirements portion of a request for proposal (RFP) which the government typically publishes prior to commencing design work. The various types of specifications (Type A, Type B, and Type C) are defined in Chapter 8. Prime contractors responding to the RFP estimate costs for the remainder of the project based on the requirements described in the functional baseline and on the items required by the government's statement of work (SOW). Changes to these requirements, as with all baselines, are still possible but may affect the contract cost and/or schedule. This serves to protect the interests of both the government and the prime contractor.

The *allocated baseline* is established at the Software Specification Review, which normally corresponds to the end of the demonstration and validation phase.   The allocated baseline consists of the development specifications (Type B) that define the specific performance requirements for each configuration item in the system.   If the project is large (by government standards) and a design competition approach (flyoff) is being used on the procurement, a new request for proposal (RFP) may be issued at this point for the next stage of work. This allows contractors to estimate costs for detailed design work with a clear understanding of the system level requirements (the functional baseline) and of the configuration item performance requirements (the allocated baseline). If the prime contractor will not be given an opportunity to modify cost estimates for later work based on the allocated baseline, the allocated baseline should be designed to fit within the previously bid costs. If this can not be accomplished while still meeting the requirements of the contract, you must renegotiate the contract.

The *product baseline* is established at the end of the full scale development phase. The product baseline consists of the detailed design documentation (Type C) and source code for each configuration item. If possible, the product baseline should be designed to fit within the previously bid costs.

Acceptance by the government of a baseline means:

- the government has accepted that one phase of the project is successfully completed to their satisfaction. Many contracts make partial payments to contractors based on acceptance of baseline documents (conditional acceptance).

- the baseline fully describes the developing system as it currently exists. Any changes to the baselined requirements must be approved by the government, and may impact on the cost and/or schedule for development.

The discussion thus far has included more than just the *software* engineering process. In the following section we will describe specifically how software engineering fits into the system engineering picture.

2.6   From System Engineering to Software Engineering

In this section, we will provide specific guidance describing how to relate software development to the government's system life cycle and hierarchies. The naive assumption is simply that the system life cycle model parallels the software life cycle and the software portions of the system hierarchy represent the software design in the sense of modular structure and calling relationships. We will see that the relationships are not nearly this simple. Remember, the government designed the system life-cycle model and the system hierarchy primarily to assist with management of the project, not as an abstraction mechanism for the system design.

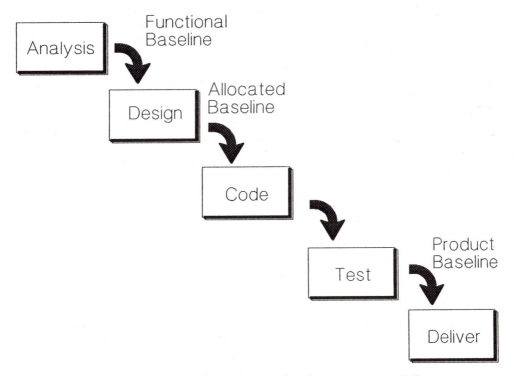

Figure 2.7 Classic software development waterfall.

Let's start by discussing the concept of baseline management as described in the previous section. It is often difficult to reconcile software development with the concept of baselines as used by the government. Figure 2.6 shows how the classic waterfall model of software development fits into the baseline management concept. Good software designs tend to be much more iterative than suggested by this model. This failing is typically overcome in one of the following ways:

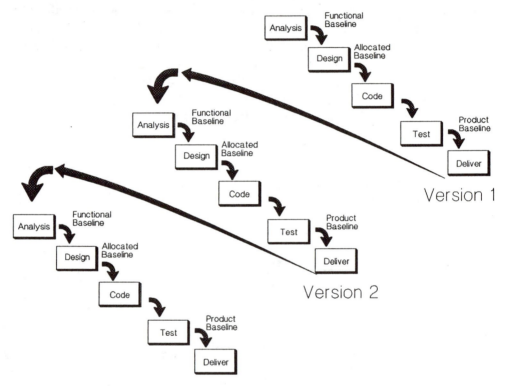

Figure 2.7 Fitting in prototyping.

- If a prototyping approach to software development is used, *each major prototype version* may have an abbreviated functional, allocated, and product baseline (see Fig. 2.7). I am using the term prototyping to refer to an iterative approach to building software, where each iteration refines the software based on user feedback. Other types of prototyping are possible. For example, a prototype may be developed just to clarify user requirements, in which case there will not be a baseline for the prototype software at all.

- If the software is technically complex, an incremental baseline is often used. This approach typically applies to the allocated and product baseline, and involves incrementally approving portions of the baseline as they become firm. For example, at the end of the demonstration and validation phase all of the Type B specifications (one per configuration item) should be completed. Incremental baseline approval allows some of these specifications to be fully approved and incorporated into the system's allocated baseline, some may be reviewed but not incorporated into the system's allocated baseline yet because of anticipated changes during detailed design, and some may include portions which are fully approved and portions which are not yet approved.

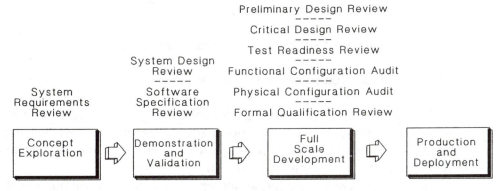

Figure 2.8 System life cycle reviews.

Figure 2.8 shows the reviews which are normally conducted during system life cycle. Chapter 11 addresses this review process in more depth.

Figure 2.9 illustrates how the various components of structured software development fit into the phases of development. Note that structured software development as defined in Roetzheim (11) consists of:

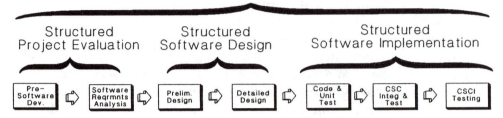

Figure 2.9 Structured software development.

- structured project evaluation

- structured project management

- structured software design

- structured software implementation

- structured software maintenance

Finally, Fig. 2.10 shows the documents that you may be tasked to produce, and the phase during which they are written and approved. During the remainder of this book we will be spending a considerable amount of time talking about the documents shown in this figure.

The government system hierarchy represents the software portion of a system as a collection of software configuration items consisting of computer software components (CSCs) and computer software units (CSUs). Computer software units are leafs in the hierarchical structure, that is, they have no elements under them. This system hierarchy is referred to as the *static structure*. At first, it might be tempting to equate computer software components and computer software units with program modules and expect that the hierarchical relationship between these items represents calling relationships. In fact, *the static structure is simply a hierarchical allocation of functional requirements to configuration items.* The static structure is a tool for management of the project, clarification of functional requirements in terms applicable to the end users (Sec. 2.2), and partitioning of respon

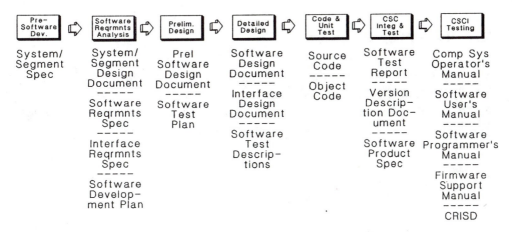

Figure 2.10 Documents produced.

sibilities. From this perspective, the static structure is better than program representations such as data flow diagrams, entity relationship diagrams, and so on, in that:

- It closely parallels the software work breakdown structure, facilitating estimating, scheduling, and tracking.

- It is well suited to the widely accepted technique of top-down functional decomposition during the analysis stage.

- It logically defines the scope and content of various documents, which typically deal with an individual configuration item.

- It allows the baseline management and configuration control to be decoupled from the detailed software design and implementation.

Chapter 4 provides more specific guidance regarding the integration of software design with government system engineering. Chapter 9 provides additional information about the specific expectations of DOD-STD-2167A, and Appendix B describes a software development environment, *Teamplan*, supporting software design under DOD-STD-2167A.

2.7 Chapter Review

We began by discovering that DOD-STD-2167A and related documents, or locally prepared documents that are very similar, are used by most government agencies and many large contractors for software development. We learned that a typical government project involves:

- End users

- Program sponsors

- Prime contractors

- Subcontractors

- Independent consultants

We learned the roles these groups play during the system engineering process, with an emphasis on their motivations.

We found that the government decomposes projects hierarchically into a static structure. This static structure consists of systems, segments, HWCIs, and CSCIs. HWCIs are broken down into subassemblies and parts. CSCIs are broken down into computer software components and computer software units.

We looked at the government system life cycle, and saw how baselines fit into this life cycle. We concluded with an overview of documents and reviews produced during the system life cycle, with an emphasis on software related documents.

2.8 Questions

1. What edition is MIL-STD-1521B?

2. Which of the following system characteristics is an end user likely to be concerned about?

a.   The menu hierarchy

b.   The data base structure and relationships

c.   Data entry screens

d.   Program modular structure

3. You are the prime contractor on a government project. During the detailed design stage of the project, you discover that making some minor changes in the programs top-level design should provide greatly improved program performance. The changes increase the risk somewhat, but the current plan would still be possible as a fall back position. What do you do?

4. What are the four phases of a government program?

5. What are the various baselines used for configuration management? Where do they fit into the four program phases (Question 4)?

Chapter 2 Answers

1.   Third edition.

2.   a and c.

3.   You should push the program sponsor to allow you to make the changes. Although the risk is increased, a valid fallback position exists. If the changes do, in fact, result in a better final product for the same amount of money/effort, your company looks better. You should emphasize to the program sponsor that the improved performance is *tentative*, and all reports and documents should describe performance based on both success with the changes and failure with the changes causing reversion to the fallback position. In many cases, the fallback position should be briefed as what will be delivered, with a footnote that better performance may be achievable.

4.   Concept exploration

Demonstration and validation

Full scale development

Production and deployment

5.   Functional baseline: after concept exploration

        Allocated baseline: after demonstration and validation

        Product baseline: after full scale development

2.9 Discussion Topics

1.   What advantages do you see to all major software projects (state and federal government, and private industry) being developed using one common set of standards?   What disadvantages do you see?

2.   If you were the program sponsor on a major project involving several hundred individuals and two dozen companies, what information would you like to see presented to you? How often? In what format? What information would you not want to see? Why not?

3.   The chapter emphasizes that the system static structure is *not* the same as the system or software design. Are the two related in any way? How? Using your favorite method of representing a program design, in what ways is the static hierarchical structure superior to your program design representation?   In what ways is your program design representation superior to the static hierarchical structure?

3 Smart Proposals

Every day, the official procurement document of the federal government, the *Commerce Business Daily* (CBD) lists over 30 computer software development procurements and well over 100 computer hardware procurements. State and local government computer related procurements double these numbers.   Finally, many of the larger federal procurements generate hundreds of spin-off subcontracting jobs for small computer companies working with the prime contractor. It should be apparent that no growing company can afford to lightly dismiss market segments this vast.   This chapter will familiarize you with the federal procurement model, showing you how to win new government contracts.   But first, let's discuss the importance of proposals.

   Writing proposals is the responsibility of the marketing department . . . right? If you agree with that statement, you may be walking a tightrope right now and not even know it. Let me tell you a story about a project team that said, "Our job starts after the project marketing is complete."

   Jim (the project manager) and his project team were extremely competent software engineers specializing in government systems. Their current project was successful and the customer was satisfied. As the project came to an end, they were not worried about the absence of a new project to start work on, because "The marketing department will take care of us." Besides, it gave them a chance to catch up on paperwork and organize program libraries.

Much of this chapter is taken from the author's book, *Proposal Writing for the Data Processing Consultant.* (9)

After a couple of months charging to overhead, they began to stop by the marketing department to find out what their next assignment would be. It became apparent that most of the marketing department was busy finalizing proposals with large financial institutes for COBOL based business programs, projects which the government team was not qualified to work on. The Marketing Director explained that commercial programming had lost a major contract and they were trying to get work for the commercial technical staff. Two junior marketing staff members had been working the government area.

Three months later, it became apparent that Jim's company was not winning any new government work. Jim finally took a recent proposal home and was shocked at the total lack of understanding about the system's requirements and the needs of the user. It was apparent that whoever wrote the proposal had no comprehension of the job that needed to be performed.

Jim realized too late that relying on others to find new projects for you to work on can be fatal. He was laid off one month later, along with most of the government programmers.

This chapter will provide you with the information *you* need to win government contracts.

3.1 The Importance of the Proposal

Webster's defines a proposal as "a plan [or] scheme ... proposed." I define a proposal as a written marketing document that:

- defines exactly what you intend to do for the customer, with particular emphasis on items that will be delivered,

- convinces the customer that what you propose to deliver will meet their needs better than what other companies can deliver,

- tells the customer how you intend to produce these deliverables, including sufficient detail to assure them that you understand the problems involved,

- leaves no doubt in the customer's mind that you are fully capable of producing the promised results,

- includes all necessary information to allow this document to stand alone in selling your project.

Although a proposal is a legal agreement (at least in government work) and a valuable project-planning document, you must never forget that a proposal is primarily a marketing tool. A proposal must sell your idea, your company, your experience, your employee's capabilities, and your costs.

One common trap many computer firms fall into after discovering the benefits of written proposals is to evaluate their proposals based on internal criteria. Its almost as if the proposal were a term paper that had to be graded. A major aerospace defense contractor once asked me to review a proposal that the company had prepared as an example of the desired format for a proposal I was writing. One illustration caption was: "A vibrant display beautifully designed for maximum convenience and versatility." The picture showed a tactical antisubmarine warfare display. I asked if they really wanted me to write in that style. "Of course. A lot of effort went into that proposal. It was very well done."

"Did it really win the contract?" I asked incredulously. Somehow I couldn't picture crusty old Navy captains falling for those flowing lines. My client replied, "Well no, but it was a good proposal."

There is no such thing as a good proposal that did not win the contract! The proposal world is made up of winners . . . and losers. The winners win contracts, the losers kid themselves into believing that "it was a good proposal." There are no Cs, and no Bs, not even any B+s. The winning proposal gets an A. The rest of the proposals get Fs.

Winning proposals not only meet the government's needs but also demonstrate a significant advantage to the government over the competitor's proposals. This advantage (or *differentiation strategy*) is woven into the proposal text as the *proposal theme*. Some common themes might be lowest risk solution, technical superiority, lower cost, or faster delivery of the final program. The development of a proposal theme is the key to winning the contract and will be stressed throughout this chapter.

3.2 The Federal Procurement Model

Imagine the difficulty of marketing to diverse market segments if every agency, every state, even every company developed and used their own procurement techniques. Competition on a national scale would grind to a standstill overnight. Luckily, a model is available which has been adopted by every major market segment: the *Federal Procurement Model* (FPM). Like the U.S. Constitution, the FPM has been able to stand the test of time because of its inherent flexibility and simplicity. The typical procedures involved in a procurement using the FPM are:

- A statement of needs, specifications, and terms is generated.

- The availability of this statement is advertised as widely as possible, soliciting competitive written responses by a certain date and time.

- After evaluation of the responses, a contract is formed based on the statement of needs and the accepted written proposal.

The Federal Procurement Model is designed around three categories of procurements: (1) *advertised* procurements; (2) *negotiated* procurements; and (3) *miscellaneous* procurements.

Advertised and negotiated procurements are further broken down into one-step, two-step, and four-step procurements. Miscellaneous procurements include requests for quote, research and development sources sought, and unsolicited proposals. The types of procurements are summarized in Fig. 3.1. Each will be discussed in depth, beginning with an overview of advertised procurements.

3.2.1 Advertised Procurements

Advertised procurements are based on the traditional "lowest bidder takes all" concept of competition. The government uses advertised procurements when the product or service can be clearly and quantitatively defined prior to contract award. For example, if the government wanted to purchase 750,000 double-sided, double density soft-sectored 5 1/4-inch floppy disks, an advertised procurement would be appropriate. The government would

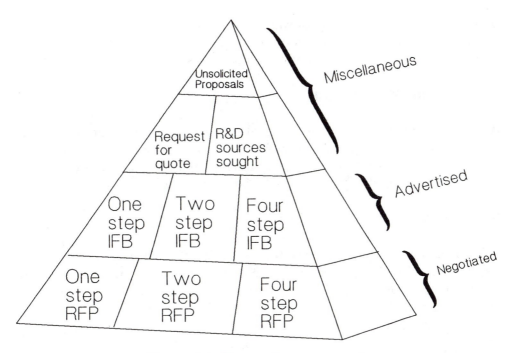

Figure 3.1 Types of procurements.

put together a detailed description of its requirements, called an *Invitation for Bid* (IFB), which would be sent to interested suppliers. These suppliers would submit a sealed bid back to the government on or before the deadline designated in the IFB. The government would qualify the bidders to ensure that they complied with the terms of the IFB; that their product did meet the specifications; and that the company appeared able to deliver the product as promised. From the list of qualified bidders, the lowest bottom-line price would be accepted, thus forming a binding contract.

3.2.2 Negotiated Procurements

Negotiated procurements allow vendors to describe *their* proposed solution to the government's needs. The government is free to evaluate each solution and the vendor's abilities to implement the solution, when selecting the winner. On negotiated procurements, price is not necessarily, or even normally, the most important factor. The statement of the government's needs is called a *Request for Proposal* (RFP) if the solicitation is a negotiated procurement. Virtually all software development and system integration work is advertised as a negotiated procurement to allow alternate solutions to a problem to be evaluated and to allow noncost factors to be considered.

3.2.3 Request for Quote

A *Request for Quote* (RFQ) is identical to a Request for Proposal used as part of a one-step procurement, with the minor exception that the government may not accept your offer without conducting negotiations, thus allowing you to modify your original offer, if desired.

3.2.4 R&D Sources Sought

Approximately every other day the government publishes research and development (R&D) projects that are of interest to computer businesses. If you are an industry leader in a particular high-technology area, you will want to watch these announcements for valuable leads to government R&D money. Publication of a project implies that funds are either available for the work or are expected to become available in the near future. Contractors with experience in the published area and with an interest in obtaining government contracts or grants are encouraged to submit their qualifications for review. The government will select the most qualified company or companies from the sources thus identified and negotiate actual research and development contracts.

3.2.5 Other Approaches

Software acquisition is particularly difficult for the government, primarily because it is difficult to evaluate the suitability of the final product on the basis of the proposal. One approach which is to split the contract into two phases, one to perform the design work and develop prototype software, and the second to develop the final system. The initial contract covers software design and development of prototypes of particularly critical software areas along with significant portions of the user interface. Two (or more) contractors are awarded the contract under this initial phase. The contract includes an option which may be exercised by the government to have the final system developed. The option is only executed for one of the contractors. This offers at least four advantages to the government.

1. The contractors are still in a competition mode during the initial stage (design), and are thus more cooperative with the government.

2. The proposed system design can be much more detailed by the time a final contractor must be selected.

3. By attending design reviews, the government evaluation team will understand the competing designs more thoroughly than is possible from just a proposal.

4. The competence of the individuals working on the project can be more effectively evaluated by observing them during the design process than by simply reading a resume bound into a proposal.

3.3 Writing Better RFPs

I've had the opportunity to work on both sides of the procurement process. As the Senior Project Manager for Honeywell, I wrote proposals responding to government RFPs and then managed the projects resulting from the awarded contracts. Working with a different company, I helped the government write RFPs and evaluate contractor proposals. During this process, I've developed the following guidelines for writing software related RFPs.

1. Contracts involving a significant amount of software development should use a multistage procurement when possible. The first stage is a contract for the software design, preferably with two different contractors. Include an option in the contract to have one of the two contractors perform the actual software development (coding, testing, and integration). The contractor you select to do the software implementation (the second stage of the contract) may be determined after you have a good grasp of the design and an appreciation for the relative abilities of the two contractors doing the design work.

2.   Require prototyping, especially of the user interface. Make the design process in general, and the prototyping process in particular, iterative throughout the contract.

3.   Focus the RFP on *what* the system must accomplish, not *how* it will be accomplished. State requirements in terms of required results and capabilities. To the greatest extent possible, describe results in operational or mission terms.

4.   Provide the software requirements in electronic form (using tools similar to those available with *Government Standards Toolbox*, so that contractors can easily integrate the government developed requirements into their automated software development tools.

5.   Software development is always extremely risky. Emphasize requirements for effective risk management in your RFP.

3.4 Improving the Evaluation Process

I believe that a quantitative approach to analyzing and evaluating contractor proposals is both possible and desirable for the majority of procurements. This quantitative analysis is based on a value-contribution model. Although the value-contribution model must be tailored to each individual procurement, the steps required to prepare the model are common for all procurements (see Fig 3.2).

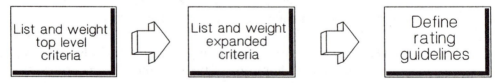

Figure 3.2 Value-contribution approach.

1.   List and weight the procurement's top-level project evaluation criteria.

2.   List and weight expanded evaluation criteria.

3.   Define utility curves or other rating guidelines at the lowest level of your evaluation hierarchy to add consistency to the evaluation process.

We begin the process of developing a value-contribution model by listing our procurement's top-level proposal evaluation criteria. For our example procurement (Fig. 3.3), we will evaluate proposals using three top-level criteria: (1) technical factors; (2) management factors; and (3) cost factors. Each of these evaluation criteria is then assigned a weight between 0 and 1 representing its relative importance on this procurement. The numbers must be assigned such that the total of all weights is exactly 1. In our example, we have assigned technical factors a weight of 0.5, risk factors a weight of 0.3, and cost factors a weight of 0.2. Note that 0.5 + 0.3 + 0.2 = 1.0.

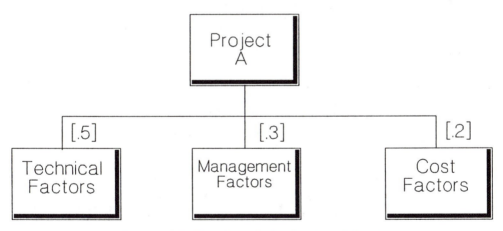

Figure 3.3 Top-Level Evaluation Criteria

The next step is to take each of these top-level evaluation factors and decompose them as necessary. Weights between 0 and 1 are then assigned to each of these detailed evaluation factors. Note that the weights for all detailed factors *under a given top-level factor* must add up to 1. This process can then be repeated until the lowest (most detailed) level of the evaluation hierarchy represents discrete evaluation factors which can be measured based on the contractor's proposals. It is important to decompose your evaluation factors such that each identified factor is independent of all others, and the set of all identified evaluation factors fully define the evaluation criteria. Figure 3.4 shows a complete value contribution weighting hierarchy for a sample procurement.[1]

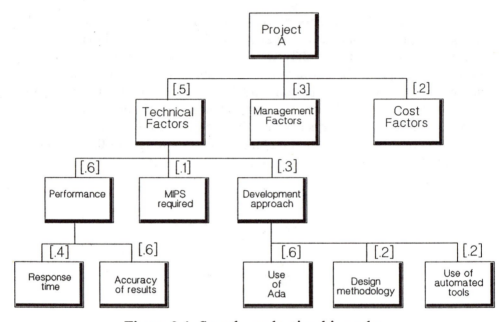

Figure 3.4 Sample evaluation hierarchy.

Our final step in developing the complete value contribution model is to provide rating guidelines for the lowest (most detailed) level of our

---

[1] Assigning the weighting factors to these evaluation criteria is often the most difficult part of the process. One method (described in Russon (13) [1985]) that is extremely effective is to use pair-wise comparisons. Data input sheets are completed that compare attributes at each level on a one-to-one basis. Data is entered into a computer, where it is analyzed, consolidated, and normalized into matrix form. Eigenvector analysis is then applied to the normalized matrix to determine the relative weightings of all components at each level.

evaluation hierarchy. These rating guidelines should assist the evaluation team in assigning to each proposal a value between 0 and 100 for each detailed evaluation factor. It is also at this point that we might define a minimum level of performance. Contractors at the minimum level of performance would receive a score of 0 but still be evaluated. Contractors below the minimum level of performance would be rejected outright. The evaluation criterion are represented as follows:

- For factors which are either present or not present, proposals with the factor present receive a score of 100 while proposals without the factor receive a score of 0. If the factor *must* be present for the proposal to be acceptable, then proposals which are acceptable receive a score of 100 while proposals which are unacceptable are rejected outright. Figure 3.5 shows a *utility curve* representing this evaluation criteria.

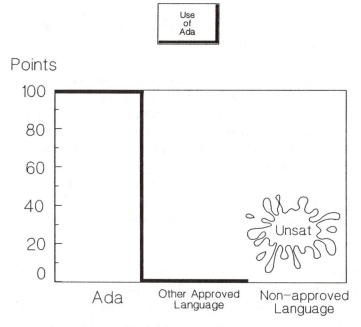

Figure 3.5 Binary utility curve.

- Some factors may involve a step function. For example, we might be contracting for software development. The system might be designed to use any one of three central processing units (CPUs). One rated at 2 Million Instructions per Second (MIPS), a more expensive one rated at 4.5 MIPS, and a very expensive one rated at 9 MIPS. Based on the proposal specified number of MIPS for the software to function properly, our evaluation criteria might be:

    - less than 2 MIPS: 100

    - 2 MIPS to 4.5 MIPS: 50

    - 4.5 MIPS to 9 MIPS: 0

    - Over 9 MIPS: Unacceptable

    Figure 3.6 shows a utility curve representing this factor's evaluation criterion.

- Many factors will receive a final score read from a continuous scale based on the proposed functionality of the contractor's system. Figure 3.7 shows some sample utility curves representing this type of evaluation factor. A contractor's score is determined by reading across the bottom to match the contractor's proposed performance, moving up to the utility curve, then reading the contractor's final score from the left axis. Utility curves such as these would be included in the proposal evaluation criteria.

Proposals are rated at the lowest level of the hierarchy. For each evaluation factor, a value between 0 and 100 is assigned (using the utility curves). The best possible project would receive a score of 100 for each factor, the worst possible (acceptable) project would receive a score of 0 for each factor. The previously assigned weights for each criterion are then used to determine the project's score for each higher level evaluation factor. This process is continued until the weights assigned to each top-level evaluation factor is used to determine the proposal's overall score. Using

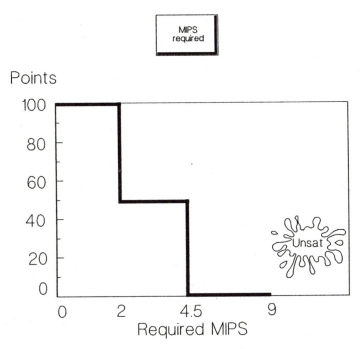

Figure 3.6 Step function utility curve.

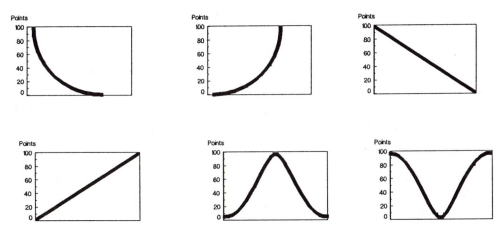

Figure 3.7 Sample utility curves.

this technique, each contractor will receive an overall rating of between 0 and 100, showing the overall acceptability of its proposal.

3.5 Writing Better Technical Proposals

The remainder of this chapter views the procurement process from the perspective of a contractor attempting to win the procurement. We focus on the proposal itself, discussing each of the three volumes:

1. technical

2. management

3. cost

On most proposals, these three volumes will be integrated and bound together. For example, Chap. 1 might be a proposal overview, Chaps. 2 to 4 your technical proposal, Chaps. 5 to 7 your management proposal, and Chap. 8 your cost proposal. On larger proposals, these might each be submitted as a separately bound volume. This section focuses on your technical proposal. For a given procurement, you will find the exact proposal format described in Section L of the Request for Proposal (RFP). You *must* follow this format exactly for your proposal to be acceptable. The following sections cover the management and cost proposals.

Your technical proposal must show the government that you understand the problem, that you have a solution to the problem, and that your solution will work. In addition, in at least one area of your technical solution, your approach must be clearly superior to competitors' approaches. The area is your proposal *differentiation strategy*.

Although I am presenting a recommended technical proposal outline, you must understand that *the government's required proposal format (in Section L) takes precedence over this outline*. Feel free to modify and change my recommended outline to meet the needs of your specific proposal.

The summary section often makes up approximately 10 percent of your technical proposal, the statement of the problem normally requires about 30 percent, and your description of the proposed solution uses the remaining 60 percent.

Recommended Technical Proposal Outline

1. Summary
    1.1   Technical Proposal Executive Summary
    1.2   Technical Response Matrix
    1.3   Overview of the Technical Proposal

2. Statement of the Problem
    2.1   Background of the Problem
    2.2   Problem as Described in the RFP
    2.3   Fundamental Problem as We Perceive It (if different)
    2.4   Significant Difficulties in Solving the Problem
    2.5   Summary of the Proposed Solution

3. Proposed Solution
    3.1   Description of the Proposed Solution
    3.2   Possible Problems and How the Proposed Solution
           Overcomes Them
    3.3   Alternatives Considered and Why They Were Rejected
    3.4   How the Proposed Solution Will Be Implemented
    3.5   Possible Risks with the Proposed Solution and How They
           Will Be Minimized

The summary section is often the only thing read by senior managers in the government's organization. This section should present your solution clearly and in nontechnical terms. The summary section is normally divided into three areas:

1.   an executive summary

2.   a response matrix

3.   an overview of the technical proposal

The executive summary should present your solution in overview form, with primary emphasis on benefits to the government from your approach, as opposed to technical features and specifications. The executive summary should be written from a sales rather than an informative perspective.

The response matrix is your key to success on large procurements. Your technical response matrix is actually a table. Along the left-hand edge you should list each requirement as shown in the RFP, including chapter, section, and paragraph number. You then answer the requirements by referencing a page in your proposal where you address the requirement, along with a brief description of your response.

The final item covered in your summary section should be an overview of the format and organization of the technical proposal.

The statement of the problem section should prove to the government that you thoroughly understand the problem. You will normally cover

- the background of the problem,

- a statement of the problem as described in the RFP,

- a statement of the actual problem, if different,

- major difficulties in solving the problem,

- a summary of your proposed solution.

Background information is included to demonstrate an in-depth understanding of the government's needs. The problem, as stated in the RFP, is then described in your own words. It is important that you describe the problem in your own words, as opposed to repeating the statement of the problem from the RFP. This will assure the government that you understand the problem as it was described. If you have identified a fundamental underlying problem that is more significant than the problem expressed in the RFP, you will want to bring this out into the open. If you are wrong in your analysis, you will probably lose the RFP. If you are right and no other bidder has accurately identified the true problem, you will often be rewarded with the contract.

You should include a detailed discussion of the difficulties you foresee in solving the problem. This will demonstrate to the government that you have anticipated the difficulties and have allowed for them in your planning and costing. In addition, this is an area that competitors often neglect, thus leading the government to believe that your company has a better understanding of what is involved in solving the specific needs. Finally, you will want to summarize your proposed solution as a lead-in to the next section of your proposal.

When presenting your proposed solution, you must convince the government that your solution will work, will meet their needs fully, and can be accomplished. To do this, you will want to include the following discussions:

- a statement of your proposed solution

- possible problems with your proposed solution and how you intend to overcome them,

- alternative solutions and why they were rejected,

- how you will implement the proposed solution,

- possible risks with the proposed solution, and how they will be minimized.

While the executive summary stated your technical solution from an overview standpoint, this section of your proposal will discuss your technical solution in exacting detail. These are the pages that the government's technically oriented personnel will read to gain a full understanding of your approach.

You will want to identify all possible problems with your proposed solution, and the methods you will use to overcome them. This will greatly strengthen your position by serving as a rebuttal to arguments against your ideas. If you ignore a weak point in your solution, you can bet that a competitor or member of the evaluation team will bring it up, leaving the impression that you did not think of and plan around the potential problem area.

You should discuss all possible solutions that were considered, including a summary of your reasons for rejecting each of them in favor of your final solution. This offers two advantages. First, it strengthens your proposed solution by demonstrating that you made a thorough analysis of possible solutions and selected the proposed solution as the strongest. Second, and even more important, it provides you with an opportunity to tear down a competitor's approach if another bidder was unfortunate enough to choose a solution that you rejected as inferior.

You must discuss your plan for implementing your solution in great detail. Remember, you must convince the government not only that your solution will work, but also that it can be accomplished. Your implementation plan will normally include Gantt charts and descriptive statements for each task element.

Finally, you will want to discuss risks associated with your solution, along with your plans for minimizing these risks. Once again, the idea is to short-circuit your competitors from tearing down your plan. It is far better to own up to any risk factors and present your best rebuttal up front than to have someone else bring it up with no chance of rebuttal from you.

3.6 Writing Better Cost Proposals

Your cost proposal must present your prices for the services and products offered in your technical proposal. An effective cost proposal will be clear, complete, and reflect your costing strategy. For each cost item, you will be asked to describe your direct costs, your burden rate, your mark up rate, and your final cost to the government. Burden is your overhead, although the government has very strict requirements covering exactly how this overhead is calculated. For example, many overhead expense items may not be allowed or may be restricted (e.g., marketing expenditures). The exact requirements are contained in the latest edition of the Federal Acquisition Regulations (FAR). Mark up, or profit, is normally much more straightforward.

Contracts can be awarded with various payment options and incentive clauses. For example,

- *Fixed Price*: You receive a fixed price for all work. If you complete the job cheaper, you make a larger profit. If you run over, your bottom line suffers. These contracts are rare for software development projects, although I believe that they should be used much more often.

- *Cost Plus Fixed Fee*: You are reimbursed for your project related costs throughout the project, and receive a fixed fee (profit) upon completion. If you overrun the project, you will be reimbursed for your costs on the overrun portion but you will not make a profit on the overrun. This type of contract was used extensively for software in the early 80's and was partially at fault for the large overruns seen on some government projects. When used now, they often include a cap on the amount of cost overrun which will be covered.

- *Cost Plus Incentive Fee*: You are reimbursed for your project related costs throughout the project, and receive a fee based upon your performance upon completion.

It is not unusual for the Request for Proposal to imply (or state) that all costs and fees are paid on completion of the project. You should be sure to include a request in your cost proposal for progress payments throughout the project. Some methods of awarding progress payments are

- *Periodic Payments*: You are paid a proportionate share of the final amount in periodic installments throughout the project.

- *Cost Reimbursement, Fee on Delivery*: You are reimbursed for your costs during the project, but receive your entire fee upon delivery.

- *0-100*: For each identified (and approved) task in your Work Breakdown Structure, you receive payment for that task upon completion.

- *50-50*: For each identified (and approved) task in your Work Breakdown Structure, you receive 50 percent payment for that task when the task is started, and the remainder on completion.

For most government contracts, you will be required to justify your cost estimates to the government. You will be required to explain your costing methodology and show how you applied the methodology to this particular project to arrive at your proposed cost.

Good cost proposals require that you: (1) cost your proposal in accordance with the requirements identified in the Request for Proposal,

(2) carefully check and re-check each item in the cost proposal to be sure that everything is accurate and that nothing was left out, and, (3) reduce your costs as much as possible to be competitive. When preparing cost proposals, there are two alternate, although not mutually exclusive, techniques for reducing costs:

- actual cost-reduction efforts,

- "paper" cost reductions.

Actual cost reductions involve changes in design or approach that result in an actual reduction in cost to the government, while still meeting the specifications. These changes are specific to each proposal effort and involve items such as modifying the software design to use existing software packages, substituting lower priced hardware in the system, reducing maintenance costs by proposing an innovative maintenance plan, and so forth. These types of changes are an ongoing item throughout the proposal effort, although it is often worthwhile to occasionally call a proposal meeting just to brainstorm about cost saving ideas. A kickoff question such as, "What can we do to reduce hardware costs to the government while still meeting the specifications?" is all that is needed to start one of these meetings.

Reducing paper costs can sometimes be less ethical but is often very effective. When reducing paper costs, it is important that your cost reduction plan not be apparent to the government, or your bid may be disqualified. In fact, I encourage government contractors to review these techniques and use this knowledge to write RFPs which prevent these techniques from being used! Nevertheless, you should be aware of these techniques if you are to successfully compete in the government marketplace. The four techniques I will cover are:

1.   low-balling unused cost categories,

2.   "playing the come",

3.   the change-request game,

4.   lowest bidder with options.

Low-balling unused cost categories is extremely common on Basic Ordering Agreement (BOA) contracts for services. A BOA simply means that the agency or company involved signs a contract with you for a fixed amount of money for skilled labor, with delivery to be as required over a period of time (normally one year). For example, you may be asked to fill out a costing form as follows:

Labor Category	Estimated Hours	Hourly Cost
Project Manager	1,000	_____
Senior Programmer	4,000	_____
Programmer	12,000	_____
Junior Programmer	10,000	_____

The standard approach would be to fill in your hourly price for each category. This would result in an honest, and probably losing, bid. To play the low-balling game, you would bid your junior programmer and programmer at their proper hourly rate, bid your senior programmer at a reduced rate, and probably bid your project manager at zero cost, claiming that you would perform project management out of overhead funds. During the year, when you were asked to estimate work involved for specific delivery orders, you would estimate that the job required lots of junior programmer and programmer hours, but very few senior programmer and project manager hours. Your goal is to end the year with the programmer and junior programmer hours (on which you make a profit) fully spent, but as few as possible of the project manager and senior programmer hours (which cost you money) spent. Government contractors can avoid this game by stating in the RFP that all costs must be bid at actual rates and that during the contract hours must be used in proportion to the stated cost category estimates.

"Playing the come" (also called "buying in") is a more ethical method of bidding projects at lower costs while not reducing actual costs. This specific RFP is bid at or near your break-even point, or even at a loss, while your technical proposal is written to ensure that no other contractor can reasonably perform follow-on work (software maintenance, etc.) that is sure to be required. Although somewhat risky (they may never do the follow-on work, or you may go broke in the meantime), this technique is successfully used by many large contractors. It is not uncommon in government contracting for follow-on contracts to amount to ten times the value of the original contract, thus allowing you plenty of opportunities to make up for this short term loss. Government contractors can turn this ploy to their advantage by ensuring that the technical work does not lock the government into a single source for future work. For example, the RFP can be written to require an open architecture for all work performed. Proprietary items which are slipped in during the technical proposal can sometimes be negotiated out during contract negotiations prior to contract award.

Playing the change request game is easy. You bid the project with little or no profit, designing the system to barely meet the government's stated requirements. Specifically, you ensure that your technical solution will not be completely satisfactory in its proposed form. During the project, you "suggest" several changes to the contract to "improve" the system (to make it usable, in reality). These change requests are quoted with ample profit margin to compensate for the reduced profit on the original contract. Government contractors can avoid this situation by writing RFP requirements in top level (but testable) terms which put the burden for deciding *how* to meet the requirements on the contractor. For example, it is better to describe a testable scenario and state that the radar shall "acquire and track the target with 93% accuracy" rather than describing specific radar characteristics which you believe will give you the required performance. One other thing I believe the government could and should do is to track contractor performance and use this information as a significant criteria when awarding future contracts. The current procurement approach prohibits government evaluators from considering past performance on other contracts in awarding a new contract, although I can't for the life of me figure out why this rule exists.

Another common technique in government contracting is to use the lowest bidder with options technique. The idea is simple: You base your quoted price on a system that just barely meets the specifications, knowing full well that the proposed system is not even close to what the government really wants or needs. As optional extras, you propose enhancements to the system, at additional cost, which bring the system up to the level required to win the technical evaluation. These options may then be used by the government to purchase a system more in line with the actual needs. This technique is extremely valuable, as it allows you to quote a low price in your cost proposal, while at the same time allows you to write a glowing technical proposal as you describe the wonderful options that may be purchased if you are selected as the winning contractor. With some careful wording of your proposal, you may find your proposal rated highest in both the cost competition and the technical competition, simply because the two evaluations are based on different configurations! Obviously, it is important during your technical write-up that you clearly indicate which items are optional. I believe that this approach is the most ethical and often the most effective.

3.7 Writing Better Management Proposals

The management proposal in general, and the management strategy in particular, are two of the most neglected areas in proposal preparation today. I think it's because the management proposal doesn't have a sponsor. Think about it a minute. Your technical volume is vigorously sponsored by your company's computer gurus, each of them anticipating a new, challenging, fun project to work on. The cost volume is sponsored by the comptroller, fearfully visualizing your company (and his or her career) going down the tubes if the costs are not reasonably correct. But whoever heard of a manager pushing for a good management proposal so some new and exciting managing can be accomplished, or job protected? The poor management proposal thus exists, woefully neglected, waiting patiently until the last few frantic moments of proposal work when somebody slaps a few pages together and calls it a "management proposal".

Ah, but where there's neglect, there's opportunity. Just because the vendors place a low importance on the management proposal doesn't necessarily mean that the government is similarly inclined. Although I will concede that most government's place the management proposal at a lower priority than the technical volume or the cost volume, it is definitely a close third. Quite often, your carefully contrived technical and cost strategy will be evaluated relative to your competitors' equally carefully contrived strategies. On many procurements, it will be difficult, if not impossible, to really shine in either of these two areas. The competition is simply too fierce. On the other hand, a well thought-out and carefully written management proposal will often be orders of magnitude better than the management proposals of your competition, thus winning the procurement for you.

A well written management proposal will provide:

- evidence that the firm is financially stable enough to complete the work,

- some assurance that the individuals doing the actual work will be qualified,

- a reasonable plan for managing the project to keep it on time and budget, along with experienced management personnel to implement this plan,

- evidence that the full intricacies of the work at hand are fully understood and planned for,

- evidence of past history with this type of work.

I will present a recommended management proposal outline for use on proposals for which the RFP does not specify a rigid format.

3.7.1 Management Proposal Summary

The management proposal summary section is normally divided into three sections (although the requirements of Sec. L take precedence)

1.   Executive summary

2.   Management response matrix

3.   An overview of the management proposal

The executive summary presents an overview of your management approach, with a strong orientation toward the benefits to the government rather than to details. The management response matrix is identical to the technical response matrix described in the previous section of this chapter; it presents your response, point by point, to all management requirements mentioned in the RFP. Your management proposal overview describes the format and layout of the remainder of the management proposal.

Recommended Management Proposal Outline

1. Summary
    1.1   Executive summary
    1.2   Management response matrix
    1.3   Overview of management and facilities

2. Corporate organization, management, and facilities
    2.1   Background and organization
    2.2   Company experience
    2.3   Company facilities

3. Personnel qualifications

4. Project management policy and techniques

5. Training plan, quality assurance plan, etc.

3.7.2 Corporate Organization, Management, and Facilities

This section discusses your corporate organization, management, and facilities and is normally divided into the following three sections:

1.   Background and organization

2.   Company experience

3.   Company facilities

No matter what size your company is, you will want to include a section called, "background and organization" to introduce your company to the government. You should present a brief corporate history, along with a description of your company's areas of interest. Obviously, it is worthwhile for you to tailor your company's areas of interest to the project at hand.

Your "company experience" refers to past projects that are in some way similar to the present project. This might include projects with the same or a similar customer, projects working with similar applications, or projects of a comparable scope and size. You should extensively tailor this section to the proposal at hand, being careful to emphasize talents that will be relevant and impressive to the government.

It is a good idea to include a brief description of "company facilities" and equipment. Pay special attention to equipment that you have in-house or that is available from another source that will be relevant to this project. One area that is required for most projects but is often neglected is access to graphic arts and reproduction facilities.

3.7.3 Personnel Qualifications

Your personnel qualifications section is used to convince the government that you have qualified personnel available to work on or advise for the project at hand. You should describe your personnel qualifications in summary form, followed by a table showing employee qualifications applicable to this project. Finally, you normally include resumes for key project individuals. Resumes should be tailored to this particular project.

3.7.4 Project Management Policy and Techniques

This section of your proposal should describe your company's general approach to project management on projects of this type. You should be careful to demonstrate

- adequate control throughout the life of the project,

- short lines of communication between senior management and project managers within your organization,

- government involvement throughout the life of the project, designed to convince the customer that adequate control of the final product will be maintained.

In addition to your generalized company project management style and organization, this section of your management proposal should describe your planned approach for managing this specific project.

Finally, you will want to include one or more specific plans. Each of these specific management plans is designed to describe your method of controlling a specific potential problem area. Some examples of management plans are:

- A cost-reduction plan, designed to show management techniques and attitudes that you will use throughout the project to minimize the government's costs.

- A quality-control plan, demonstrating a realistic approach to ensuring the highest quality possible.

- A schedule-control plan is used when on-time delivery is especially important to the government. This plan describes how senior management will monitor progress of the project, and describes actions or procedures that will be taken to make up for lost time if the project falls behind schedule.

- The document-control plan describes how you will control the quality and content of the documents produced as part of the contract.

- The financing plan is especially important for small companies, and describes how you will handle the financing of any capital requirements or temporary negative cash flows during the life of the project.

- The staffing plan describes how you will staff the project, and often includes detailed statements of how you will hire qualified individuals to supplement your current labor force if the need arises.

- On projects in which you team with another company, you will want to include a subcontracting or teaming plan that describes how you will handle the intercompany interfaces and responsibilities necessary to accomplish the job.

- The installation plan describes how you will ensure proper installation of all components.

- The training plan describes how you will ensure that the customer receives adequate training, normally including detailed course outlines or lesson plans.

- The maintainability plan shows how you will control the project at the early stages to ensure that the final software or hardware is easily maintained over the life of the system.

- The security plan describes how you will control access to classified or sensitive information you receive from the government as part of the project.

3.8 Using Proposal Libraries

Proposals consist of 50 to 70 percent existing material describing your company, your project management techniques, presenting your employee resumes, and so on. These must be tailored to each specific proposal, but should certainly not be rewritten. Proposal libraries normally consist of files formatted for your specific word processor and designed to be read into the master document. The following types of proposal-oriented word processing files should be maintained:

- complete proposals

- project planning materials

- key employee resume files

- company qualification files

- management plan files

- cover information files

3.8.1 Complete Proposals

Every proposal file should include disks containing the entire text of the proposal and all spreadsheets with formulas. Besides the obvious value as a reference, this will enable you to rob entire sections form one proposal to include in a different proposal, which may then be tailored as required.

3.8.2 Project Planning Materials

I'm going to let you in on a little secret that I've had to learn the hard way. During the frantic proposal preparation effort, cost estimates are made based on information that is often of an informal nature. For example, you may need to locate a source for a particular computer board. You call several suppliers and obtain verbal quotes for the quantity contemplated. Being a sharp person, you also ask for a written confirmation of the price. From here, things go down hill. In the last minute, hectic rush to finish the proposal, you do your costing based on the verbal quote. The written confirmation is either never received or is lost. With the proposal completed, everyone sits back, takes a breather, then moves on to other matters.

Four months later you are notified that you have been selected as the winning bidder. A project manager (often not the person on the original proposal team) is assigned and the champagne corks fly. Before the champagne has a chance to go flat, the new project manager finds that he or she is in trouble. The lowest price on those boards you bid at $525 is $900. The project manager tracks you down, but at this point you can't remember everyone you called, much less which of the companies you finally based your estimate on. The end result is the all too common problem of the project manager being burned because information used by the proposal team is no longer available. We illustrated the example with a hardware component, but the result is equally common with software projects where the intermediate calculations that resulted in the bottom-line cost are no longer available. The project manager is then left asking, "How in the world could you possibly tell them it would only cost $350 thousand?"

The solution to these problems is the inclusion of all project planning-type materials in the master proposal file. For hardware, this should take the form of a table showing each item costed, the supplier contacted, the point of contact, and the price agreed to. This table can be used as a checklist to confirm receipt of written price quotes. For software, planning materials consist of all notes and preliminary calculations that went into the final cost.

3.8.3 Key Employee Resume Files

Your employee resume file must be designed with sufficient flexibility and detail to allow a proposal manager to quickly build a resume tailored to each proposal. This can be accomplished by setting up a file for each employee that includes the following three subsets of information:

1. A standard header, which should include employee name, academic training, publications and patents, and professional memberships.

2. A job description section, which should include at least three descriptions of the employee's current job, written from different directions of emphasis. If a new tailored job description must be written for a specific proposal, add the new description to this file for future use.

3. A list of examples of professional experience covering every angle possible, grouped into subheadings applicable to your type of work. In addition, examples with different levels of detail should be available to allow the final tailored resume to match the government's needs exactly. For example, my resume file might include the following professional experience subheadings.

   a. Military software applications experience

   b. Project management experience

   c. Hardware specific experience

   d. Operating system specific experience

   e. Programming language specific experience

f. Real-time programming experience

g. Electronic networking and communications experience

h. System design and analysis experience

Under one of the headings, for example, operating system specific experience, the following personal descriptions might be found.

- Mr. Roetzheim is a published authority on the Unix operating system, with extensive firsthand experience with the Hewlett Packard implementation of Unix.

- Mr. Roetzheim has led several major software development efforts using the Hewlett Packard 9845, 9836, and 9020, and is intimately familiar with the HP-DOS operating system on each of these computers.

- Using the Wang VP operating system, Mr. Roetzheim designed and implemented a tactical characteristics database management system, and an interface between remote Wang computers and Navy telecommunications networks.

- Mr. Roetzheim has done extensive software development under the MS-DOS operating system, and has worked in a consulting capacity to assist users and other programmers in understanding the intricacies of the MS-DOS Basic Input-Output System (BIOS).

- Mr. Roetzheim is a leading expert on the Unix and HP-DOS operating systems, and is familiar with the Wang VP and MS-DOS operating systems.

3.8.4 Company Qualification Files

In a similar fashion, you will want to categorize and list your company's experience and qualifications, including major contracts and types of work undertaken. Once again, these should be available in various levels of detail for easy customization.

3.8.5 Management Plan Files

Management plans involve short write ups of your approach to quality control, subcontractor management, cost control, and so on. Each of these plans should be kept in your proposal library after they are developed.

3.8.6 Cover Information Files

You should develop a standard proposal cover page that protects your company by including copyright information and proprietary information notices. These cover pages should be kept in your proposal library.

3.9 Proposals Are a Starting Point

A tremendous amount of system design and project management effort goes into writing the proposal. A good proposal will include a top level system design, a project work breakdown structure, risk analysis, and detailed algorithms for critical system functions. It is vital to the project that this work be used as a starting point for the actual software engineering effort. As a minimum, the same individuals who participated in writing the technical proposal should be involved in the project after the contract is awarded. Ideally, the proposal team should use the same automated tools to prepare the technical proposal that will eventually be used during the software engineering phase to design the actual software. This allows the proposal generated design work to be easily used and refined during the software engineering activities after contract award.

3.10 Chapter Review

Proposal Checklist

_____ Is the differentiation strategy introduced early, and presented clearly throughout the proposal?

_____ Is the technical approach clearly defined, including a convincing discussion of how it will be implemented?

_____ Is the writing clear, unambiguous, and to the point?

_____ Does the writing and idea presentation flow smoothly?

_____ Are graphics and resumes used to best advantage in the proposal?

_____ Are costs accurate and complete?

_____ Does the transmittal letter present the flavor of the proposal in the best possible light?

_____ Does every section have a good lead-in, a body, and a closing that provides both a conclusion and a lead-in to the next section?

_____ Have you included the correct quantity of copies in your delivery?

_____ Is the transmittal letter included and signed?

_____ Are the proposal volumes addressed properly?

_____ Are all required forms included and signed?

_____ Are all cost figures double-checked for accuracy?

_____ Is the overall appearance of the proposal professional?

_____ Is the table of contents included and accurate?

_____ Have you inserted the proposal response matrix?

_____ Are all cost tables included and double-checked for accuracy and completeness?

_____ Are all illustrations inserted?

_____ Are all pages, especially illustrations, right side up in the final copies?

_____ Are any pages out of order or missing?

_____ Have the appendices and manufacturers' spec sheets been included?

_____ Were employee resumes bound in, if desired?

3.11 Discussion Questions

1. Suppose you (as a member of the government procurement team) prepare a detailed proposal evaluation hierarchy complete with utility curves. What advantages do you see to providing this information to the contractors as part of the procurement package? What disadvantages?

2. What members of a typical company should be part of a proposal team (responsible for writing a proposal)? What roles should they play in the proposal effort?

3. Suppose you are in the marketing department of a large company. The people best qualified to help you write the technical portion of your proposals (the company's sharpest technical individuals) are all "too busy" to work on the proposal. When they do work on proposals with you, the work is done between important interruptions (from the paying project they are responsible for), and the resultant work is not especially impressive. You have an opportunity to make a presentation to senior management in your company arguing for more technical support during the proposal process. What will you ask for? What arguments will you make to convince senior management to give it to you?

4. Suppose that senior management grants your requests from Question 3. You are now responsible for making a presenta-

tion to the senior technical individuals who will be assisting you. What will you ask for? What arguments will you make to convince the senior technical individuals to give it to you? Will you end up with complete support or people resentfully "going through the motions"?

4 Start With a Solid Foundation

To effectively compete in the government software development arena, it is vital that your organization operate as efficiently as possible. This efficiency can be achieved through:

1. *Strategic planning*: to ensure that your organization as a whole is working in a market segment which you can penetrate effectively.

2. *Managing your people*: discussed in the context of establishing an effective software engineering environment, encouraging team attitudes, and enhancing the quality of your people.

3. *Selection of appropriate methods*: ensuring that you select and use software development methods which are particularly well suited to government software development.

4. *Selection of appropriate tools*: ensuring that you select and use software development tools which will speed up and simplify software development to government standards.

This chapter will provide some background information for this process, then conclude with an overview of the government standards which will be dealt with in the remainder of this text.

Portions of this chapter are taken from the author's book *Structured Computer Project Management*. (10)

4.1 Strategic Planning

Department of Defense mission critical software costs are currently approximately 25 percent of total U.S. software costs. (1) Other software development within the government pushes this figure past 50 percent. This is a market segment of such a vast size that no software development company can ignore it out-of-hand. Where do you start?

The first question is: Do you want to be a prime contractor or a subcontractor? Prime contractors are responsible for writing the proposal (in response to a Request for Proposal), are awarded a contract, and then work directly for the government. Subcontractors work for prime contractors. In general:

- The larger your company, the more likely you are to be a prime contractor.

- The longer you have been working in the government marketplace, the more likely you are to be a prime contractor.

- The more significant your government work is (as a percentage of your overall business), the more likely you are to be a prime contractor.

- The more comfortable you are with *system* level thinking the more likely you are to be a prime contractor.

Of course, most prime contractors will still be subcontractors on some projects.

Your next task is to determine your area(s) of specialization. You may choose to focus on *system* engineering, with much of your work involving integration; *hardware* engineering; or *software* engineering. You may decide to focus on one or more application areas (e.g., anti-submarine warfare, fire department dispatch systems, electronic warfare systems, etc.) Finally, you may decide to focus on one specific aspect of the project (e.g. independent verification and validation (IV&V), quality control, configuration management, documentation, etc.) It is important that you select your areas of specialization carefully. They should be broad enough that you will be able to obtain adequate work, yet narrow enough that you can obtain a significant market share and establish a company reputation within the given specialization.

Having a strong company reputation will benefit your company in several ways, including:

- Your company will be asked to provide constructive criticism of RFPs that are about to be released. This will allow you to provide input that ensures your ability to compete on the procurement, and also gives you advance warning of the solicitation.

- Selling the customer on your technical qualifications to do the job will be greatly simplified.

- Government agencies will approach your company asking for technical advice in your area of specialization, thus opening the door for submission of an unsolicited proposal to a receptive government official.

- Agencies will forward solicitations to you well before you even write requesting a copy, thus giving you a significant time advantage over your less fortunate competitors.

Building an impressive company reputation takes determination and persistence, not spectacular technical expertise. Technically competent, even outstanding, companies are a dime a dozen. The company that stands out from the pack is the firm that has taken the effort to build name recognition. This normally involves these steps:

- Write articles for trade publications that will be read by your potential customers to build your reputation. There are hundreds of computer related trade journals floating around, all hungrily looking for worthwhile, interesting articles to fill each issue. If you aren't a hot-shot writer yourself, hire someone to write the article under your technical direction.

- Speak at conferences. This is a valuable reputation-building technique, if you are careful to select conferences in which your potential customers will be represented in the audience.

- Offer live demonstrations to your potential customers; a favorite method of proving to the customer that your product is superior to the competition's.

- Offer training programs to potential customers. This will build your credibility, if you ensure that you really are providing valuable training, and not simply making a marketing pitch.

- Undertake subcontracting work with larger prime contractors to build your credibility and experience base.

There is one more technique that is often used by the top government contractors, both large and small. You can hire a reputation. This does not necessarily mean hiring an individual with an impressive resume to work for you, although that is an acceptable solution. Instead, try to locate individuals with an impressive reputation in your area of interest, using local college professors as a good starting point. Retired professionals are another excellent source of talent. Talk with these individuals about the possibility of their working for you on a consulting basis. If they are interested, ask if you can pay them a retainer ($1,000 a year seems to be fairly typical) in exchange for an agreement that you can use their resume when marketing and that they will assist you as needed during the year for an agreed-to hourly rate. In this way, you can legitimately use these individual's qualifications to further your own company's reputation.

4.2 Is Your Organizational Structure Appropriate

In general, a project oriented approach is necessary for government software development projects. This is apparent if we examine the five criteria used when evaluating the desirability of formal project management. (10)

- Does the job involve the integration of many components into a functioning, operational whole? The interaction between these components is best handled by a single individual having ultimate responsibility for the project. The very nature of modular software development is a classic example of this factor. In addition, most computer hardware and systems projects involve this type of complex interaction.

- Is the job large or technically complex? Large or complex projects normally require and deserve the close management attention available with formal project management. The technical complexity of most software projects is best handled by formal project management.

- Does top management strongly feel that a single individual should be available to serve as a focal point for information and responsibility? Are tight budgetary, fiscal or schedule controls necessary or desired?

- Is the project being developed in an environment of changing requirements? A project management approach to solving the problem will allow more rapid responses to changing needs and result in greater customer satisfaction.

- Does the task require that a diverse group of professionals be brought together to work toward a common goal? Many software development projects require software professionals to work hand in hand with application specialists and end users of the final system. The interactions between these groups is often best handled in a project management environment.

It should be apparent that a project oriented organizational structure is well suited to software development in general and software development for the government in particular. Unfortunately, many companies attempt to incorporate all aspects of software development into a project oriented structure. At least two software development functions should be performed using a traditional department oriented organizational structure

1. Quality control (often combined with configuration management)

2.   Software library management

Quality control should always be a function which is external from and independent of all project organizations. This allows the quality control personnel to maintain their independence and objectivity during their activities. It is also a requirement on many government contracts.

Software library management is a somewhat different story. Most projects designate a software librarian as part of the project team. This is adequate if the goal of the software librarian(s) is simply to control and archive software modules. This approach will also cost your company a fortune in lost cost saving opportunities!

The real goal of the software librarian(s) is to *work with the software engineers to maximize the amount of design components (including code) which is captured from previous projects.* One of your most valuable resources is your company's vast library of existing program design and code. The problem usually is finding what you want, when you want it. I've often found that it is cheaper and easier to develop the software again than to pay someone to wade through a mass of code hoping to find a few gems. The solution is to maintain a well-organized, well-documented library of design solutions and source code. I firmly believe that for most organizations of any size, development and maintenance of this library is a full time job for a skilled technical person. I recommend that any organizations with 20 or more software engineers on staff assign at least one individual this responsibility full time. Your software librarian can be paid for out of overhead or by allocating time to projects using his or her services. The common argument that talented software engineers would not be willing to accept this position is not valid if the job is properly defined. In addition to configuration management of the library, this individual will be responsible for the following:

- Participation in the early design work for all projects to ensure that the design uses existing code and techniques as much as possible and that developed software will be applicable to future projects.

- Participation in the programming stage to ensure that existing code is used where appropriate and that all new functions are documented and added to the library.

- Developing libraries of functions which will be used on future projects.

- Converting functions between languages if you do program development using more than one language.

- Locating function libraries from other divisions of your company or from other sources outside of your company.

Many programmers enjoy being able to play a key role in the design of a wide variety of projects, and have fun developing new function libraries for use within the company. These programmers should be part of a separate organizational unit.

4.3 Establishing an Effective Work Environment

Even the most motivated software engineer cannot work efficiently in a poor work environment. Software engineering is an activity which requires extreme concentration for hours at a time. Just organizing the problem in your mind prior to working on the solution can require 20 minutes or more. One interruption and the entire organizing process must begin anew. A productive work environment will minimize distractions and interruptions, allowing prolonged concentration.

As the first item on your agenda, do everything in your power to ensure that every programmer has a private office with a door. I have worked in and observed the programmer bullpen and cubicle arrangements; they are space efficient but productivity inefficient. Software engineers *need* a small place, isolated from interfering factors, in which they can work. The office does not need to be large, or fancy, or expensive, - however, it must be well lighted and private.

The next most important action you can take to improve project-team efficiency is to minimize the effect of external interruptions, especially phone calls. I cannot overemphasize the importance of having a knowledgeable, friendly receptionist screen project-team phone calls. Of course, calls which are urgent may require an interruption (including many of those to senior people), but most calls can wait for an hour or two. Establish two times per day, one mid-morning and one mid-afternoon, during which nonurgent calls will be returned (I use 10:00 a.m. and 3:00 p.m.). When a call comes in, have the receptionist ask if the subject is urgent or a call back at either of these times is acceptable. For nonurgent calls, a written message should be taken and held by the receptionist. At the two appointed times for return calls, the receptionist should distribute all messages requiring a call back at that time. You must also emphasize to project-team members that they *must* return their calls at the appropriate times so that callers will not become impatient. Project-team members should also use these times to make short personal calls, if required.

Project related interruptions must be handled slightly differently. I recommend that your company establish an electronic mail system using the same terminals used by your software engineers. Most project-related questions, comments, and so on, should be transmitted among individuals electronically. Software engineers should be encouraged to check their electronic mailbox at convenient stopping points in their work, approximately every hour. Responses can then be sent electronically when possible. *Government Standards Toolbox* (described in appendix B) supports extensive tools to control project and nonproject related interruptions.

These actions alone will make a tremendous difference in your project team productivity. Here are some other hints to create the best possible software engineering work environment

- Each programmer should have his or her own terminal, and it should be possible to electronically connect the terminal with any computer the programmer is expected to work with. It never ceases to amaze me the way companies ask programmers to share the single most important tool of their trade. It is not really much different from asking a team of carpenters to share one hammer.

- Programming involves extensive hours sitting in one place. A backache is never good for concentration and can often be avoided by investing in a very good back-support chair. I recommend that you spend the money necessary to purchase the best possible adjustable chairs for your software engineers.

- Just as it is insane for programmers to be forced to fight over terminal time, I am appalled that many companies expect programmers to fight over the hardware, operating system, and programming manuals. If each programmer spends fifteen minutes per day looking for a needed reference manual (or walking to and from a library of manuals), how long will it take to pay for a new set of manuals? Each programmer should have his or her own set of vital reference manuals for your development environment.

- Design documentation for the application being produced is often a problem. Changes do not get incorporated into programmers' copies of the design specification, and the result is a program bug. One possible solution is to maintain a central master copy which is always kept current and which should be referred to by programmers. A better alternative, when possible, is to maintain design documentation on-line and let the programmers access the latest information from their terminals. This is the approach used in *Government Standards Toolbox* (see Appendix B).

- Maintain a good central reference library with both application and software engineering reference materials.

- Encourage your project team to maintain a neat, organized environment. Insist that common areas be kept clean at all times. Have project-team members look around their personal areas and clean/organize at least once per week. Time spent looking for lost materials is wasted time.

4.3.1 Programming Tools

New software engineering tools are being developed almost daily. If you constantly strive to keep up with the state of the art in this area, you will find that your team members are spending most or all of their time reading manuals and experimenting with new toys. On the other hand, ineffective or inefficient languages, operating systems, debuggers, and so on, can drastically hamper program development. I recommend spending some time carefully evaluating tools which are available. Select the best tools for your type of work and let your software engineers learn them well. If a tool turns out to be a poor choice, get rid of it quickly and replace it. Once you have a good development environment (and not before), standardize it so everyone uses the same tools.

In addition, you should be very slow to change the standard configuration. Try to work as many projects as possible using the same operating system, the same hardware, the same language, and the same editors/debuggers/profilers, and so on. This is how you get a reasonable payback on the learning curve for complex software tools. When you must change the standard configuration for a project, be sure to factor in the additional learning time for your project team, a penalty which can as much as triple the cost of a small project.

4.3.2 Meetings

Within limits, properly conducted meetings can improve productivity. On the other hand, improperly conducted meetings can destroy productivity. It's really not that difficult, just follow these rules when planning meetings:

1. Before scheduling a meeting, ask yourself if the meeting topic could be handled using an electronic message, a memo, a telephone call, or a couple of one-on-one discussions. Schedule meetings only when absolutely necessary.

2. Always have a meeting agenda and objectives, and stick to them.

3. Limit attendance to those who absolutely and positively must attend.

4. Keep the time to a minimum. Discussions pertaining to only a portion of the meeting attendees should normally be conducted privately after the meeting.

Another technique for improving the software engineering work environment requires your admission that secretarial support for software engineering is at least as specialized as secretarial support for the legal or medical profession. Although you can not currently hire a software engineering secretary, you can certainly train one (or more). I recommend selecting a sharp secretary for this area and getting him or her involved in supporting all aspects of the project. This person should be responsible for taking notes at meetings, smoothing up all design documents, collecting and distributing program listings, assisting with the editing and preparation of the various user's manuals, and so on.

Finally, you must monitor the efficiency of each individual on your project team. Watch for patterns which might indicate drug, alcohol, or personal problems that need to be solved. If motivation is high and hours are long, pay special attention to efficiency. Falling efficiency is the first sign of burn-out, which must be dealt with promptly. On a stressful project, ensure that individuals take enough time away from work to operate efficiently. High-stress projects can also be helped with unusual activities to relax the project team. On a recent project, I walked into the project work area one afternoon and dragged everyone out to an afternoon matinee at the local theater (my treat).

For more information on effective management of all aspects of a project, I recommend my book *Structured Computer Project Management* (10).

4.4 Building the Team

A project team typically consists of a project manager responsible for all aspects of the project, a technical manager responsible for all technical aspects of the project, hardware and software engineers responsible for doing the technical work, and documentation specialists responsible for preparing technical documentation. As discussed earlier, the project team will be assisted by the quality control group and the software library management group. For the project team, I'm going to stress professional development as a method of simultaneously building team spirit and expanding the knowledge of your companies employees.

Professional development is such a good deal for companies that I sometimes pinch myself to make sure I'm not dreaming. Professional development deals with long range skill building. The first step in this process is for you to decide what skills you will need. Try to look two to four years into the future and make a list of skills which will be valuable to you. Skills will often include software development related skills (e.g., new languages, data base systems, design techniques), hardware related skills (e.g., networking, I/O port control), computer science skills (e.g., artificial intelligence, data structures), and application oriented skills (e.g., underwater acoustics, wave theory, command and control). Next to each area, put the name of one or more members of your staff. Try to avoid assigning any staff member to more than four areas. You will probably want to have one-on-one informal discussions with each individual before making your decision.

Discuss your selections with each individual, stressing the professional opportunities the new knowledge will open up. Present examples of how the knowledge will be useful. Convince them that becoming an expert in these areas is of benefit to them. Then make it easy for this person to become an expert in the designated areas, using the following suggestions as a starting point:

- Find appropriate evening classes (or short duration day classes) taught in your area at a reasonably priced school. Help the individual(s) register for these classes (one per semester), with your company paying for tuition and books.

- Find and order (at company expense) appropriate books. Allow the individual(s) to read the books at home (on their time), then place them in a common library in your company.

- Locate and subscribe to technical journals appropriate to each area of specialization. Ensure that the appropriate people are on a route list to read the journal. Encourage employees to take the journals home to read at their leisure. After everyone has read an issue, add it to your common library.

- Find appropriate technical books in your library, the local university library, or the local public library. Check them out and lend them to an appropriate individual to read. If an occasional book is lost, replace it with company funds if possible.

- Look for cheap personal computer software programs which involve the desired skills. For example, a low-cost ($49) Prolog compiler might pertain to AI expertise, a low-cost Ada compiler ($99) might pertain to Ada knowledge, and so on. Buy appropriate software for the use (at home) of your employees with personal computers. Give a programmer a

$49 Prolog compiler and manual, and a chance to play with it at home, and I'll show you a new Prolog programmer trained for next to nothing.

- Encourage your employees to use your computers at night to perform school and personal work. The added familiarity with the computer will greatly assist them in their work for you, while the added cost in electricity and wear and tear is insignificant.

- Attempt to identify projects or project tasks which will allow the employee to apply his or her growing talents in this new area.

- Encourage each employee to act as an in-house expert in his or her designated areas. The process of researching and answering the questions will educate, increase confidence, and motivate the employee.

Working as a project manager, my interests in professional development were purely selfish; I wanted to develop a set of experts tailored to my requirements. I know of no company that can find, or afford, all of the experts required to perform a top-notch job. I know of no company that can afford *not* to pay the small price in money and effort required to encourage their employees to become these required experts. In addition, I *guarantee* that you will be astounded at how motivated, ambitious, and productive your employees become in this environment. People in general, and software engineers in particular, *crave* just this type of challenge and opportunity. Professional development really is one of those few good deals where everyone wins.

4.5 Consistency Is Critical

One common mistake made by many contractors is to apply government standards only when absolutely required, and then to the minimum possible extent. Although this may result in short term savings, the long term costs associated with this short sighted viewpoint can be staggering. These companies are trading short term cost savings in document preparation for long term costs in software capture, extended learning curves, inadequate tools, and lost marketing opportunities. Let's look at each of these areas individually.

1. *Software capture*. If you apply government standards equally to deliverables on all projects, you can be sure that all software produced by your organization is fully documented, and that the documentation is compatible from one project to the next. This allows portions of the software (including design) from one project to be reused on another project with minimal changes to the documentation.

2. *Extended learning curves*. If your software engineers never know what documents will be required from one project to the next, they will be constantly learning a "new" set of requirements. It is much more efficient to consistently use exactly the same set of documentation requirements so that your software engineers will know what is expected of them.

3. *Inadequate tools*.   Documents prepared to government standards are ideally suited to automated production. If you apply these standards inconsistently, you will find that automated tools are not able to produce the modified documents you require. If you consistently develop your software to the government standards, it will be cost effective to purchase (or develop) the tools you need to produce the documentation you require. See Appendix B for a description of one tool (*Government Standards Toolbox*) tailored to government software development.

4. *Lost marketing opportunities*. During the proposal evaluation process, the government puts a lot of thought into determining if your company will be able to properly apply DOD-STD-2167A (and related standards) to their project. Is your company adequately familiar with the standard? Will you properly apply the standard? Will previously developed software be documented to the standard? These difficult questions are easily answered by the companies which are able to state that "All software developed by our company,

including internal programs, is developed to DOD-STD-
2167A." I can assure you that companies able to make this
statement have a significant marketing edge during proposal
evaluations.

The following section presents a brief overview of the most
significant documents used by the government to define software engineering
requirements. These documents will be covered in much more detail during
the remainder of this text.

4.6   Government Standards Applicable to Software Development

The primary documents applicable to government software development (in
order of priority) are:

- DOD-STD-2167A

- DOD-STD-2168

- MIL-STD-490A

- MIL-STD-1521B

- MIL-STD-483A

- DOD-HDBK-287

- *System Engineering Management Guide*

All of these documents can be ordered by contacting the Superinten-
dent of Documents, Government Printing Office, Washington, DC 20402.
The *System Engineering Management Guide* is not an official document, but
this textbook from the Defense Systems Management College is widely used
as a guide for system engineering during government work.

DOD-STD-2167A: DOD-STD-2167A (Defense System Software
Development) defines a set of activities to be accomplished during software
development.   In addition, DOD-STD-2167A includes 17 data item

descriptions (DIDs) which describe each document produced during a large development effort. DOD-STD-2167A is discussed in Chap. 9.

DOD-STD-2168: DOD-STD-2168 (Defense System Software Quality Program) describes how to develop, document, and implement a software quality program. DOD-STD-2168 is discussed in Chap. 10.

MIL-STD-490A: MIL-STD-490A (Specification Practices) is the primary document used to guide system and segment procurements. Because of this, any software project that is part of a larger system or segment will likely be required to follow MIL-STD-490A guidelines. The primary impact of MIL-STD-490A on software developers is as follows:

- You will receive a type "A" System/Segment Specification which describes the top-level requirements of the system, some of which must be met by software.

- You will be required to produce a type "B5" Software Development Specification, which is simply a combination of the Software Requirements Specification and Interface Requirements Specification prepared under DOD-STD-2167A.

- You will be required to produce a type "C5" Software Product Specification, which is simply a combination of the Software Design Document, Interface Design Document, and source and object code listings of the final software. Each of these documents is required by and defined in DOD-STD-2167A.

MIL-STD-490A is discussed in Chap. 8.

MIL-STD-1521B: MIL-STD-1521B (Technical Reviews and Audits for Systems, Equipments, and Computer Software) describes procedures for conducting the following program reviews:

- System Requirements Review

- System Design Review

- Software Specification Review

- Preliminary Design Review

- Critical Design Review

- Test Readiness Review

- Functional Configuration Audit

- Physical Configuration Audit

- Formal Qualification Review

Each of these reviews/audits is required by and described briefly in DOD-STD-2167A, but MIL-STD-1521B contains the detailed descriptions and checklists that will be used when conducting the reviews. Many software and system requirements are implied by the sample meeting agendas itemized in this standard. MIL-STD-1521B is covered in Chap. 11.

MIL-STD-483A: MIL-STD-483A (Configuration Management Practices for Systems, Equipment, Munitions, and Computer Programs) is normally invoked only on contracts requiring concurrent software and hardware development. MIL-STD-483A requires slightly more stringent configuration management of the software development effort than that required in DOD-STD-2167A, in that computer software configuration identification and configuration management records/reports are required. MIL-STD-483A also provides guidance about controlling changes to baselines during the project. MIL-STD-483A is covered in Chap. 12.

DOD-HDBK-287: Although DOD-HDBK-287 (A Tailoring Guide for DOD-STD-2167A) is not invoked as a contractual requirement on software projects, this official guide amplifies and clarifies many of the requirements contained in other military standards. DOD-HDBK-287 also includes algorithms for determining which of the data item descriptions described in DOD-STD-2167A apply to a specific project. These algorithms are beneficial both to government employees writing contracts and to members of industry trying to justify reductions in software documentation requirements. DOD-HDBK-287 is covered in Chap. 12.

4.7 Chapter Summary

Small to midsized software development projects will normally use DOD-STD-2167A with tailoring to combine required documents, eliminate unneeded documents, or eliminate unnecessary portions of documents. Review meetings will normally be conducted in accordance with DOD-STD-2167A guidelines and may also be combined. Large software development projects are normally conducted to DOD-STD-2167A guidelines, with all or most deliverables required in accordance with the DOD-STD-2167A data item descriptions. Review meetings are normally more formal and are often conducted to MIL-STD-1521B specifications.

System projects are normally conducted to MIL-STD-490 requirements, with software developers also required to follow DOD-STD-2167A requirements. System projects virtually always conduct reviews in accordance with MIL-STD-1521, and software developers should be prepared to meet all software related requirements in that document. System projects are normally conducted in accordance with the guidelines in the System Engineering Management Guide, so knowledge of this document is required. If configuration management is expected to be a problem, the configuration management guidelines in MIL-STD-483A will be required, although tailoring in the software area is often allowed.

4.8 Discussion Questions

1. Refer back to the market niches identified in Sec. 4.1. Can you identify any others?

2. Rank the market niches identified in Sec. 4.1 (and those you identified in Question 1) by relative size. Which market niches is your company currently in? Which market niches *should* your company be in?

3. We stated that quality control and software library management should be organized along functional rather than project management lines. What other areas within your organization should be organized along functional lines?

4.   What disadvantages do you see to using government
        standards for all software development projects, as recom-
        mended in Sec. 4.5? Can you identify any advantages to this
        approach other than those identified in the text? Do you
        agree with the recommendation?

5 Allocating Costs . . . Reducing Costs

This chapter begins by comparing government software development to commercial development. We then describe the hierarchical decomposition of government software costs. The resultant cost hierarchy starts with the entire project at the top, then progressively decomposes the work into categories and assigns a percentage of the total cost to each category of work. Any differences between this cost hierarchy and cost hierarchies you may be familiar with are related to the size of the government projects. Cost savings will also be discussed which can be achieved using libraries, tailoring of standards, and automated production of documents.

5.1 Government versus Commercial Development

Let me begin by stressing that software development to government standards need not cost more than developing *equivalent* software to commercial standards. The widely held misconception that government software development must cost much more than commercial software (some say double) has arisen for the following reasons:

1. Government systems are often *much* larger than commercial systems. Programs involving 20 to 50 million lines of code are currently operational. There are substantial problems developing systems of this size efficiently, whether commercial or government.

2. Government systems are often technically more complex than commercial systems, frequently pushing the state-of-the-art.

Developing technically complex software is always more expensive.

3.   There is a substantial cost associated with entry into the government software arena in terms of both marketing dollars and the learning curve while your employees become familiar with the government standards.   Inconsistent use of the standards can greatly lengthen this learning curve.

4.   Similarly, there is a significant cost for each document required by the standard *the first time you do the document*. This document specific learning curve is caused by the time to learn the document Data Item Deliverable (DID) requirement and the time to become familiar with the document format. After the document has been prepared once, subsequent tasks preparing the same document (for a different software configuration item) will have a sample to work from and will often be able to directly copy much of the document content.

5.   Developing software to government standards can be *very* expensive if a contractor does not make effective use of automated tools, especially in the document production area.

6.   Many costs which show up on commercial projects as "maintenance" (after completion of software development) are pushed forward in time on government projects and show up as software development costs.

It can be argued that developing software to government standards *will* cost somewhat more than developing equivalent software for the commercial world because of additional testing requirements imposed by the government. I believe that this additional up-front cost for testing actually *saves* money over the life of the software because of reduced maintenance costs.

Figure 5.1 Cost estimating steps.

5.2 Types of Costs

As shown in Fig. 5.1, software cost estimating typically involves the following steps:

1.   Estimating the program's size and/or functional complexity using an accepted metric. Examples of common software costing metrics are lines of code (lines of code-based costing models) and functionality delivered (function-based costing models).

2.   Adjust your estimate based on project and company characteristics, including staff experience, project environment, hardware resources, and so on. Many estimating models combine steps 1 and 2 as part of the estimating process.

3.   Allocate the resulting costs to specific tasks to be performed during the project life cycle.

It is also possible to estimate costs from the bottom up, estimating the costs for each task to be performed and aggregating these costs to arrive at a final cost.

This text will not attempt to describe methods of estimating what a given project will (or should) cost. Interested readers may wish to refer DeMarco (2), or Putnam (8) for a detailed treatment or Roetzheim (10) for an overview of this initial costing process. What we *will* describe in this chapter is how to allocate the project funds to various tasks which must be accomplished.

As shown in Fig. 5.2, software costs can be broken down into software development costs, documentation costs, and management costs. On large government projects, software development costs typically consume 68 percent of your budget, documentation costs 12 percent of your budget, and management costs 20 percent of your budget. Documentation costs include preparation of system oriented user manuals and *production* of other documents using technical inputs from other areas. Software development can be further broken down into system design (13%) and system implementation (55%). These figures assume that the contractor is provided with a reasonable set of system requirements in the government generated Request for Proposal.

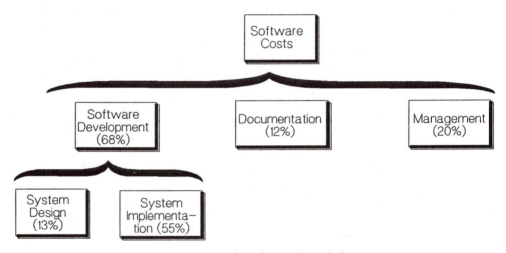

Figure 5.2 Top level cost breakdowns.

How much should you increase your cost estimates to allow for the fact that the software must be developed to DOD-STD-2167A? Not one penny! You should, however, modify your cost estimates based on factors such as

•   travel and coordination costs,

•   technical difficulty,

- your experience with the application, language, and hardware,

- whether the equivalent commercial software also required extensive documentation and testing designed to reduce long term maintenance costs. These factors can add approximately 25 percent to the initial development cost of a system.

One interesting question is: "How much should we allow to learn the government standards if we have never worked with them before?" The costs involved will be roughly equivalent to the costs to begin using a new method of software design, varying from 10 percent for large projects where the start-up costs can be recovered during the project all the way up to 100 percent on small projects. This learning curve cost is the likely source of the rumors that developing software to government standards costs twice as much as commercial development.

5.3 Estimating Software Development Costs

As previously stated, software development tasks can be divided into system design related tasks and system implementation related tasks. On typical government software development projects, system design will consume 13 percent of your total project budget, leaving 55 percent of your total project budget for system implementation. Remember, *all* percentages in this chapter are reasonable starting points but *they must be tailored to your company*. As shown in Fig. 5.3, system implementation can be further decomposed into Detail Design (12%), Coding (13%), Unit Testing (10%), Integration Testing (17.5%), and Software Configuration Management (2.5%).

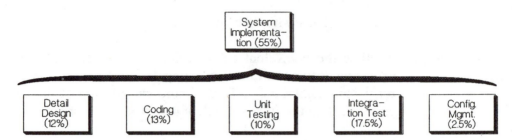

Figure 5.3 Software development tasks.

On larger projects, we will want to decompose our cost hierarchy even further. The following additional cost elements can be used to provide some guidance (the format and content of the Data Item Deliverables (DIDs) and reviews discussed are covered later in this text):

Management Costs (20%)   As shown in Fig. 5.4, management costs fall into the general areas of Data Item Deliverables, Reviews, and Management functions.   Data Item Deliverable (DID) costs include all costs associated with writing the appropriate DID, although the actual cost of producing the final report falls under documentation expenses (discussed later).   Management DIDS typically require 8 percent of your project resources. Four management oriented DIDs may be required on government contracts:

- A *Software Development Plan,* prepared in accordance with DID number DI-MCCR-80030A from DOD-STD-2167A, typically requires 3 percent of your budget. These funds are necessary to do software development planning functions even if a formal DID is not required in this area.

- A *Software Quality Program Plan,* prepared in accordance with DOD-STD-2168, requires 1.5 percent of your budget.

- A *System Engineering Management Plan,* prepared in accordance with DID number DI-S-3618/S-152, will typically require 3 percent of your budget. Even if the SEMP is not formally called for in the Contract Data Requirements List (CDRL), you should budget this 3 percent of resources to

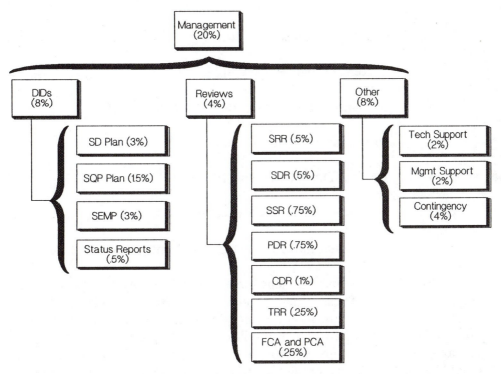

Figure 5.4 Management costs.

cover the trade studies and various reports which would normally be delivered as part of the SEMP.

- *Project status reports,* often required monthly during the contract, will require approximately 0.5 percent of your project resources.

Your management budget will also be required to pay for the various reviews and audits conducted during the project. These costs include the meeting preparations, expenses associated with preparing meeting minutes, and the costs associated with having members of the project team attend the meetings. The costs of preparing technical material for presentation at these meetings is not a management expense and is paid for out of the appropriate software development budget category. The costs of actually having the meetings is typically 4 percent of your project budget, broken down as follows:

- System Requirements Review: 0.5%

- System Design Review: 0.5%

- Software Specification Review: 0.75%

- Preliminary Design Review: 0.75%

- Critical Design Review: 1%

- Test Readiness Review: 0.25%

- Functional and Physical Configuration Audit: 0.25%

Finally, other management functions will require 8 percent of your project resources. These functions are as follows: 1. Technical support, which is used to pay internal or external consultants to assist members of your project team when required, should be budgeted for 2 percent; 2. Management support, paying for your time and the time of your staff, should be budgeted for 2 percent; and 3. Contingency funds of 4 percent of the project budget should be set-aside.

System Design Costs (13%) As shown in Fig. 5.5, system design costs can be broken down into time writing required DIDs and time preparing for reviews. Note that from a management perspective, the process of writing the DIDs and preparing for the reviews *is* the process of designing the system. This is true because each project task identified in the Work Breakdown Structure *must* have an identifiable product upon completion. The actual design work leading up to the production of the physical document is considered (by management) to be *part* of writing the DID. Actual document production will be covered out of documentation expenses and the actual cost of attending the reviews will be covered out of management expenses. You should plan to allocate 9 percent of your project funds to preparing the system design related documents. This money should be further broken down as follows:

- The *System/Segment Specification,* prepared in accordance with DID number DI-CMAN-80008A, will require 1.5

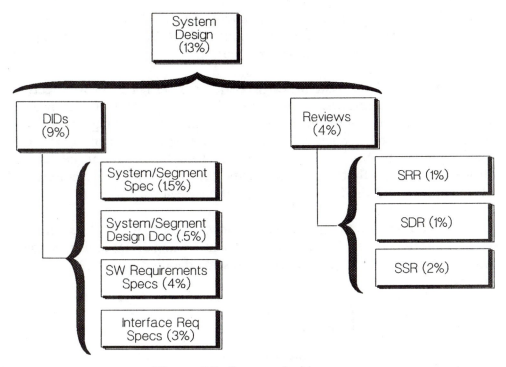

Figure 5.5 System design costs.

percent of your project resources. This document is an updated version of the System/Segment Specification (or Type "A" specification) which should have been available as part of the Request for Proposal. The System/Segment Specification is modified at this point to reflect changes to (or clarifications of) the requirements developed by the government.

- The *System/Segment Design Document,* prepared in accordance with DID number DI-CMAN-80534, will require 0.5 percent of your resources.

- The *Software Requirements Specification(s),* prepared in accordance with DID number DI-MCCR-80025A, will require 4 percent of your resources.

- The *Interface Requirements Specification(s),* prepared in accordance with DID number DI-MCCR-80026A, will require 3 percent of your resources.

As part of the system design work, your design team will need to prepare for three reviews. You should allocate 4 percent of your project resources to preparing for these reviews, including performing design work which is not directly associated with one of the previously mentioned DIDs but which will be presented at a review. This 4 percent can be further divided among the System Requirements Review (1%), the System Design Review (1%), and the Software Specification Review (2%).

Detail Design Costs (12%) As shown in Fig. 5.6, detail design costs can be further broken down into time spent writing DIDs and time spent preparing for reviews. The requirements for detailed design DIDs are as follows:

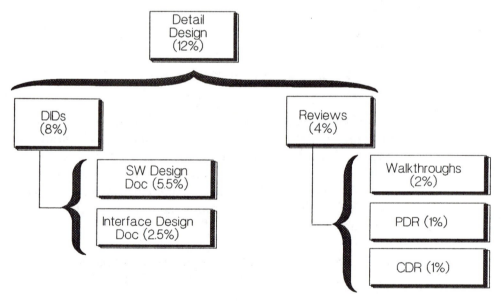

Figure 5.6 Detail design costs.

- The *Software Design Document(s)*, prepared in accordance with DID number DI-MCCR-80012A, must be prepared using approximately 5.5 percent of your resources.

- The *Interface Design Document(s)*, prepared in accordance with DID number DI-MCCR-80027A, must be prepared using approximately 2.5 percent of your resources.

Reviews required during the detailed design work are internal design walk-throughs (2% of resources); the Preliminary Design Review (1% of resources); and the Critical Design Review (1% of resources).

Coding Costs (13%) As shown in Fig. 5.7, coding costs can be broken down into five categories:

1. *Coding environment definition* (0.5%) involves defining specific programming hardware and software tools which will be required. Trade-off decisions between hardware, operating systems, languages, etc. also fall into this category.

2. *Resource acquisition* involves purchasing, installing, and learning the new hardware, operating systems, languages, etc. identified in item number 1 above. This typically costs much more than many managers suspect, with 2.5 percent of the project budget being a figure I use with some success.

3. I like to budget 7 percent of the project resources to *code development.*

4. *Internal code walk-throughs* typically require an additional 2 percent of the project budget.

5. Finally, preparation of the *Software Product Specification* prepared in accordance with DID number DI-MCCR-80029A, will require 1 percent of your project resources.

Component Testing and Debugging (10%) Component testing and debugging can be divided into module testing and CSU testing. Module testing (9%) is often performed by the individual programmers and involves

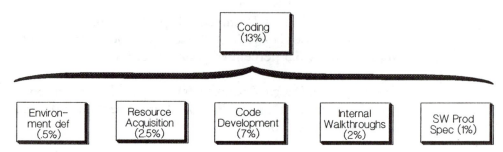

Figure 5.7 Coding costs.

testing and debugging individual modules of code. A CSU is a detailed functional requirement which must be met by one or more modules. CSU testing means combining modules as necessary and testing individual low level functionality. CSU testing (5.5%) may be done by the individual programmer, but is more often done by independent testing teams.

Integration and Testing (17.5%) - Integration and testing involves integrating CSUs together into Computer Software Components and integrating Computer Software Components into Computer Software Configuration Items (CSCIs), then testing the completed CSCI to ensure that it meets the requirements allocated to it during the functional allocation. As shown in Fig. 5.8, this typically involves preparing DIDs (10%), writing test drivers or simulators (4.5%) and preparing for reviews/audits (3%). The DIDs prepared as part of this process are the *Software Test Plan*, prepared in accordance with DID number DI-MCCR-80014A (2%); the *Software Test Description(s)*, prepared in accordance with DID number DI-MCCR-80015A (4%); and the *Software Test Report(s)*, prepared in accordance with DID number DI-MCCR-80017A (4%). Remember that the costs of actually performing the tests is tied to the corresponding Software Test Description and Software Test Report.

I typically budget 4.5 percent of my project resources to writing the appropriate test drivers, simulators, and test data to allow the tests to be conducted. In addition, I budget 2 percent for preparation for the Test Readiness Review and 1 percent for preparation for the Functional and Physical Configuration Audit.

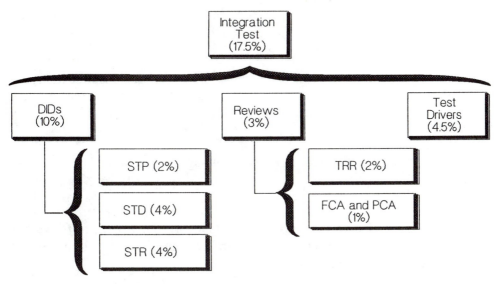

Figure 5.8 Integration and testing costs.

Software Configuration Management Costs (2.5%) As shown in Fig. 5.9, software configuration management costs involve:

- Preparation of the *Version Description Document*, prepared in accordance with DID number DI-MCCR-80013A (1.5%).

- Status accounting throughout the project (0.5%).

- Maintenance of the software development files (the software library) (0.5%).

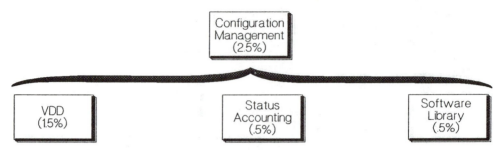

Figure 5.9 Configuration management costs.

There will also be some up-front costs involved in procuring/develop-
ing configuration management software and training your people in proper
configuration management practices.

Documentation Costs (12%)   I consider documentation costs to
include preparation of some documents which are system level and primarily
oriented to the end user (as opposed to documents produced as part of the
development process). I also consider documentation costs to include the

actual production and maintenance of final documents when the technical
content comes from a different budget category (the design team, for
instance). As shown in Fig. 5.10, I typically allocate 6 percent to user
oriented documents and 6 percent to document production and maintenance.

User oriented documents (by my definition) include:

- The *Computer System Operator's Manual*, prepared in accordance with DID number DI-MCCR-80018A (0.5%). This
  document typically consists almost entirely of manuals
  provided by the manufacturer of your computer.

- The *Software User's Manual*, prepared in accordance with
  DID number DI-MCCR-80019A (2%).

- The *Software Programmer's Manual*, prepared in accordance
  with DID number DI-MCCR-80021A (0.5%) typically consists
  almost entirely of manuals provided by the manufac

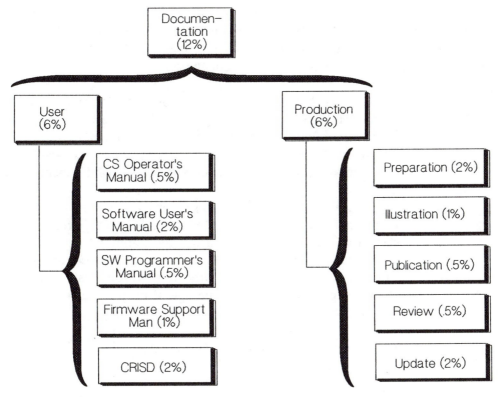

Figure 5.10 Documentation costs.

turer of your computer, operating system, language, and other development tools.

- The *Firmware Support Manual,* prepared in accordance with DID number DI-MCCR-80022A (1%).

- The *Computer Resources Integrated Support Document,* prepared in accordance with DID number DI-MCCR-80024A (2%).

Document production and maintenance typically includes: preparation (typing, copy editing, etc.), 2 percent; illustration, 1 percent; publication (printing, proofing, collating, etc.), 0.5 percent; review (internal and external), 0.5 percent; and update and maintenance, 2 percent.

These percentages have worked well for me, but feel free to adjust them as you see fit. I should also point out that:

1. These costs do not include travel expenses. Travel costs can dramatically skew these percentages in unpredictable fashions. I prefer to initially cost the project ignoring travel expenses. A line item is then added for travel costs based on my estimate of the actual travel costs which will be incurred.

2. These costs assume that you are using a software development methodology which is compatible with government standards. Use of an incompatible development methodology, including many of the methodologies used for commercial software development will greatly increase your costs (in both absolute terms and as a percentage of project resources) in the following areas:

    • Document expenses (production, illustration, and update).

    • System design and detailed design (caused by the difficulties in maintaining traceability of requirements from the functional baseline through the allocated baseline and finally, to the product baseline).

    • Component and integration testing.

3. These costs assume that you are using automated tools to produce and maintain your documentation. Failure to use appropriate tools can easily double the cost of actually producing and updating each of the documents.

4. These costs assume that your company is familiar with developing software to government standards. Costs must be increased to allow for the learning curve if this is not the case.

5.4 Cost Reduction Through Libraries

The single most important cost saving measure you can take is to establish and maintain a usable library of software computer software units (CSUs). These modules should include not just the code required to implement the CSU, but also the design and test documentation. By making a conscientious effort to develop reusable components, and to reuse these components on multiple projects, I was able to reach the point where most of our software development projects involved less than 25 percent new code!

Because of the rich potential for cost savings by reusing existing software, *Teamplan* (described in Appendix B) includes built in features to encourage engineers to build from existing software design components, making modifications as necessary to fit the already developed components into the new system.

5.5 Cost Reduction Through Tailoring

The Federal Acquisition Regulations (FAR) defines tailoring as

> the process by which individual sections, paragraphs, or sentences of the selected specifications, standards, and related documents are reviewed and modified so that each one selected states only the Government's minimum requirements. Such tailoring need not be made a part of the basic specifications or standard but will vary with each application, dependent upon the nature of the acquisition.

Many contractor's believe that it is in their best interest to have the standards tailored so that they are required to produce as few documents as possible. As we discussed earlier in this book, this approach may save money in the short run but will cost money in the long run. It is your objective to tailor the requirements so that your costs are as low as possible *while still producing all of the documentation necessary to ensure that future projects will be able to reuse components developed during this project without writing any new documentation.* This can be accomplished using the following tailoring guidelines:

Tailoring Guidelines

1. For *system* level documents, attempt to: have the document eliminated; have two or more system-level documents combined; or have the content of the document reduced. Examples of system level documents are the System/Segment Design Document, the Version Description Document, and the Computer Resources Integrated Support Document.

2. For documents whose required content is closely duplicated by existing documentation, either from another program or from the manufacturer, attempt to have the existing documentation be declared acceptable for delivery without change. Examples of this type of document typically include the Computer System Operator's Manual, the Software Programmer's Manual, and reused software components which were documented using an older standard (such as DOD-STD-2167 or MIL-STD-1679).

3. For other documents, attempt to maintain and deliver the documentation on-line (using a tool such as *Government Standards Toolbox*), avoiding the significant costs associated with keeping a hard copy document current.

In addition, you should always attempt to reduce the time spent in reviews to the greatest extent possible. The government will normally not allow reviews to be skipped, but will often be receptive to the idea of combining multiple reviews into one meeting. Because much of the material presented at reviews tends to be redundant from one review to the next, combining reviews can save a considerable amount of time and expense.

Tailoring is also discussed Chaps. 9 and 11 of this book.

5.6 Cost Reduction Through Automated Production

Developing software to government standards requires painstaking attention to detail in producing documents, tracing requirements between documents, tracking of results, and configuration control. These tasks are ideally suited to automation using a software development environment (SDE). Cost effective development of software to government standards absolutely *requires* that you use automated tools tailored to this type of work.

5.7 Reducing Travel Costs

It is always in your best interest to schedule as many meetings and reviews at your facility as possible. It is much better for the government to fly four or five people to your facility than for you to fly a dozen (or more) people to a government facility.

As mentioned earlier, it is in your best interest to combine reviews and audits whenever possible. This is especially important if you will be traveling to the review. In addition, time spent actually at the review can be reduced considerably, often by as much as half, by using the following guidelines:

1.   Ensure that all parties who will be at the review have copies of all documents to be discussed well ahead of the review. When possible, it is also a good idea to provide copies of the viewgraphs you will be using at the review ahead of time.

2.   Request that questions about the documents be provided to you, in writing, prior to the review. Answer as many questions as possible over the telephone before the review. Use the review to discuss controversial questions only.

3.   Limit your presenters to their allotted time. Insist that they practice the talk ahead of time to find out how long their talk will last.

4.   During the review, be prompt to identify when the discussion is off-track. This is often a sign that you should assign an *action item* based on the discussion currently under way and

move the discussion to the next topic. An action item is a short task which is committed to by the government or by a contractor.

5.8   Tracking Costs

You will want to track the following cost related items throughout the project:

- Total cost to date for each task, total planned cost for each task, variance, estimated cost to complete, and estimated final variance.

- Actual and planned cost for each major project activity (system design, detailed design, code, etc.) and variance.

- Actual and planned cost for project work to date and variance.

- Actual and planned schedule for project work completed to date and variance.

- Amount by which the project can be expected to overrun or underrun its budget.

- How early or late the project is expected to be completed.

The software development environment described in Appendix B (*Teamplan*) automatically maintains this information.

5.9   Discussion Questions

1. We talked about the learning curve associated with developing software to government standards. As a contractor, what competitive advantages do you see to this learning curve?

2. Referring back to our cost hierarchy, you will notice that most technical work (top-level design, detail design, etc.) is not

explicitly shown. Instead, these costs are associated with the preparation of the technical content of an associated Data Item Deliverable. What advantages do you see to this approach? What disadvantages?

3.   We talked about cost reductions through libraries, tailoring, automated production, and reduced travel. What other items could you add to this list?

4.   For the complete list identified in Question 3, how would you rank the items according to cost saving potential? How would you rank the items according to ease of implementation? Which areas could benefit your company the most?

6 Managing Government Contracts

This chapter begins by introducing the concept of structured project management. The phases of a data processing project are discussed from the management perspective and these are contrasted with the project phases from a strictly technical perspective. Next, how to evaluate a project *from the contractor's perspective*, and how to prepare a project plan, is covered. Finally, we talk about requirements traceability, managing risk, and controlling expectations. This chapter is oriented toward the project manager on a government software development project, and will use examples and discussions which are specific to project management.

6.1 Structured versus Casual Project Management

I would estimate that nine out of ten project managers I've met use casual project management. Every project is managed a little differently. They seldom know what aspect of the project they will be working on later that day, much less in six months. They are familiar with many of the tools available to them but use them inconsistently. Projects often degenerate to the point where crisis management is the rule rather than the exception. Effective delegation of project management tasks is truly impossible because the tasks are not sufficiently well defined. The only way to train new project managers is a baptism by fire, starting with small projects and graduating to larger projects as experience is gained.

Portions of this chapter are taken from the author's book *Structured Computer Project Management*. (10)

This is not to say that the project managers I'm referring to are not successful. Quite the contrary, many of them are leaders in their field using just this approach. Their experience gives them the intuition needed to get the job done in this fluid environment. In spite of this, I contend that casual project management should be banished from the industry! Although the casual approach takes less work on your part, I believe that the formal techniques outlined in my book *Structured Computer Project Management* are worth the effort. Let me explain why I am so strongly opposed to an apparently successful approach to project management and why I wrote that book.

The cost and complexity of computer software has been increasing geometrically over the past 15 years, and I see no sign of this trend changing in the near future. Computer programs 250,000 to 2,000,000 lines of code long are common, and larger programs are not unheard of (some 25 million lines of code or longer). The cost of developing this code is rapidly outpacing the cost of the computer hardware it is designed to run on. WIth frightening regularity, I see lengthy, complex software development projects which are requiring two to five times the original estimate in terms of time and cost. Although some of this increase may be caused by estimation errors, much of the error is simply poor management during the project.

Reason 1: The increasing size and complexity of computer software development projects is rapidly making effective casual project management impossible.

Even the most successful project managers using casual project management are inconsistent. On one project they will be on time and on budget, while on the next project they may be 100 percent overrun before the project is completed. Large organizations are increasingly demanding consistent and predictable performance by their software teams.

Reason 2: Consistent, predictable performance is not possible using casual project management.

Using casual project management, delegation of project management responsibilities is virtually impossible. The tasks to be performed are simply not sufficiently well defined. In addition, the urgency of the need prevents a less experienced, and hence slower, individual from performing the work. The end result is that typical software development project managers work 60 to 70 hours per week and are under tremendous work-related stress.

Reason 3:   Using casual project management, to effectively delegate project management tasks while still retaining adequate control over the project is not possible.

Finally, the explosive growth of the computer software industry has created a tremendous demand for new project managers. Many organizations do not have the five to ten years required to allow a technical staff member to learn project management skills from experience. Schools certainly cannot teach casual project management, as shown by the almost total absence of data processing project management classes in this country.

Reason 4:   The learning curve for new project managers is unacceptably long when using casual project management.

6.2 Phases of a Data Processing Project

Some of the worst data processing project managers are competent during all phases of software development. How is this possible? Project management includes tasks that are not considered part of software development. The software development life cycle typically consists of design, code, test and deliver, and maintenance. The project management life cycle consists of analysis and evaluation; marketing; design; code, test and deliver; and post completion analysis. As shown in Fig. 6.1, the project manager becomes involved well-before software development commences,

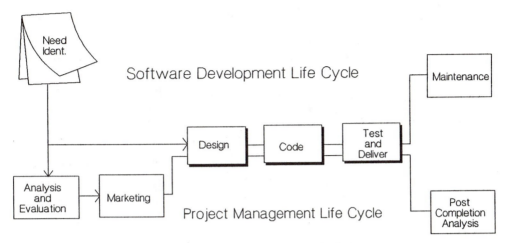

Figure 6.1 Phases of a project.

diverging from the software life cycle after system delivery. A project manager who ignores project analysis and evaluation, project marketing, and post-completion analysis is seldom successful. In the paragraphs that follow we will introduce each phase in the project management life cycle. Each is covered in depth in Roetzheim, 1988. (10)

6.2.1 Analysis and Evaluation Stage

It has been my experience that up to half of all potential software development projects are born losers. For example, some projects (as envisioned by the customer) are not technically feasible. Other projects are possible, but not within the framework of time and money that the customer is willing to accept. Some projects are so vaguely defined that the requirements cannot even be approximated. It is my belief that, in terms of bottom-line profitability, my most significant job as Senior Project Manager is to analyze and evaluate new projects to determine if it is *possible* to successfully accomplish the work at a profit. Even the best project team cannot perform adequately if the ground rules make a win impossible.

Figure 6.2 shows the significant actions accomplished during the analysis and evaluation stage. Information is obtained from customer documents and interviews with personnel in the customer's organization. During project analysis you will be expected to provide the following:

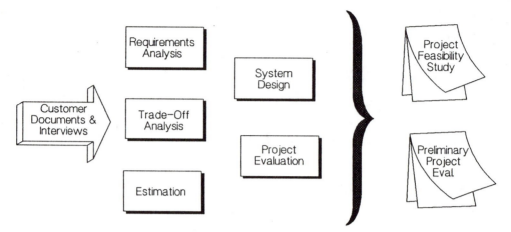

Figure 6.2 Analysis and evaluation.

- *Requirements analysis.* Determine major functional requirements, data sets, and information flows of the system. Examine the initial technical and economic feasibility of the proposed system.

- *Trade-off analysis.* Examine alternate ways of meeting the requirements that were identified. If a preferred alternative involves changes to the hardware or software configuration, try to convince the customer of the validity of the modification. If the preferred alternative points away from a computer solution – a fairly common result – present this alternative to the customer also.

- *Estimation.* Provide initial rough estimates of the system cost, delivery time, and functional capabilities. It is important to determine as early as possible whether the customer's expectations regarding these factors are realistic.

- *System design.* Select an initial system design which best meets the customer's objectives.

- *Project evaluation.* Estimate the expected value to your organization of performing the work, and prepare your initial estimate of the risks involved.

At the conclusion of the analysis and evaluation stage, you should prepare a *Project Feasibility Study* and a *Preliminary Project Evaluation.* Both documents are relatively informal and are typically prepared for internal use only (with summaries briefed to the customer). The Project Feasibility Study describes the major requirements, data sets, and information flows of the system along with your conclusions about the project's technical and economic feasibility. This report will also include the alternative approaches to meeting the requirements which were considered, and your reasons for accepting or rejecting each alternative. The proposed initial system design which forms the basis of your cost estimates is also included.

The Preliminary Project Evaluation references the Project Feasibility Study and presents initial rough estimates of the system cost, delivery time, and functional capabilities. In addition, the expected value to your organization of performing the work is included in this document.

6.2.2 Marketing Stage

During the marketing stage, you will normally prepare, or assist in the preparation of, the *Project Proposal.* Preparing a proposal is a vital step in project management, as discussed in Chap. 3.

6.2.3 Design Stage

A senior technical individual is primarily responsible for effective technical work. If you were a senior program designer, you would simply be concerned with preparing good design documents. You *are not* simply a senior technical individual. As a project manager, you must never forget that you are also a manager of people. During the program design stage, your efforts are normally primarily technical in nature. You may be actively participating in the work, and the people you work with are normally senior, mature individuals. Nevertheless, you should not neglect the management aspects of your position even during this stage. Some rules of thumb and hints which I have found useful in managing the program design team are:

- Create an atmosphere that promotes healthy competition among team members. Encourage peer pressure and rewards (as opposed to pressure from above) to promote productive, quality work.

- Make it clear throughout the project that every project team member fails if the project fails. Hard work by an individual is necessary but not sufficient for advancement and official rewards. Even the best performer loses if the project does not meet its goals.

- Communicate the project goals to project team members. Help them understand why the goals are important. Explain seemingly illogical requirements, even if the reason involves describing political-type decisions. In short, ensure that the project's goals become the project team's goals.

- When dealing with senior technical individuals, lead but do not push. I have a reputation as a hard driver because some projects were saved from failure only because the project team worked 16-hour days, seven days a week. Yet I can honestly state that I never told anyone to work overtime – I never needed to. The project team know the goals, why they are important, and they *want* to achieve those goals every bit as much as I. The only orders I ever gave were to take a weekend off to prevent total collapse from some dedicated individuals!

- Give people as much responsibility as they can handle. People in the computer field thrive on responsibility. Take every opportunity possible to publicly express total faith in the ability of individuals working for you.

- Trust your people. Have faith in their abilities and sense of responsibility. Expect 100 percent from everyone working for you, but let them decide what 100 percent is for them based on their current energy, health, and personal life. Do not watch the clock or nag your project team.

- If someone lets you down, have a long, frank discussion to express your disappointment. Actual threats are not necessary or appropriate, although implied threats should be clear. After receiving a commitment from the employee for improvement, forgive totally as if nothing happened. Look especially hard for ways to publicly praise this employee.

- If someone lets you down a second time, hammer hard and fast. It is true that one bad apple can spoil the whole barrel. The atmosphere of trust and teamwork you must foster cannot work with employees who do not function in that environment. In addition, marginal or bad employees will require significantly too much of your valuable time to justify the effort. I normally insist that such an individual be removed from my project, and recommend that he/she be fired or demoted.

- Healthy conflict focuses on an issue rather than personal attacks. For example, a conflict about the best method of designing or coding a function is healthy, while a conflict involving insults about a person's design or coding abilities is unhealthy. Avoid getting involved in a healthy conflict unless it is prolonged, in which case you should step in and resolve it one way or the other. On the other hand, you should never tolerate *any* unhealthy conflict. Talk to both parties about the conflict in private and put a complete and emphatic stop to it.

It is during this stage that you must thoroughly understand the concept of *scope*. Government software projects tend to grow in functionality as the development progresses. The design is reviewed by a large number of people, each of whom tends to add some features or otherwise modify the design somewhat. Managers who acquiesce to every requested modification will find the software has grown far beyond the money/time allocated to its development. Suggested changes must be divided into three categories:

1. Those that are within the original requirements described in the contract.

2.   Those that are not within the original requirements described
        in the contract but whose implementation has little or no
        impact on the system's cost and development effort.

3.   Those that are not within the original requirements described
        in the contract and whose implementation does have a
        significant impact on the system's cost or development effort.

Category 1 suggestions must be implemented under the contract.
Category 2 suggestions should be implemented in the interest of good will
and fairness. Category 3 suggestions should be clearly identified as being *out
of scope*, and hence should only be implemented if additional time and
dollars are provided.

6.2.4 Code, Test, and Deliver Stage

During earlier project stages, your success or failure was primarily dependent
on your technical skills and ability to plan and organize. During the code,
test and deliver stage your capability as a leader and manager will be the
primary factor in your success or failure. As project manager, you will not
normally be responsible for writing any actual code, but you *will* be
responsible for ensuring an accurate implementation of the design. You will
also be responsible for tracking the project in terms of cost, manpower, and
schedule. In addition, you will spend a significant amount of time managing
the customer, marketing for future work, and performing quality control
activities.

6.2.5 Post-Completion Analysis Stage

All too often, a project ends when the software is delivered. This shortsight-
ed approach to project management leads to repeated mistakes within the
organization, static estimating and planning tools which do not improve with
experience, lost marketing opportunities, and project team members who are
unfairly denied performance evaluations by the only individual truly qualified
to recognize their achievements.

As shown in Fig. 6.3, during the post-completion analysis stage you
will normally produce

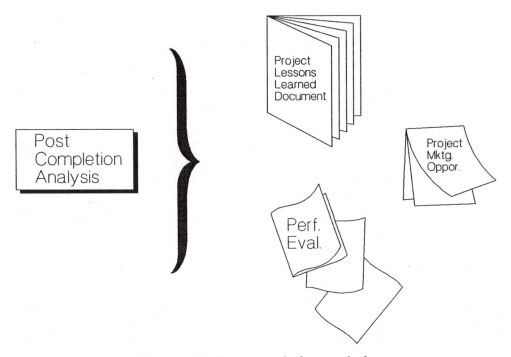

Figure 6.3 Post-completion analysis.

- a *Project Lessons Learned* document, which is an informal, internal report for use by other project managers in your organization. This report is primarily used to document major problems encountered and their solutions. The first chapter normally presents an assessment of the success of the project in terms of levels of satisfaction by all concerned parties. The Project Lessons Learned document should describe technological and other advances which might be valuable to current or future projects within the organization. Finally, an appendix is normally included to promulgate updates to various estimating and planning tools used in your organization.

- A *Project Marketing Opportunities* report which documents marketing opportunities identified during the project which should receive follow-up attention. This report is normally provided to the marketing department for action.

- *Performance evaluations* for each project team member should be prepared at the conclusion of the project. Project team members have a right to expect an evaluation after even the shortest project. These evaluations are normally informally reviewed with each team member, then delivered to the manager responsible for the individual's performance reviews. Project evaluations are sometimes made part of the employee's permanent file but more often serve as written input to the employee's supervisor for use during periodic evaluations.

6.3 Project Evaluation

While working as the Senior Project Manager for a midsized computer company, I was called in by the Chief Executive Officer (CEO) to discuss a new project. Our parent company had requested that we develop software to automate the process of measuring ocean bottom depth readings and producing navigation charts. Our CEO had given an "off the top of his head" estimate that the work would cost $50,000 and require three months to complete. He asked me to manage the project.

I spent the next week evaluating the project. I read several documents describing the proposed work. I talked to the end users of the system to find out how the work was currently performed and how they envisioned the new system working. Finally, I quantified the task to be performed in a top-level functional design, prepared a rough work breakdown structure, and used a function-based estimating model to cost the system. I concluded that the software should cost $225,000 and take nine months to deliver if we used an accelerated development schedule. *If I did everything RIGHT, I would deliver the system with a 350 percent overrun!* Preventing disasters like this is what project evaluation is all about.

Because my evaluation was quantitative, I was able to defend my analysis to senior management and the customer. In the end, the new estimate was accepted, allowing the project to be brought in on time and on budget. A sure disaster was turned into a victory. Careful project evaluation is the only way to avoid those career killing project failures.

6.3.1 Three Critical Decision Points

A *critical decision point* is a milestone in the project's life at which the project is evaluated and a decision is made whether to proceed to the next stage of development or to shelve the project. Computer projects normally have three critical decision points: (1) whether to proceed from feasibility to design (whether to start work on the allocated baseline), (2) whether to proceed from design to development (whether to start work on the product baseline)c and (3) whether to proceed from development to operation (see Fig. 6.4). Each of these decision points has the following characteristics:

- Revised project cost and performance estimates can be significantly more accurate than previous estimates.

- Substantial additional funds must be committed to the project in order to proceed to the next stage.

- The project is at a logical stopping point. Project-related documents produced as part of the current stage are complete and can be archived for later use. Organizational disruptions are minimized, because one group of professionals is completing its work and a second group has not begun.

The documents produced as part of a contractor's project evaluation stage will be used as a basis for the first critical decision – whether or not to bid the project.

6.3.2 Completing the Project Financial Analysis

I will never forget the first formal analysis of a large project which I conducted. Our company was bidding on a contract to supply 95 minicomputers plus maintenance to the U.S. Forest Service. A junior project manager had written the proposal, the costing was complete and approved, and I was asked to review the numbers in preparation for a corporate brief describing the project. Because standard profit rates and equipment costs were used throughout, the project review was considered a mere formality. I ran the project through an evaluation model and was shocked to discover that, although the total revenue and net income figures were very good, the return on investment (ROI) was a totally unacceptable 4 percent. Worse yet, I projected that the negative cash flow during the first year would result in a peak capitalization requirement of over $5 million just to keep the project afloat! The project analysis allowed us to adjust maintenance pricing and lease terms to improve the ROI to an acceptable level. Because we were able to demonstrate a favorable ROI and long-term positive cash flow, we were able to obtain the needed capital from our parent company to meet the initial shortfall. That one day spent modeling the project's financial performance prevented us from making a mistake which might have been fatal to our division!

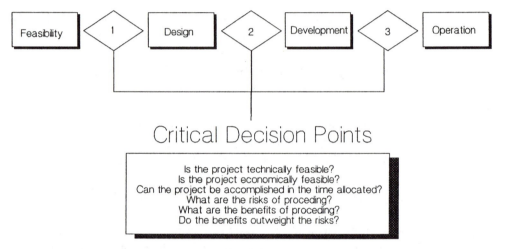

Figure 6.4 Three critical decision points.

The procedure to compute the basic project statistics is straightforward but tedious. Some basic accounting knowledge is certainly helpful, although not required. For all evaluation models the project is treated as an independent cost center, which means that the project is evaluated as a small entity separate from the remainder of your company. The goal is simple:

This process is described in detail in Roetzheim. (10, 11) In addition, *Teamplan* (described in Appendix B) will perform this analysis automatically.

Treating the project as an independent cost center, predict the month-end status of all relevant accounts for the cost center throughout the expected life of the project.

6.3.3 Preparing a Project Risk Evaluation

No project evaluation is complete without some estimate of the overall risk to which your company will be exposed by accepting the project. Although techniques are available to deal with project risk (see Sec. 6.6), we would prefer to avoid high-risk projects to begin with. In addition, most companies expect to receive a higher profit margin on riskier projects. As shown in Fig. 6.5, estimating a project's risk involves three steps: (1) estimate the likelihood-of-failure factor, (2) estimate the consequence-of-failure factor, and (3) combine these factors to determine the project risk factor. Failure is a nonspecific term which means that the project was not able to meet its technical, cost, or schedule goals by a significant margin. The definition of "significant margin" varies from project to project and customer to customer. Once again, this process is described in detail in Roetzheim (10) and *Government Standards Toolbox* will assist in performing a project's risk analysis.

Figure 6.5 Project risk evaluation.

6.4 Preparing the Project Plan

The *project plan* is a formal or informal document which is both a tool used by you throughout the project and a deliverable item submitted to your management. It is also common for the project plan to be submitted to the customer, and for relevant portions of the project plan to be available to your project team. On government projects, the software oriented project plan is called the *Software Development Plan* (SDP) and the system oriented project plan is called the *System Engineering Management Plan*, or SEMP. The SEMP normally includes:

- definitions of project activities and required results (deliverables)

- dependency definitions for tasks

- resource estimates for each project activity, often expressed in staff-days for people

- risk estimates for each activity, and plans to reduce the risk or the impact of failure for high-risk tasks

- activity schedules which include the highlight milestones and other checkpoints for formal progress reviews

- resource budgets and loading estimates (resource requirements by time period) for personnel, equipment, and other resources which must be tracked.

The software team may also be required to contribute to one or more specialty plans which support the SEMP, including:

- *Technical performance measurement*, which allocates critical factors such as CPU cycles, storage space, input-output bandwidth, or accuracy constraints among project components. Technical performance measurement is covered in more depth in Chap. 7.

- *Maintainability*, which analyzes the ease of maintaining and enhancing the final system. The software team may be required to demonstrate an approach to building maintainability into the software using techniques such as modularity, table driven software, built in hooks for future expandability, and so on.

- *Quality*, which requires an explanation of your company's software quality control procedures.

- *Human engineering*, which involves describing your approach to designing the software human interface. It may be valuable to include prototypes of the human interface to support this specialty plan.

- *Safety*, which may involve demonstrating how the software will be designed so that critical components will include safeguards to prevent the software from failing in a catastrophic fashion.

- *Reliability*, which requires that you document your method of measuring and documenting software reliability.

As a minimum, each of these specialty plans will include the following information: (1) objective, (2) activity definition, (3) responsibilities, (4) schedules, and (5) resource definition (manpower requirements, etc.)

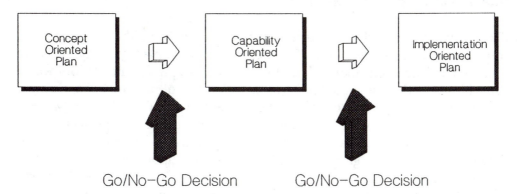

Figure 6.6 Software planning.

Software planning must be an iterative process. As shown in Fig. 6.6, software planning is normally accomplished in three stages

- A *concept-oriented plan* is prepared based on a rough under-standing of the system concepts (top-level requirements). The concept oriented plan will typically be prepared as part of the proposal effort.

- After the system requirements are clearly defined and well-understood, a *capability-oriented plan* can be prepared.

- When the program detail design is complete, an *implementation-oriented plan* can be prepared.

The implementation-oriented plan is then used during software production to track the project, with adjustments made to the plan as necessary. Although there will be significant carryover from one stage to the next, it should be clear that the amount of detail and accuracy is significantly higher at each stage. The transition periods from one plan to the next correspond to the go/no-go decisions discussed in Sec. 6.3.1. Each of these software planning stages will be briefly discussed.

6.4.1 Concept-Oriented Plan

The concept-oriented plan can be prepared as soon as the rough system requirements are understood. The concept-oriented plan typically includes detailed information about all tasks through completion of the Software Specification Review and top-level descriptions of the detailed design, coding, and testing related tasks. The concept-oriented plan will, however, include all known major milestones throughout the entire project. The concept oriented plan is typically based 80 percent on inputs from the project management group and 20 percent on inputs from the project technical staff. Total software cost estimates at this stage are "ballpark figures" and can be expected to be accurate plus or minus 50 percent.

6.4.2 Capability-Oriented Plan

The capability-oriented plan revolves around the functional capabilities identified in the Program Functional Specification, with schedules and cost estimates based on these functional capabilities. Detailed time and cost planning for both design and coding stages are possible, although the task breakdowns for these areas are based on functional capabilities only. The capability-oriented plan normally takes the project through the Critical Design Review. At this stage, rough functional and/or data element costing metrics become available, allowing total software cost estimates to be prepared which are accurate to plus or minus 25 percent. The capability-oriented plan is typically based 50 percent on inputs from the project management group and 50 percent on inputs from the project technical staff.

6.4.3 Implementation-Oriented Plan

The implementation-oriented plan can be prepared after completion of the detailed program design and is based on coding, testing, and integration of specific program modules. For the first time, the plan will have a true one-to-one correlation with a physical unit of software. Finally, true functional and data element metrics are available, allowing total software cost estimates to be prepared which are accurate to plus or minus 10 percent. In addition, it is only at this point that reasonable use can be made of Lines of Code (LOC) based costing models. The implementation-oriented plan is typically based 20 percent on inputs from the project management group and 80 percent on inputs from the project technical staff.

6.4.4 The Planning Process

The actual planning process during each of the three scheduling stages is identical. As shown in Fig. 6.7, the steps required are as follows:

1.   Decompose the tasks to be performed.

2.   Define the dependency relations between the tasks.

3.   Estimate the resources required to perform each task.

4.   Perform a risk analysis for each task.

5.   Schedule the project by scheduling all tasks to be performed.

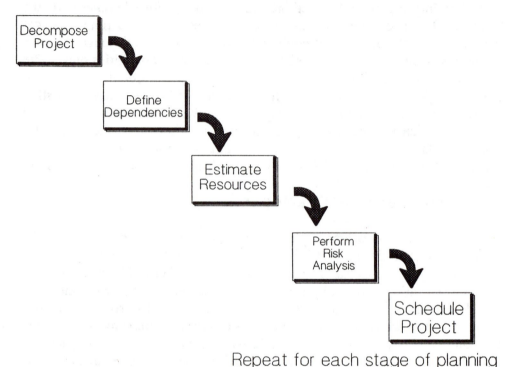

Repeat for each stage of planning

Figure 6.7 Software planning process.

        This process is then repeated for each stage of software scheduling.
Of course, the fact that each successive plan is based to a large extent on the
previous plan implies that each is really a revision to the project plan (as
opposed to a new plan).   How these steps are performed, and the tools
necessary to accomplish each task successfully, are described in Roetzheim.
(10)

6.5 Requirements Traceability

One critical aspect of government software development projects that is not normally present in commercial projects is requirements traceability. The issue is really one of accountability. Remember the three baselines identified in Chap. 2? The functional baseline described the functions the system must accomplish. The allocated baseline identified which configuration item would be responsible for implementation of each function identified in the functional baseline. Finally, the product baseline was a finished specification of the final product. The government insists that the functional requirements which are identified as part of the functional baseline be traceable directly to specific capabilities within the allocated baseline, which must then be directly traceable to specific capabilities within the product baseline. This requirements traceability through the three configuration baselines must be specific and well-documented, including detailed testing of the product baseline to verify claims. One important aspect of any software development environment designed to assist with software development to government standards is the ability to automatically document this requirements traceability.

6.6 Managing Risk

Risk management is extremely important on virtually every government project. Performing a detailed risk analysis is useful to you for the following four reasons

1. Resources (time, money, and management attention) can be allocated based on each task's risk.

2. Candidate tasks for prototyping can be identified. Prototyping risky software functions or modules is often the most powerful method available to you to reduce risk.

3. A risk-optimized schedule can be generated. A risk-optimized schedule attempts to schedule risky tasks as early as possible in the project to allow sufficient time for recovery in the event of failure.

4.   Contingency planning is possible.

6.6.1 Process of Risk Analysis

Software development projects typically have four types of risk associated with each task: (1) network risk, (2) technical risk, (3) schedule, and (4) cost risk. Schedule and cost risk are often considered together because schedule delays and cost overruns nearly always go hand-in-hand. For each of these types of task related risk, we will want to determine the task's overall *task risk factor* (R_t). This will often involve first calculating the likelihood-of-failure factor (L_f) and consequence-of-failure factor (C_f). Fig. 6.8 summarizes this process. Specific guidelines for calculating these factors can be found in Roetzheim. (10)

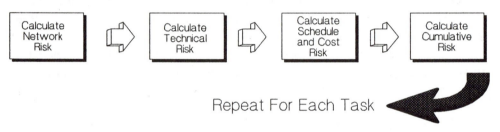

Figure 6.8 Task risk analysis.

6.6.2 Products of Risk Analysis

To document your risk analysis, you will normally produce a ranked table of each task's risk factor in the risk areas of network, technical, schedule/cost, and cumulative. You will normally want to document risk-reduction planning and contingency planning efforts for high-risk tasks. Be sure to discuss high-risk tasks with your technical staff to determine if the task can be modified to eliminate or reduce project risk. Finally, be sure to discuss high-risk areas with the most important member of your project team – your customer.

If the project is unusually high risk, the government may require that you prepare a *Risk Management Program Plan* and/or a *Risk Handling Plan*. A Risk Management Program Plan might use the outline suggested by DSMC. (3)

Risk Management Program Plan
Suggested Outline

I. Introduction
   1. Overview
   2. Applicable documents/definitions
   3. Management organization/responsibilities
   4. Scheduled milestones/reviews

II. Identification and Assessment
   5. Survey and identification
   6. Risk assessment models
   7. Flow/level assessment/treatment
   8. System hierarchy and risk tree

III. Analysis and reduction
   9. Reduction methods
   10. Analysis methods
   11. Risk abatement plan
   12. Prototyping/simulations/tests

IV. Appendices
   A. Survey form
   B. Report format and content
   C. Assessment tables/graphs
   D. Plan format and content

The Risk Handling Plan is submitted for each high risk task, and typically addresses the following items:

- nature of the risk,

- consequences of failure,

- alternatives considered along with the impact of each alternative,

- recommended approach to reducing the risk and the impact of this approach on the project's cost, schedule, and technical performance,

- organization and personnel responsible for monitoring this item and for implementing the risk reduction plan,

- schedule for implementation of the risk reduction plan, including key decision points at which the success (or failure) of components will be measured and appropriate actions taken.

6.7 Controlling Expectations

You must remember that you are responsible for managing the customer's expectations. No customer has a clear, complete, and firm concept of *exactly* what the final product will be like at the end of a project. Their expectations for the final product develop and mature during the project, primarily based on discussions with you and your programming team. If you emphasize the bells and whistles of your design during development, they will expect those bells and whistles and be disappointed or mad if they are not delivered. If you emphasize the functional aspects of your program, they will be pleasantly surprised when you deliver what you promised along with some beneficial additional features. In short:

Keep the customer focused on the steak, not the sizzle!

6.8 Chapter Review

Project Management Checklist

_____   Were project engineers, software designers, and programmers heavily involved in the planning?

_____   Was the project decomposed into activities, each with a tangible output?

_____   Were the resource requirements for each activity estimated?

_____   Are responsibilities for each activity clear?

_____   Are status points included for measurement of progress and resource consumption?

_____   Is contingency funding planned for, either implicitly or explicitly?

_____   Was the schedule adjusted to obtain a plan optimized in terms of time, cost, risk, or some combination?

_____   Was approval of the plan obtained from all people who must support the plan (or not oppose it) in order for the project to be successful?

6.9 Discussion Questions

1.   Does your company use structured or unstructured project management? Why or why not?

2.   What criteria do you think your company should use when evaluating new projects? Rank them in relative order of priority.

7 Special Topics

Several topics are covered in this chapter which government software development projects emphasize. These topics are

- Configuration management

- Independent verification and validation

- Software quality assurance

- Technical performance measurement

We conclude by describing some "tricks of the trade" which will improve the quality of your work when developing software to government standards.

7.1 Configuration Management

Configuration management is an extremely important topic on government projects. Government projects are typically quite large and complex, often involving concurrent development by multiple vendors. The government insists that configuration control procedures be carefully followed throughout the project. This section will discuss government configuration management procedures, including the following topics:

- The four basic aspects of configuration management

- Classes and priorities of changes

134

- Change control forms and procedures

- The configuration control board

- Configuration management general requirements

7.1.1 The Four Basic Aspects of Configuration Management

We stated previously that the government bases configuration management on a principle called *baseline management*. Software will be divided into three baselines during development

1. *Functional Baseline*: defines the functions the software will perform

2. *Allocated Baseline*: identifies a specific configuration item (CSCIs and CSCs) which will perform each function

3. *Product Baseline*: the approved or conditionally approved software

Each configuration item will be baselined and placed under configuration management to control the product (design or code) until it is ready for the next baseline. This configuration management involves:

1. *Configuration identification* (documented in the appropriate Data Item Description and approved at the appropriate formal review),

2. *Configuration control* (formal change control procedures),

3. *Configuration status accounting*,

4. *Configuration audits*.

Changes to a baselined configuration are not discouraged, they are simply controlled. Let's start by looking at the classes of changes as identified by the government.

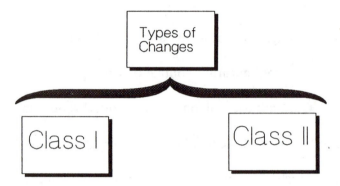

Figure 7.1 Categories of changes.

7.1.2 Classes and Priorities of Changes

As shown in Fig. 7.1, changes are divided into two major categories:

1.   *Class I Changes*

2.   *Class II Changes*

Class I changes have a significant impact on the software's user interface, technical performance, efficiency, cost, or schedule. In addition, any changes involving modifications to the interfaces between configuration items would normally be considered Class I changes. Class I changes must be approved by a configuration control board (discussed later).

Class II changes are considered minor changes. Examples include editorial changes to documentation, changes to the internal structure of software if the impact is localized and not apparent to the user, and material substitutions for hardware. Remember that changes impacting the program's cost or schedule would not be Class II changes. Although the government must still approve these changes, the changes do not need to go through the configuration control board. Approval can be granted by the government contracting officer technical representative (COTR) or by a government plant representative if available.

The contractor is responsible for determining if a change should be considered Class I or Class II, but the government representative approving the Class II changes may determine that the proposed change should be treated as a Class I change.

Both Class I and Class II changes are further prioritized as emergency, urgent, or routine according to the criticality of the change.

7.1.3 Change Control Forms and Procedures

When each document is completed, a number is assigned which is unique to this program. Changes to the document are then carefully controlled. As shown in Fig. 7.2, five forms may be used during the change control process

1. The *Engineering Change Proposal* (ECP) is used by the contractor to propose Class I changes. This form includes a description of the change, justification for the change, configuration items effected by the change, the impact on integrated logistic support and operational effectiveness, impact on the project's cost and/or schedule, and results of trade-off analyses looking at alternate solutions, if appropriate. ECPs are submitted to the configuration control board.

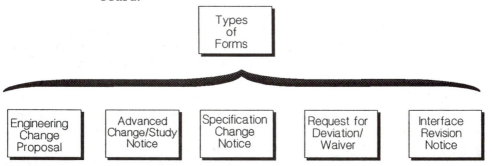

Figure 7.2 Change control forms.

2. The *Advanced Change/Study Notice* (ACSN) form is used to seek government approval to expend engineering effort to prepare a formal Engineering Change Proposal. It includes the need for the change, the configuration item(s) effected, alternatives to be considered, and a rough cost estimate. A preliminary ECP may be used in place of an ACSN. In either

case, the form is submitted to the government which may reject the change or authorize the necessary engineering effort to prepare a formal ECP. Note that the "approval" is authorization to prepare an ECP, *not* approval of the change itself.

3.   The *Specification Change Notice* (SCN) is used to propose, transmit, and record changes to a specification. ECPs which will affect a specification (System/Segment Specification, for example) must have an SCN form attached. Section 8.4 addresses changes to specifications in more detail.

4.   A *Request for Deviation/Waiver* is used to request and document temporary departures from the specifications when a permanent departure would not be acceptable. Although this form primarily applies to hardware, software development projects may use a Request for Deviation/Waiver if you plan to make preliminary or phased deliveries where the software as initially delivered will not meet the full requirements.

5.   The *Interface Revision Notice* (IRN) is used to propose, transmit, and record changes to an approved Interface Requirements Document or Interface Design Document. ECPs which will affect one of these two documents must have an IRN form attached.

Figure 7.3 summarizes the change control process. A change is initiated by the contractor, government, subcontractor, or one of the working groups. If the change is a Class I change and will involve significant expenditure of effort to prepare the ECP, an ACSN or preliminary ECP is prepared and submitted to the government for approval. If approved, a formal ECP is prepared. For Class I changes, the ECP will include:

- a description of the problem and the proposed change,

- alternatives considered and a trade-off analysis, if appropriate, to show why the selected alternative is the best,
- analysis showing that the proposed change will solve the problem and will not introduce new problems,

- an estimate of the impact on the project's cost and schedule,

- impact if not implemented.

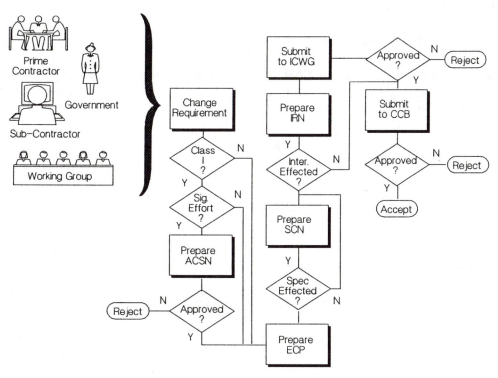

Figure 7.3 Change control process.

For Class II changes, the ECP may be shortened to include as little as simply a description of the problem and the proposed change.

If the ECP affects any approved specifications, a Specification Change Notice form is prepared. This applies to both Class I and Class II changes.

If the ECP affects an Interface Requirements Specification or Interface Design Document, an Interface Revision Notice is prepared. The Interface Revision Notice is submitted to the Interface Control Working Group (ICWG), which will review and approve or disapprove the change.

This step simply ensures that the change to the interface will not adversely impact others. If the change is approved by the ICWG, it is passed on to the configuration control board for final action. If the configuration control board approves the ECP, then the attached Interface Revision Notice is automatically approved at the same time.

7.1.4 The Configuration Control Board

The Configuration Control Board (CCB) is responsible for reviewing and approving changes to the configuration baseline. The CCB typically includes a representative from the

- program office (chairman),

- end users of the final system,

- government contracting office.

In addition, representatives from the training command, logistics command, manufacturing, and engineering may attend.

7.1.5 Configuration Management General Requirements

Within the contractor's organization, a configuration management system must support

- a software *and documentation* library management system which supports check in and check out capabilities, change tracking, access control, and archiving,

- tools to export or reference common information from one document to another, and to ensure that each of these documents referencing common information stays current and accurate throughout the change process,

- tools to support requirements traceability through multiple documents,

- the ability to do version control and baselining,

- internal or external approval of changes electronically prior to incorporation in the final documents/source code,

- configuration status accounting. Configuration status accounting provides traceability of configuration changes, Engineering Change Proposals, and related forms.

7.1.6 Configuration Management Checklist

_____   Does senior management recognize the importance of configuration management?

_____   Do the configuration management procedures adequately encompass the entire software life cycle?

_____   Is an automated configuration management system installed *and used* throughout development?

_____   Are all project team members aware of the importance of configuration management and the proper procedures to be followed?

_____   Are the configuration management procedures and the current product baseline periodically audited by the project manager?

_____   Are all concerned individuals, including subcontractors, properly integrated into the configuration management procedures?

7.2   Independent Verification and Validation

The government's strong interest in independent verification and validation, or IV&V, is a natural consequence of its desire for requirements traceability throughout the project. IV&V is normally included in the approval process for the three configuration baselines (functional, allocated, and product).

Verification matches the new baseline against the requirements identified in the previous baseline to ensure that all requirements have been satisfied. *Validation* matches the new baseline against the original requirements for the system to ensure that the final product will meet the end user objectives. Verification and validation are normally performed by an organization not directly involved in the product development, hence the term *independent*.

IV&V relies on documentation reviews, contractor test monitoring, and independent testing to evaluate the products making up each of the baselines. Obviously, much of the work involved in IV&V relies on the results of test and evaluation. This testing is divided into two categories.

1. *Development Test and Evaluation*, which is conducted to verify that design objectives have been meet, minimize risk, estimate the functional performance of the final system, and evaluate compatibility and interoperability with other systems. The emphasis during development test and evaluation is on validation.

2. *Operational Test and Evaluation*, is conducted by the end users to verify that the final system meets the end-user objectives and to determine impacts, if any, on end-user operations when the system is installed. The emphasis during operational test and evaluation is on verification.

As shown in Fig. 7.4, development test and evaluation is further divided into four subcategories.

1. *DT-0* is accomplished during the concept exploration phase to evaluate alternative system concepts, technologies, and designs.

2. *DT-I* is accomplished during the demonstration and validation phase to determine the preferred technical approach, including the identification of technical risks and feasible solutions.

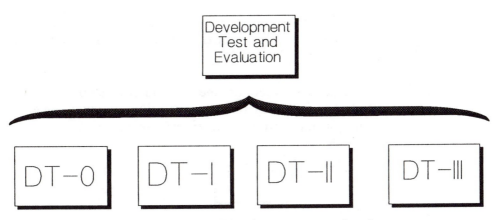

Figure 7.4 Development test & evaluation.

3. *DT-II* is conducted during the full scale development phase to demonstrate that the design meets its required specifications in all areas.

4. *DT-III* is conducted after the final system is completed.

As shown in Fig. 7.5, operational test and evaluation is further divided into five subcategories:

1. *OT-0* is conducted during the concept exploration phase to evaluate the operational impact of candidate technical approaches.

2. *OT-I* is conducted during the demonstration and validation phase to estimate the operational effectiveness and suitability of the candidate system.

3. *OT-II* is conducted during full scale development to verify the system's operational effectiveness and to evaluate tactics and procedures for operational use of the final system.

4.   *OT-III* is conducted prior to final testing of the completed system to verify that the final system meets the objectives of the end user.

5.   *OT-IV* is conducted on the completed system, and may include evaluation of the system's utility in a new environment, new application, or to meet a new need.

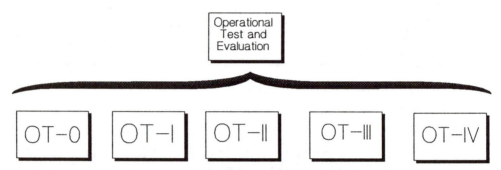

Figure 7.5 Operational test & evaluation.

The testing is coordinated using a document called the *Test and Evaluation Master Plan* (TEMP). DODI 5000.3-M-1 specifies the outline for the TEMP. In addition, IV&V will often involve system simulation both to check project feasibility and to provide results against which the "as built" test results can be compared.

Required TEMP Outline

Part I. Program Background
1. Mission background
2. System objective
3. Required technical characteristics
4. Required operational characteristics
5. Critical issues
6. Interface/coordination

Part II. Program Summary
1. Management
2. Integrated schedule

Part III. DT&E Outline
1. DT&E to date
2. DT&E planned
3. Pre-production qualification testing and evaluation
4. Production qualification testing and evaluation
5. Special requirements for system/subsystem verification
6. Critical DT&E items

Part IV. OT&E Outline
1. Critical operational issues
2. OT&E to date
3. Future OT&E
4. Critical OT&E items

Part V. Test Resource Summary
1. Test articles
2. Threat systems
3. Test targets
4. Test support
5. Computer simulations, models, and testbeds
6. Test sites
7. Special requirements
8. OT&E funding requirements

Part VI. Bibliography

7.3 Software Quality Assurance

Software defects can be divided into four broad categories: (1) requirements defects, (2) design defects, (3) code defects, and (4) documentation defects. In general, I have found that defects by category are about as
follows:

- Requirements defects: 20%

- Design defects: 20%

- Code defects: 40%

- User documentation defects: 20%

As shown in Fig. 7.6, the cost to find and repair defects is highest for
requirements defects and lowest for documentation defects. With a little
thought, the relative costs will make sense. Requirements defects normally
result in improper design, code, and documentation. Design defects result
in improper code and documentation. Code defects can be limited to code
problems.
   Requirements defects are a failure of the program requirements
documents to accurately and fully describe the customer's requirements and
needs. Requirements defects typically show up in the

- System/Segment Specification

- System/Segment Design Document

- Software Requirements Specification

- Interface Requirements Specification

Some common problems include:

- functional requirements which were left out,

- functional requirements which were inaccurately described,

- functional requirements which are technically or operationally infeasible,

- requirements which conflict with each other,

- inaccurate or missing constraints on the design,

- incorrect, incomplete, or missing descriptions of the input and output data and format.

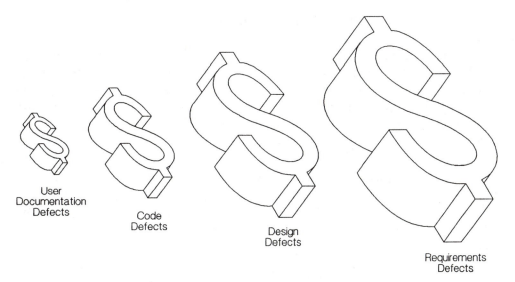

User
Documentation
Defects

Code
Defects

Design
Defects

Requirements
Defects

Figure 7.6 Defect cost.

Design defects are defects caused by a failure of the design team to properly design and document the system so that all requirements described in the requirements documents are properly met. Design defects typically show up in the Software Design Document or the Interface Design Document. Some common problems include:

- inconsistencies among or incompleteness of the derived requirements.   Derived requirements are lower level requirements based on higher level requirements identified earlier.

- a program design which omits some required function(s) or which implements the function in the wrong manner. A common example is a program design which will not operate properly over the full possible range of input data.

- a design which is incompatible with the hardware, operating system, language, or state of the art in technology,

- failure to conform to structured programming guidelines.

In addition to classifying software defects into one of these four categories (requirements, design, code, or documentation), it is often useful to assign a level of severity to defects. These defect severity ratings are especially useful when deciding if a program with known defects is impaired enough to prevent delivery. Government contracts typically use a prioritization scheme such as following:

- *Priority 1.* An error which causes an unexpected program termination; which jeopardizes personal safety; or which prevents the accomplishment of a critical function of the program.

- *Priority 2.* An error which significantly and adversely affects the ability of the program to accomplish a critical function and for which there is no alternative work-around solution.

- *Priority 3.* An error which significantly and adversely affects the ability of the program to accomplish a critical function and for which there is a reasonable alternative work-around solution.

- *Priority 4.* An error which is an operator inconvenience or annoyance and does not affect a critical program function.

- *Priority 5.* All other errors.

The primary tool you will use for quality control is the *peer review* (or program walk-through). Peer review can be an effective technique during all stages of development – requirements definition, design, and coding. Peer review during the requirements definition stage ensures that the requirements are properly defined. Peer review during the design stage initially involves review of the hierarchical program structure, followed by review of the detailed pseudocode. Peer review during the coding stage involves review of actual program listings.

Two common errors many companies make when implementing a peer review process are to ignore *accountability* and *momentum*. When a company keeps the peer review process completely informal, or has peer reviews with massive numbers of participants, each individual reviewer has little or no accountability for the effectiveness of his or her review. As with everything else in life, lack of accountability assures a mediocre-at-best performance. If a company holds infrequent peer reviews, covering completed major sections of a document (or an entire document), the momentum behind the work completed to date prevents major changes in direction from being practical. In effect, the reviewers are presented with a "fait accompli" and are forced to make the best of a possibly bad situation with minor modifications to the existing work.

To ensure that the peer review process is effective, you should follow these general guidelines:

- Reviews should involve as few people as possible, and each reviewer should be forced to accept responsibility for work accepted during the review.

- Reviews should be conducted frequently and should cover small portions of the work, guiding major decisions during their early stages. Reviews should normally cover two to five pages of design materials or one to five program modules.

- Reviews should be conducted on the raw material of requirements and design documents, emphasizing the content of the material. The individuals responsible for the actual work should then take the approved requirements/design and produce the smooth material for use in the document.

- Reviewers should have at least four hours (and perhaps up to several days) to study the material prior to the review meeting.

- Your schedule should include adequate time and hours for your senior software engineers to conduct these reviews. They should not be expected to do this work in addition to a full-time work load of their own.

- Reviews should be conducted only when the material to be reviewed is the best work the developer is capable of producing. Reviews are *not* a chance for a developer to have someone else do his or her work. Reviews which identify consistently slipshod work are a waste of time by all concerned and should not be tolerated by the reviewers or by you.

- In general, managers should not attend peer reviews. An exception is technical managers (senior technical individuals who also perform some management functions).

7.4 Technical Performance Measurement

System requirements (requirements for the performance of the final product) can be divided into allocable and non-allocable requirements. Allocable requirements can be allocated to specific configuration items or program modules. Examples include processing time, memory requirements, disk-based storage requirements, and accumulative error. Non-allocable requirements can not be divided. An example would be software development standards which must be followed by all software engineers.

Of the allocable requirements, some may be considered particularly critical to the success of the project, or of a particularly high risk. These parameters are then candidates for technical performance measurements. The purpose of technical performance measurement is to

- document actual versus planned technical performance during the project,

- identify developing problems in meeting key technical objectives,

- support the evaluation of the program impact from proposed changes,

Parameters selected for tracking should meet the following criteria:

1. they should be directly measurable during development to evaluate progress,

2. they should be significant predictors of the final success or failure of the system.,

3. it should be possible to determine time-phased values and tolerance bands for the parameters during the project life.

For each parameter measured using technical performance measurement, you will need to track each of the following values on a regular basis, normally monthly.

- *Planned value*: including tolerance band if known

- *Demonstrated value*: based on actual measurements

- *Specification requirement*: the value(s) which the specifications require be attained prior to completion of the project

- *Current estimate*: the current predicted value for this parameter upon delivery of the system

- *Demonstrated technical variance*: the difference between the planned value and the demonstrated value at this time

- *Predicted technical variance*: the predicted difference between planned value and demonstrated value at completion of the system.

Government Standards Toolbox (described in appendix B) supports all aspects of technical performance measurement.

7.5 Tricks of the Trade

The following hints may improve the quality of your work when developing software to government standards

- The quality assurance team within your organization should be independent from the project team. When this is not possible, an independent quality assurance task force should be formed *at least* once per year to "audit" the project from a quality assurance standpoint.

- Be sure that your quality assurance efforts encompass all software developed during the project, including software tools which are not intended for eventual delivery to the customer.

- Be sure that requirements identified in the functional baseline are testable.

- When time is short, make the interface requirements and design your number one priority.

- Whenever possible, try have one person "write" each document to be delivered. This person will obviously receive considerable input from other engineers, but will be responsible for tieing the whole thing together. This approach will produce documents which are much smoother and professional sounding.

- Be sure to follow the format and content requirements of the Data Item Descriptions exactly. Use automated tools to produce the documents to the greatest extent possible.

- Keep documents as short as possible. Make extensive use of appendices and references to other documents.

- Try to set up your library function as an independent organizational unit. Involve the software librarian in the project early during the functional allocation (top level design) stage to tailor the design to existing code.

- Maintain your design documentation on-line, and insist that your software engineers use the on-line documentation when working. This will avoid the very common problem of engineers developing software to out-dated versions of the requirements specifications.

8 The Role of MIL-STD-490A

Government projects involving system engineering use MIL-STD-490A, *Specification Practices*, to define the documentation requirements for each of the system's configuration baselines. Although software engineers working with DOD-STD-2167A will find that MIL-STD-490A does not impose any additional documentation requirements on the software engineering effort, it is important for software engineers to be familiar with the terminology and overall content of MIL-STD-490A.

The following aspects of MIL-STD-490A will be covered:

- MIL-STD-490A defined specifications

- Configuration identification

- Format requirements

- Specification configuration control

8.1 MIL-STD-490A Defined Specifications

Figure 8.1 illustrates the various documents defined by MIL-STD-490A. Only the following subset of these documents is applicable to the software engineer.

1. Type A specification

2. Type B5 specification

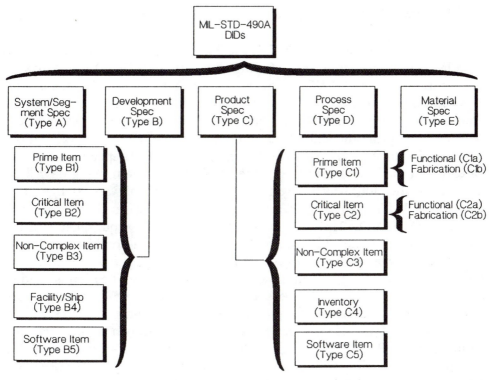

Figure 8.1 MIL-STD-490A documents.

3.   Type C5 specification

8.1.1 Type A Specification

MIL-STD-490A requires a description of the detailed system requirements (hardware and software). This document is called the *Type A* specification. You will often hear people talking about the system's 'A Spec' when referring to this document. The Type A specification is identical to the *System/Segment Specification*. Simply remember that the Type A specification and System/Segment Specification are two names for the same document. A Type A Specification is prepared for each *system* and for each *segment* of a system, so a program to develop a segment (most projects) will have only one Type A Specification.

8.1.2 Type B5 Specification

After the requirements identified in the Type A Specification are allocated
to individual Computer Software Configuration Items (CSCIs) and Hardware
Configuration Items (HWCIs), this allocation is documented in the *Type B*
specification, or 'B Spec'. One Type B specification is prepared for *each*
configuration item (HWCI or CSCI) in your system or segment, so a
development program will typically have multiple Type B specifications
associated with it. MIL-STD-490A divides the Type B specifications into
categories based on the nature of the configuration item being described.
Type B specifications which are describing a computer software configuration
item are called Type B5 (Software Development) specifications. Although
no single DOD-STD-2167A document fully meets the requirements of the
Type B5 specification, the requirements are met by a combination of the
Software Requirements Specification and the *Interface Requirements Specification* for each CSCI. If one Interface Requirements Specification is used to
describe multiple CSCIs, the B5 specification for each CSCI will reference
the appropriate Interface Requirements Specification.   MIL-STD-490A
states that the Type B5 specification consists of these two documents. If a
Contract Data Requirements List (CDRL) requires you to deliver a Type
B5 specification, you would simply prepare the Software Requirements
Specification and the Interface Requirements Specification as defined in
DOD-STD-2167A (and described in Chaps. 17 and 18), prepare a cover
sheet identifying this document as the Type B5 specification, and attach the
cover sheet to the two software documents without making any changes to
the documents themselves.

8.1.3 Type C5 Specification

The *Type C* specification is a complete description of the configuration item
(CSCI or HWCI). A Type C specification is prepared for *each* configuration
item, so a development program will typically have multiple Type C
specifications associated with it.   MIL-STD-490A divides the Type C
specifications into categories based on the configuration item category. For
computer software configuration items, the Type C specification is called the
Type C5 (Software Product) specification, or "C5 Spec". The Type C5
specification consists of all documents required by DOD-STD-2167A which
describe the software itself. Specifically, the Type C5 specification consists of

the Software Product Specification, which contains the Software Design Document, the Interface Design Document (if required), listings, and source code.

Each of these documents is described later in this text.

Figure 8.2 summarizes the relationship between MIL-STD-490A required documents and DOD-STD-2167A software documentation.

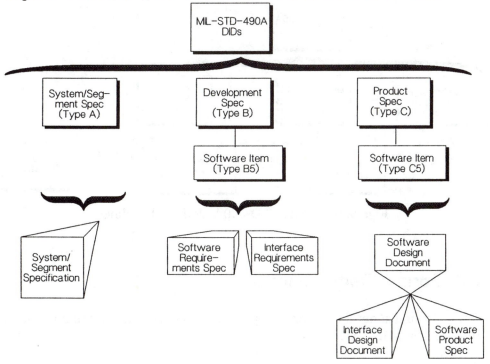

Figure 8.2 MIL-STD-490A versus DOD-STD-2167A.

8.2 Configuration Identification

Figure 8.3 shows how the MIL-STD-490A defined documentation is used to define the three configuration baselines. The Type A specification defines the functional baseline for the system or segment. The Type B specifications then define the allocated baseline for each system or segment. There must be clear traceability from each requirement identified in the Type A specification to one or more requirements in the Type B specifications.

Finally, the Type C specification defines the product baseline for each configuration item. There must be clear traceability from each requirement identified in the Type B specification to a function delivered in the Type C specification. In addition, the functions described in the Type C specifications must be actually demonstrated using appropriate tests.

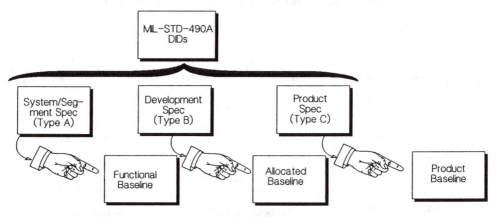

Figure 8.3 MIL-STD-490A defined baselines.

8.3 Format Requirements

The following general guidelines apply when preparing any of the documents required by MIL-STD-490A.

- Use consistent terminology to refer to material.

- Abbreviations and acronyms are spelled out in full the first time they are used with the abbreviation or acronym shown in parenthesis after the word or phrase. It is best to spell the abbreviation or acronym out again in full the first time it is used within each major section of the document.

- The use of trade names or other proprietary names shall be avoided when possible. When necessary, the words "or equal" must be inserted after each reference to a trade name or proprietary name.

- When referencing other requirements in the specification, it is normally better to use the phrase "as specified herein" rather than a specific reference to a page.

- When appropriate, use phrases such as "no greater than" or "no less than" rather than absolute requirements.

- *Shall* means that a requirement is binding. *Will* is a declaration of purpose on the part of the government. *Should* implies a requirement which must be followed unless an alternative is backed up by trade studies and the government approves. *May* implies a preference only.

- Paragraph numbering shall be limited to seven levels of indentation.

- Figures shall be placed in or after the paragraph which references them. If numerous figures are used, they may be placed in numerical sequence at the end of the document.

- Submission of specifications in electronic format is encouraged on most contracts.

8.4 Specification Configuration Control

Changes to specifications are controlled using Specification Change Notices (SCNs) and revisions. SCNs describe specific pages in the document which must be changed. SCNs are prepared at the same time an Engineering Change Proposal (ECP) is prepared which affects an approved specification. When the ECP is approved, the SCN is automatically approved. SCNs are numbered sequentially for each document, starting with 1. If the ECP will require extensive changes to the specification, then revisions are used. Revisions are an updated version of the specification. When a specification is revised, the specification number is amended to include a trailing letter to show the revision number (A, B, C, etc.)

Updated specification pages are complete reprints of the pages with all corrections incorporated on the reprinted page. Inserted pages use the original page number followed by lowercase a, b, c, and so on. Changes from the previous version are shown using a vertical bar along the right hand margin for changed text.

Revisions are a complete update of the entire document. Once again, changes from the previous version are shown using a vertical bar along the right hand margin for changed text. If the changes are extensive, the following note may be included at the start of the document in place of the vertical markings:

> Symbols are not used in this revision to identify changes with respect to the previous issue, due to the extensiveness of the changes.

9 The Role of DOD-STD-2167A

DOD-STD-2167A, *Defense System Software Development*, is the principle guiding document for developing software to government standards. This is the document which

1. describes software specific requirements of system engineering,

2. shows how software fits into the "big picture,"

3. provides detailed descriptions of all documents (Data Item Descriptions) which must be produced by the software engineering team.

DOD-STD-2167A *does not* attempt to recommend or require any specific software development methodology. It includes an appendix which lists requirements for contractor generated coding standards. It does not require any particular programming language (although other government instructions do). The emphasis of DOD-STD-2167A is on *activities* to be performed during software engineering, with the activities more oriented toward *managing* the software development effort throughout the development lifecycle as opposed to technical approaches to software engineering. DOD-STD-2167A will be discussed as follows:

• We begin with a brief description of the physical organization of the standard itself.

- Then discuss the documents required by DOD-STD-2167A, and present a dependency network showing each of these documents and associated reviews and audits.

- Each of the phases in the software development life cycle are discussed next, as identified in DOD-STD-2167A.

- Followed by some special requirements imposed by DOD-STD-2167A, including: risk analysis, defect analysis and tracking, software development files, and internal reviews.

- We conclude by discussing tailoring of DOD-STD-2167A requirements.

Before starting the remainder of this chapter, quickly review the system static hierarchical structure (Fig. 9.1) as defined by DOD-STD-2167A. From a software perspective, a system is divided into segments. Segments are divided into Computer Software Configuration Items (CSCIs). CSCIs are decomposed into Computer Software Components (CSCs). CSCs are decomposed into other CSCs or into Computer Software Units (CSUs). CSUs are the lowest level in the static hierarchy, corresponding to leafs in the hierarchical tree.

9.1 Organization of DOD-STD-2167A

DOD-STD-2167A begins with discussions of general requirements which apply to all phases of software development. These general requirements fall into the following categories:

- *Software development management*, including discussions of project reviews/audits, planning, risk management, security, maintenance of a software development library, and problem reporting.

- *Software engineering*, including discussions of software engineering methods and environments, decomposition of the functional requirements into the software static structure, requirements traceability, and design and coding standards.

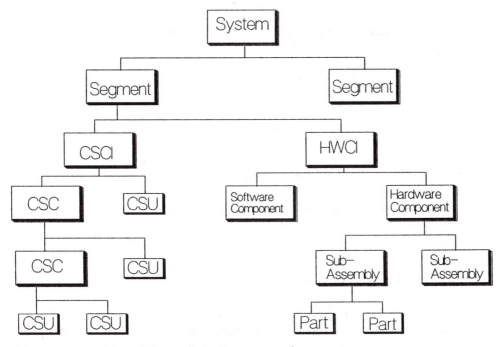

Figure 9.1 System static structure.

- *Formal qualification testing*, including discussions of test planning, and traceability of requirements to specific tests.

- *Software product evaluations*, including requirements for independent evaluations, record keeping, and evaluation criteria.

- *Software configuration management*, including configuration identification and control, configuration status accounting, and use of engineering change proposals.

- *Transitioning to software support*, including transition planning and required transition documentation.

DOD-STD-2167A then discusses detailed requirements for each phase in the software development life cycle. These phases are

- System requirements analysis/design

- Software requirements analysis

- Preliminary design

- Detailed design

- Coding and CSU testing

- CSC integration and testing

- CSCI testing

- System integration and testing

For each of these phases, DOD-STD-2167A discusses requirements in the areas of software development management, software engineering, formal qualification testing, software product evaluations, and configuration management.

Appendix A of DOD-STD-2167A lists acronyms and abbreviations. Its Appendix B gives a set of requirements which must be addressed in software coding standards generated by each contractor, and Appendix C contains categories and priority classifications for problem reporting. Finally, Appendix D contains general evaluation criteria applied to all documents required by DOD-STD-2167A. These documents are described in the following section.

9.2 DOD-STD-2167A Documentation Requirements

Figure 9.2 shows the DOD-STD-2167A required documents broken down by category. The standard requires the following management oriented Data Item Description (DID).

- *Software Development Plan*: One Software Development Plan is prepared for the project (system or segment). The

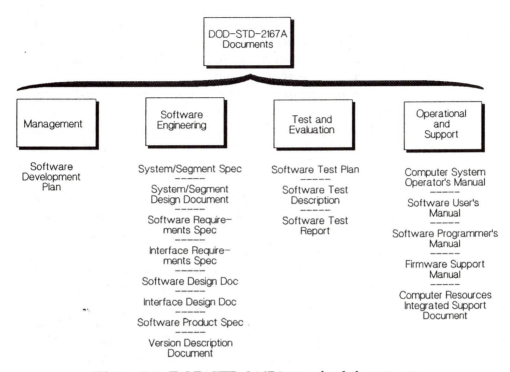

Figure 9.2 DOD-STD-2167A required documents.

Software Development Plan describes the contractor's plans for conducting software development and is used by the government to monitor the procedures, management, and contract work effort of the contractor(s) performing software development. This document is described in Chap. 16.

The standard requires the following software engineering oriented Data Item Descriptions (DIDs):

- *System/Segment Specification*: One System/Segment Specification is prepared for the system and one system/segment specification is prepared for each segment. On most contracts, the entire project will be a single segment so only one System/Segment Specification needs to be prepared. It is important to note that if a segment is erroneously termed a system, this will result in additional paperwork to prepare System/Segment Specifications for each of the *segments* under the system. The System/Segment Specification specifies the requirements for a system or a segment. These requirements then become the Functional Baseline for the system or segment. The System/Segment Specification is also used to provide an overview of the system or segment to training personnel, support personnel, or users of the system. This document is described in Chap. 14.

- *System/Segment Design Document*: One System/Segment Design Document is prepared for each system and each segment. On most contracts, the entire project will be a single segment, so only one System/Segment Design Document will need to be prepared. The System/Segment Design Document describes the decomposition of the system/segment into Hardware Configuration Items (HWCIs), Computer Software Configuration Items (CSCIs), and manual operations. This information is then used as the basis for developing the various requirements specifications for each CSCI and HWCI. This document is described in Chap. 15.

- *Software Requirements Specification*: A Software Requirements Specification is prepared for each CSCI to describe the specific requirements which will be met by that particular CSCI. The Software Requirements Specification for a CSCI may contain several requirements all designed to satisfy a single requirement in the System/Segment Specification. This document is described in Chap. 17.

- *Interface Requirements Specification*: The detailed requirements for interfaces between each CSCI and other CSCIs/-HWCIs is described in the Interface Requirements Specification(s). If the CSCI organization of the segment requires either tricky or extensive interfaces between CSCIs and other configuration items, then one Interface Requirements Specification will normally be prepared for *each* CSCI. If the interfaces are relatively straightforward, one Interface

Requirements Specification may describe the interfaces to/from multiple CSCIs. This document is described in Chap. 18.

- *Software Design Document*: One Software Design Document is prepared for each CSCI to describe the complete design of the CSCI. This includes the functional decomposition of the CSCI requirements into Computer Software Components (CSCs) and Computer Software Units (CSUs); the allocation of CSCI requirements to CSCs and CSUs; and the detailed design of the CSCI software to meet the allocated requirements. This document is described in Chap. 19.

- *Interface Design Document*: An Interface Design Document is prepared for each previously prepared Interface Requirements Specification. The Interface Design Document contains the detailed design for the interface, including electrical characteristics, protocols, error correction schemes, data formats, and so on. This document is described in Chap. 21.

- *Software Product Specification*: A Software Product Specification is prepared for each CSCI. The Software Product Specification consists of the up-to-date Software Design Document for the CSCI and source code listings. This document is described in Chap. 30.

- *Version Description Document*: A Version Description Document is prepared for each formal release of each CSCI. This document is basically a "packing list" of what is included in the release. This document is described in Chap. 24.

The standard requires the following software test-oriented Data Item Deliverables (DIDs):

- *Software Test Plan*: The Software Test Plan describes the software test environment, test resources required, and test schedule for one or more CSCIs. If a CSCI has extensive or difficult testing requirements, a Software Test Plan will be prepared for that specific CSCI. If testing requirements are less complicated, one Software Test Plan may be used to describe testing for several CSCIs. This document is described in Chap. 20.

- *Software Test Description*: One Software Test Description is prepared for each CSCI. The Software Test Description contains the test cases and test procedures to be conducted for the CSCI. This document is described in Chap. 22.

- *Software Test Report*: One Software Test Report is prepared for each CSCI. The Software Test Report describes the results of testing the CSCI. This document is described in Chap. 23.

The standard requires the following operational and support Data Item Deliverables (DIDs):

- *Computer System Operator's Manual*: One Computer System Operator's Manual is prepared for the entire segment, unless the segment consists of multiple different computer systems (in which case one manual is prepared for each set of hardware). This manual describes how to start, operate, and shut down the computer hardware. This document is described in Chap. 25.

- *Software User's Manual*: One Software User's Manual is prepared for each computer program. The entire segment may be a single computer program, or one or more CSCIs may be a separate computer program requiring a separate Software User's Manual. The Software User's Manual describes how to operate the computer program. This document is described in Chap. 26.

- *Software Programmer's Manual*: One Software Programmer's Manual is prepared for each different type of computer in the segment. For most segments, this means that only one Software Programmer's Manual will need to be prepared. The Software Programmer's Manual provides hardware oriented information about the CPU instruction set, interrupt handling, programming tools, operating system, and so on. This document is described in Chap. 27.

- *Firmware Support Manual*: One Firmware Support Manual is prepared for the entire segment. The Firmware Support Manual describes how to load or initialize firmware devices (ROM, EPROM, etc.) This document is described in Chap. 28.

- *Computer Resources Integrated Support Document*: One Computer Resources Integrated Support Document (CRISD) is prepared for the entire segment. The CRISD documents the contractor's plans for transitioning support of delivered software to the government. This document is described in Chap. 29.

9.3 Software Engineering Dependencies

The nine reviews/audits required by MIL-STD-1521B are typically considered milestone tasks when defining your dependencies. The following four figures [Fig. 9.3 (a) (b) (c) and (d)] summarize the relationship between software documents and project reviews and audits. The sample project shown consists of a single segment and two CSCIs. Figure 9.4 shows how the DOD-STD-2167A software development phases fit into the review and audit schedule.

These phases will be discussed, including the documents produced during the phase, in the following sections.

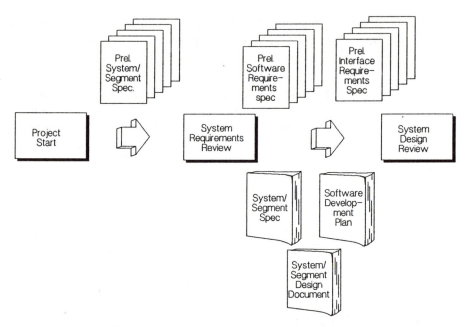

Figure 9.3 (a) Document dependencies.

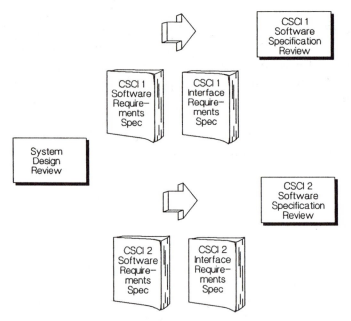

Figure 9.3 (b) Document dependencies (continued).

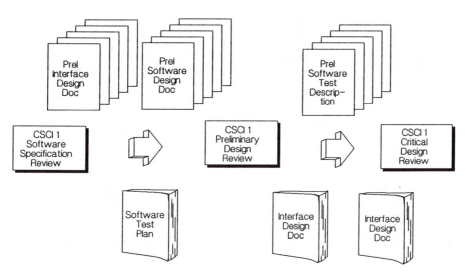

Figure 9.3 (c) Document dependencies (continued).

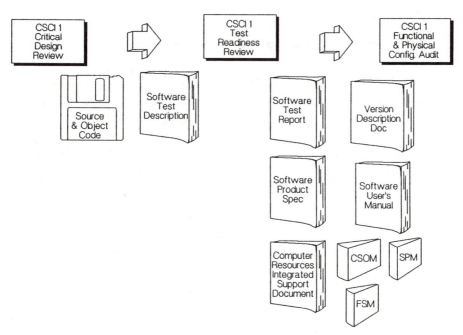

Figure 9.3 (d) Document dependencies (continued).

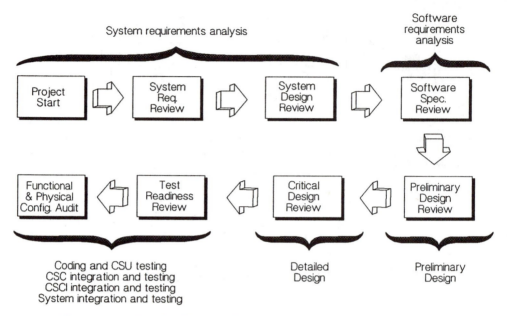

Figure 9.4 DOD-STD-2167A software development phases.

9.4 System Requirements Analysis

The system requirements analysis phase covers all activities through the System Design Review, and culminates in an approved functional baseline. The functional baseline describes the specific capabilities which the system must be designed to meet. The System Requirements Review and Software Design Review are conducted during this phase. Both of these reviews cover the entire system or segment. The following documents are produced during this phase:

- *System/Segment Specification*

- *Software Development Plan*

- *System/Segment Design Document*: requirements must be traceable to requirements in the System/Segment Specification.

- *Software Requirements Specification*: (preliminary) requirements must be traceable to System/Segment Specification, must be consistent with the Interface Requirements Specification, and all requirements must be testable.

- *Interface Requirements Specification*: (preliminary) requirements must be traceable to System/Segment Specification, consistent with the Software Requirements Specifications, and must be testable.

Each of these documents must be placed under configuration control prior to delivery to the government. Changes to these capabilities must be formally submitted as Engineering Change Proposals (ECPs) and approved by the government.

9.5 Software Requirements Analysis

The software requirements analysis phase covers all activities through the Software Specification Review. Unlike the System Requirements Review and Software Design Review, one Software Specification Review is held for *each* CSCI. If one Software Specification Review is held to deal with multiple CSCIs, these items are still treated individually during the meeting. The following documents are produced during this phase:

- *Software Requirements Specification* (final)

- *Interface Requirements Specification* (final)

After successful completion of each Software Specification Review (and approval of the appropriate Software Requirements Specification and Interface Requirements Specification), the system functional requirement allocations for the covered CSCI are frozen as the allocated baseline for use during design. After *all* CSCIs have been approved, the system allocated baseline is fully defined (at least as far as software is concerned). Each of these documents must be placed under configuration control prior to delivery to the government.

9.6 Preliminary Design

The preliminary design phase covers all activities through the Preliminary Design Review. During this phase, the top level software design is completed and initial plans for testing the final software are developed. A Preliminary Design Review is conducted for each CSCI, or for a group of functionally related CSCIs. The following documents are produced during this phase:

- *Software Design Document*: (preliminary) requirements must be properly allocated to the Computer Software Component (CSC) level

- *Interface Design Document*: (preliminary)

- *Software Test Plan*: Data recording, reduction and analysis methods must be adequately covered.

Each of these documents must be placed under configuration control prior to delivery to the government. After completion of the Preliminary Design Review for a CSCI, detailed software design work can begin.

9.7 Detailed Design

The detailed design phase covers all activities through the Critical Design Review. During this phase, the detailed software design is completed, and detailed test plans are developed. A Critical Design Review is held for each CSCI, *and* one Critical Design Review is held for the entire system after successful completion of all CSCI and HWCI Critical Design Reviews. The following documents are produced during the detailed design phase:

- *Software Design Document*: (final) design must be consistent in definition and use of data. Data accuracy and other descriptive information must be included. Automatic checking of data flows is encouraged.

- *Interface Design Document*: (final) data flows along interface must be consistent with data flows in Software Design Document.

- *Software Test Description*: (part one only)

Each of these documents must be placed under configuration control prior to delivery to the government.

9.8 Coding and CSU Testing

The coding and CSU testing phase covers the actual writing of code and testing to the CSU level. Remember that a CSU is a detailed *functional* requirement, not necessarily a program module. It is quite possible that one program module will satisfy the requirements of several CSUs, or that several program modules will be required to satisfy one CSU requirement. Individual programmers are typically responsible for testing the modules they code, but separate individuals should perform CSU testing. The CSU testing is totally under contractor control, i.e., the government is not involved in CSU testing at all. The Software Product Specifications are prepared during this phase and placed under configuration control. CSU test results are documented in the Software Test Reports.

9.9 CSC Integration and Testing

The CSC integration and testing phase covers all activities from completion of coding and CSU testing through completion of CSC level testing. Software modules are integrated together to form CSCs, and testing is performed to verify that the software meets the requirements at the CSC level. CSC test results are documented in the Software Test Reports.

9.10 CSCI Integration and Testing

Software CSCs are integrated together to form complete CSCIs, and testing is performed to verify that the software meets all requirements at the CSCI level. The contractor must perform a dry run of all CSCI tests prior to the formal testing with the government present. CSCI test results are docu-

mented in the Software Test Reports. During this phase, the following
reviews are conducted for each CSCI:

- Test Readiness Review

- Functional Configuration Audit

- Physical Configuration Audit

9.11 System Integration and Testing

The system integration and testing phase covers all activities from completion of CSCI integration and testing through final system acceptance.
During this phase you will be expected to deliver the following documents:

- *Software Test Report(s)* (final)

- *Version Description Document(s)*

- *Software Product Specification(s)*

- *Computer System Operator's Manual*

- *Software User's Manual*

- *Software Programmer's Manual*

- *Firmware Support Manual*

- *Computer Resources Integrated Support Document*

In addition, updated versions of all previously submitted documents
should be submitted to accurately represent the software as delivered.

9.12 Transitioning to Software Support

The contractor must now turn the completed software over to the government. The Computer Resources Integrated Support Document is used to document the contractor prepared plan for this transition. The software development contract will typically require some contractor assistance in installing the software on one or more government sites and training government personnel in the use of the software. All software must be delivered with complete source code and all tools, including compile scripts, required to allow the government to modify and recompile the code. Smart government project managers will use the following procedure to verify that the source code which is delivered is adequate. The executable program and all object modules are saved in subdirectories. The source code is then used to regenerate the object modules and the final, linked executable program. The newly produced executable program is then compared, on a byte by byte basis, with the previously saved executable program which was saved in a subdirectory. This will quickly identify any problems with older versions of the source code being delivered by mistake.

9.13 Special Requirements

This chapter addresses the following software engineering requirements which are described in DOD-STD-2167A:

- Risk analysis

- Defect analysis and tracking

- Software development files

- Internal reviews

9.13.1 Risk Analysis

DOD-STD-2167A requires that procedures for risk management be documented in the Software Development Plan and implemented. Contractors are required to identify, analyze, prioritize, and monitor software development tasks which involve potential technical, cost, or schedule risk.   Chapter 6 of this book discussed risk analysis and risk management in more detail.

9.13.2 Defect Analysis and Tracking

DOD-STD-2167A requires that the contractor prepare a formal problem report for each problem detected in software or documentation that has been placed under configuration control. The corrective action process used to manage these problem reports must

- be closed-loop to ensure that all detected problems are reported, analyzed, and resolved. The status of all problem reports must be tracked throughout the entire process.

- be classified by category and priority. Problems are classified as software problems (coding), documentation problems, design problems, or requirements problems (the four problem categories). They are then assigned one of five possible priorities as identified in Chap. 7.

- identify identify trends in the problem reports through the analysis of summary reports.

- ensure that the problem has been corrected and that no new problems have been introduced.

9.13.3 Software Development Files

Software development files must be maintained throughout the contract using either manual or automated means. *Government Standards Toolbox* (Appendix B) is one example of a program which will automatically maintain software development files. Software development files must include, directly or by reference, the following information:

- design considerations and constraints used when making trade-off decisions during software design,

- design documentation and data,

- up-to-date schedule and status information down to at least the CSU level,

- test requirements and responsibilities,

- test cases, procedures, and results.

9.13.4 Internal Reviews

DOD-STD-2167A refers to internal reviews as *software product evaluations*. All software and documentation delivered under DOD-STD-2167A must be reviewed internally by the contractor's organization. The group responsible for conducting this internal review must have the resources, responsibility, authority, and freedom to do the job right. Obviously, people writing the documents or software can not be the same group that is responsible for reviewing the quality of the results, although they may participate in the review process. Records of the internal review process must be carefully maintained. The specific procedures to be used for the internal reviews must be clearly spelled out in the Software Development Plan.

9.14 Tailoring DOD-STD-2167A

As a contractor, it is in your best interest to propose tailoring of the total list of documents to be delivered (even though tailoring is a government responsibility). Tailoring is best accomplished during the proposal stage. In your proposal, make specific suggestions of how you feel DOD-STD-2167A should be tailored to the specific contract. This will be looked at highly favorably by the government evaluators, as it shows a clear understanding of the true intent of DOD-STD-2167A on your part. If you are concerned that your tailoring suggestions may make you non-responsive because you may not propose to deliver all documents required by the request for proposal, take the following approach:

When discussing tailoring, I will make the assumption that you are following my recommendation and using DOD-STD-2167A requirements for all software development projects. This means that it is counter-productive

> Respond by proposing to deliver all documents required by the Request For Proposal, and cost the contract accordingly. Then propose a detailed, specific tailoring approach to reduce the required number of documents. Show the cost savings associated with the tailored contract as an option in your proposal which can be executed by the government, if desired.

to attempt to tailor out software engineering documents which are necessarily to properly design and document the program. We will focus our tailoring attention on documents which will not contribute to your ability to reuse software components on future projects. Specifically, you will want to look at the following:

- Request permission to deliver all documentation on electronic media (such as that produced by *Teamplan*. This is encouraged throughout DOD-STD-2167A and should be well received by the government. It saves you printing and collating costs, and greatly simplifies the process of keeping the documentation up-to-date.

- Propose that your project be considered a segment rather than a system (it normally *should be* considered a segment, anyway). This will prevent your being required to deal with a System/Segment Specification for the System and one or more System/Segment Specifications for each of the segments.

- If the project is pure software (no hardware), and the project is not too large, propose that the entire software program be considered a single CSCI. This is quite logical and appropriate given the intent of DOD-STD-2167A authors when defining CSCIs. This will greatly reduce the number of documents you will need to produce and reviews you must schedule, given the fact that many documents and reviews are done *for each CSCI*. Use the CSC and CSU structure to decompose the program.

- Identify what manufacturer's documentation or "off-the-shelf" store bought books describe your computer hardware, instruction set, programming tools, and so on. Propose that these documents be accepted, without modification, as the deliverable requirements for the Computer System Operator's Manual, Software Programmer's Manual, and Firmware Support Manual. Of course, the documents must be verified to ensure that they are complete and accurate.

- Unless the software transition is expected to be tricky, request that the Computer Resources Integrated Support Document be replaced by transition planning information included in the Software Development Plan.

10 The Role of DOD-STD-2168

DOD-STD-2168, *Defense System Software Quality Program*, is a recently released standard which addresses quality control during software development. DOD-STD-2168 contains requirements for quality control of DOD-STD-2167A developed software, documentation, and procedures. The following DOD-STD-2168 related topics will be covered:

- General quality control requirements imposed by DOD-STD-2168

- Quality control requirements which apply to the *process* of software development

- Quality control requirements which apply to the *products* of software development

10.1 General Requirements

The requirements of DOD-STD-2168 affect *all* aspects of the software development effort, including the software engineering methods, products, and testing. Even software which is not delivered under the contract (test drivers, simulators, development tools, etc.) is covered by DOD-STD-2168. The quality control group must be separate from the development group, although the development group may obviously assist the quality control group in their actions. Ideally, the software quality control group should be a separate functional group within your organization. This group *must* have sufficient resources, responsibility, authority, and organizational freedom to do their job. It is normally best to allow direct communication between the head of the quality control group and the President of your company. All software quality control actions must be well documented either electronically (using a program similar to *Government Standards Toolbox*) or manually. As a minimum, the documentation for each quality control evaluation must include the:

- evaluation date,

- evaluation participants,

- evaluation criteria,

- evaluation results,

- recommended corrective actions.

Problems identified during the evaluation should be referenced to a formal problem report which will allow them to be tracked to resolution. The *Software Quality Program Plan* is your plan for implementing quality control procedures. If the quality control group is a separate functional group within your organization, they should be responsible for preparing this document. Your company's management is required to approve of (and support) both the Software Quality Program Plan and the on-going quality control actions.

10.2 Quality Control of the Software Development Process

The software quality control group is required to periodically audit the software development process to ensure that all work is being performed properly. This audit will typically address the following issues:

- *Management*: Is the Software Development Plan being followed? Are all contractual requirements being adhered to?

- *Software Engineering*: Are the software engineering procedures and methods being used in compliance with the Software Development Plan?

- *Software Testing*: Are all materials required to properly conduct the tests (including adequate time) available to the testers? Is the testing being performed by individuals who were not part of the original development (perhaps individuals within the quality control group)? Are all results of testing being properly recorded?

- *Configuration Management*: Is configuration management being practiced in accordance with DOD-STD-2167A, the Software Development Plan, and any other contractually required documents or standards?

- *Problem Reports*: Are problems promptly reported in writing? Are problems classified by priority and classification? Is the problem tracked through resolution, including analysis of problem trends? Are records maintained for the life of the contract? Has it been verified that problem corrective actions did not introduce additional problems?   Have corrective actions resulted in changes to the appropriate documents?

- *Documentation and Media Distribution*: Is documentation and media distribution carefully controlled in accordance with the Software Development Plan? Do all distributions include clear markings of the deliverable requirement being met, the version number, and changes incorporated (if any)?

- *Evaluation of Subcontractor Management*:   Does all subcontractor developed documentation and software meet the contract's requirements? Are requirements for quality control included in the subcontractor's contractual arrangements? Are subcontractors aware that the government must be allowed to review all software products and activities required of the subcontractor?

- *Software Development Library*:   Is the library set up in accordance with the Software Development Plan? Does it contain the most recent authorized versions of all materials? Are previous versions clearly identified and controlled to provide an audit trail which permits reconstruction of previous configurations, if necessary?

- *Participation in Formal Reviews and Audits*:   Are all required products available for review? The software quality control group may be required to present an evaluation of the status and quality of each of the development products reviewed.

10.3 Quality Control of the Software Development Products

The software quality control group must approve *all* products which are to be delivered during the contract. This evaluation must ensure that the products are properly marked, appear to be of acceptable quality, and have been updated to reflect all changes approved by the contracting agency and scheduled for inclusion. DOD-STD-2168 also provides the following specific guidance:

- *Evaluation of Deliverable Software*: The software must comply with the contract, must adhere to the Software Development Plan, and must be properly tested.

- *Evaluation of NonDeliverable Software*:   Nondeliverable software which will be incorporated into deliverable software must be evaluated to ensure that it functions properly, was placed under internal configuration control prior to its incorporation, and that data rights provisions are consistent with the contract.

- *Evaluation of Software Engineering and Test Environments*: Software used exclusively for the software engineering and test environments must be evaluated to ensure that it performs the required functions properly, complies with the contract and Software Development Plan, was placed under internal configuration control prior to use, and that data rights provisions are consistent with the contract.

- *Evaluation of Software Documentation*: Software documentation must be evaluated to ensure that both the *content* and *format* meet the requirements of the contract.

11 The Role of MIL-STD-1521B

MIL-STD-1521B, *Technical Reviews and Audits for Systems, Equipments, and Computer Software*, prescribes the requirements for the conduct of reviews and audits during the system engineering process. These reviews and audits are the cornerstone of government system engineering. They are used both to review the developing design and also to approve documentation, establish baselines, and provide guidance to the engineers.

The heart of MIL-STD-1521B is its appendices, which discuss each review in-depth. This level of detail will be reserved for our discussions in Chaps. 31 through 37. At this point, MIL-STD-1521B requirements will be discussed which are not specific to an individual review or audit. We will cover:

- MIL-STD-1521B required reviews and audits

- Contractor responsibilities during the review process

- Government responsibilities during the review process

- Tailoring of MIL-STD-1521B requirements

11.1 Required Reviews and Audits

Figure 11.1 summarizes the reviews and audits required by MIL-STD-1521B. The reviews shown are:

- *System Requirements Review*: This review looks at the *system* requirements. One System Requirements Review is con

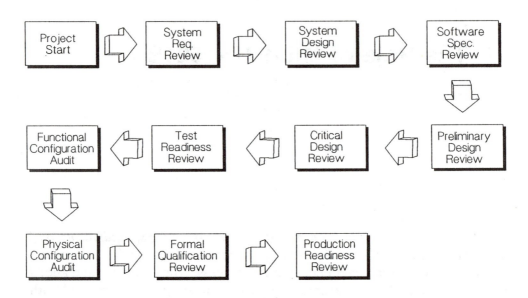

Figure 11.1 MIL-STD-1521B required reviews.

ducted for the entire system or segment. The emphasis is on understanding the problem that the system is designed to solve. Most of the material presented at the System Requirements Review is based on government work. On many programs, the System Requirements Review will be conducted by the government prior to writing the Request for Proposal, so no contractor work will be presented at all. The System/Segment Specification should be available in preliminary form and reviewed at this time.

- *System Design Review*: This review looks at the allocated technical requirements for the system. The optimization, correlation, completeness, and risk analysis which resulted in a specific allocation of requirements to configuration items (HWCIs and CSCIs) is covered. Initial system engineering considerations are covered. The system requirements which are approved during this review become the *functional* baseline configuration for the system. The CSCI and HWCI architecture approved during this review becomes the *allocated* baseline configuration for the *system*.

- *Software Specification Review*: By default, one software specification review is conducted for *each* CSCI. With government approval, software specification reviews for multiple CSCIs may be combined into one meeting when appropriate. This review looks at the CSCI's Software Requirements Specification and the Interface Requirement Specification(s) which define the interfaces to/from this CSCI. When approved, these documents become the *allocated* baseline configuration for the *CSCI*.

- *Preliminary Design Review*: By default, one preliminary design review is conducted for *each* CSCI and *each* HWCI. With government approval, preliminary design reviews for multiple CSCIs and HWCIs may be combined into one meeting when appropriate. This review looks at the top-level hardware and software design.

- *Critical Design Review*: By default, one critical design review is conducted for *each* CSCI and *each* HWCI. For CSCIs, this review looks at the detailed design, performance, test characteristics, and risk areas (technical, cost, and schedule) of the design solution.

- *Test Readiness Review*: By default, one test readiness review is conducted for *each* CSCI and *each* HWCI. This review looks at test plans and procedures, CSU and CSC test results, and informal CSCI testing to verify that the completed CSCI is ready for *formal* testing and approval. The test readiness review is conducted *prior* to formal testing of the CSCIs and HWCIs.

- *Functional Configuration Audit*: By default, one functional configuration audit is conducted for *each* CSCI and *each* HWCI. This review looks at results of formal testing of the configuration item to ensure that the results completely satisfy all requirements identified during the system requirements review and system design review. The functional configuration audit is normally conducted at the contractors site.

Typically, the contractor conducts the tests under government supervision.

One functional configuration audit is often conducted for the entire system. This review checks system level performance which can not be measured during individual CSCI testing, including inter-operation of CSCIs. Some CSCI testing may be repeated if there is concern that the performance may change after integration into the system. The system level functional configuration audit is normally conducted after the contractor has installed the system at the final (government) site where the system is to operate. Testing during this review is typically conducted by government operators under contractor supervision.

- *Physical Configuration Audit*: By default, one physical configuration audit is conducted for *each* CSCI and *each* HWCI. For CSCIs, this review ensures that the CSCI documentation matches the actual software implementation. The functional configuration audit and physical configuration audit are often combined into one audit covering both aspects of the CSCI.

- *Formal Qualification Review*: For most software projects, the requirements of the formal qualification review are met during the functional configuration audit.

- *Production Readiness Review*: The MIL-STD-1521B defined production readiness review applies to items that are manufactured, and does not normally apply to software.

11.2 Contractor Responsibilities

The following checklist may be used by contractors to ensure that they are prepared for the review or audit (additional and more specific guidance is provided in Chaps. 31 through 37):

Contractor Review Checklist

_____   Subcontractors, vendors, and suppliers aware of meeting and present when appropriate

_____   Meeting agenda prepared and distributed

_____   Conference facilities available

_____   Secretary designated to take minutes

_____   Documents to be reviewed sent to government attendees _prior_ to meeting

_____   Specialty and trade study results prepared for presentation

_____   Risk analysis results prepared for presentation

_____   Mockups, breadboards, prototype software, simulators available for demonstration

_____   Test methods and data available

_____   Meeting conducted

_____   Meeting minutes prepared and distributed

_____   Action items prepared and distributed

11.3 Government Responsibilities

The following checklist may be used by the government to be sure that they are prepared for the review or audit.

Government Review Checklist

_____   Security clearances and visit request for all attendees sent to contractor

_____   Meeting minutes reviewed daily to ensure that they are acceptable

_____   Action items reviewed to ensure concurrence

_____   Review or audit formally approved, disapproved, or contingently approved. Contingent approval is an approval contingent on completion of specific action items.

11.4 Tailoring MIL-STD-1521B

As a contractor, it is in your best interest to propose tailoring of the total list of reviews to be conducted although the actual tailoring is the responsibility of the government. Tailoring is best accomplished during the proposal stage. In your proposal, make specific suggestions of how you feel MIL-STD-1521B should be tailored to this specific contract. This will be looked at highly favorably by the government evaluators, as it shows a clear understanding of the true intent of MIL-STD-1521B on your part. If you are concerned that your tailoring suggestions may make you non-responsive by not proposing to conduct all reviews/audits required by the request for proposal, take the following approach:

> Respond by proposing to conduct all reviews and audits required by the Request For Proposal, and cost the contract accordingly. Then propose a detailed, specific tailoring approach to reduce the required number of reviews/audits. Show the cost savings associated with the tailored contract as an option in your proposal which can be executed by the government, if desired.

Specifically, you will want to tailor the reviews/audits as follows:

- If the Request For Proposal includes a System/Segment Specification (Type A specification) as an appendix or by reference, the government has performed the work which is normally accomplished prior to the System Requirements Review. Propose that you review the government furnished System/Segment Specification, submit modifications to the requirements as you feel necessary, then submit these suggested changes either as a new revision of the System/Segment Specification or as specification change notices to the existing revision. The government may then review and approve these changes. If your reading of the System/Segment Specification leads you to believe that these changes will not be too extensive, you should be able to follow these procedures and eliminate the requirement for a System Requirements Review. Alternatively, you may prefer to propose combining the System Requirements Review with the System Design Review. Much less formal program reviews (called in-process reviews) can fill any gaps.

- If the system/segment is mostly software and is not too complex, you may propose to combine the System Design Review with the Software Specification Review(s) and to conduct all of the Software Specification Reviews simultaneously. This combined review will then cover allocation of requirements to CSCIs and the specific CSCI requirement decompositions in one review.

- For the Preliminary Design Review, Critical Design Review, and Test Readiness Review, you will normally want to hold these reviews during the times suggested by MIL-STD-1521B. However, it is often a good idea to cover multiple CSCIs (perhaps all CSCIs) at a single meeting for each of these reviews.

- For the Functional Configuration Audit and Physical Configuration Audit, it is common to combine these two reviews into a single combined review. It may also be a good idea to cover multiple CSCIs during a single meeting.

- If the contract requires training (most do), it is a good idea to propose that the system level functional configuration audit be combined with training of the government operators.

- If the contract has you perform "all reviews required by MIL-STD-1521B", and this is a software contract with no manufacturing considerations, propose to eliminate the production readiness review as not applicable to software.

12 The Role of Other Standards and Instructions

This chapter provides brief descriptions of the contents of several standards, handbooks, and instructions which are applicable to software development. These documents are typically not directly called out in contracts, but they are referenced in other documents (such as DOD-STD-2167A) which *will* be called out in your contract. They are not covered in great depth because they typically do not impose additional documentation or review requirements on you. To a large extent, you can consider the information in these documents as guidance during your contract. The documents discussed are as follows:

- MIL-STD-499A, *Engineering Management*

- DOD-HDBK-287, *Defense System Software Development*

- MIL-STD-483A, *Configuration Management Practices for Systems, Equipments, Munitions, and Computer Programs*

- DOD-STD-480A, *Configuration Control – Engineering Changes, Deviations and Waivers*

- MIL-STD-481A, *Configuration Control – Engineering Changes, Deviations and Waivers (Short Form)*

- DODD 3405.1, *Computer Programming Language Policy*, and DODD 3405.2, *Use of Ada in Weapon Systems*

- MIL-STD-881A, *Work Breakdown Structures for Defense Materiel Items*

- FM 770-78, *System Engineering*

12.1 MIL-STD-499A

MIL-STD-499A, *Engineering Management*, provides suggested task statements and evaluation criteria for judging engineering planning and documents. The *System Engineering Management Plan* is described. This document is often used to establish contractual requirements for technical performance management and general system engineering procedures. Of particular interest is the following checklist (which can be derived from paragraph 4) of criteria for evaluation of individual program engineering planning and output.

_____   Do the technical objectives of the program properly balance need, urgency, risks, and delivered value?

_____   Does the program plan explicitly show the development of a functional, allocated, and product baseline?

_____   Are the technological risks implied by the technical approach acceptable?

_____   Are values for reliability, maintainability, and other support factors realistic?

_____   Is the top-level design simple and easy to understand. [A complex top-level design is almost always a sign of inadequate analysis and a portender of failure. – WHR]

_____   Is the design complete with respect to *all* aspects of the system, including hardware, facilities, personnel, computer programs, and operational procedures?

_____   Are documentation requirements held to a minimum? [Is electronic production and delivery of documentation considered? – WHR]

_____   Do trade studies factor in considerations of cost, performance, schedule, resource constraints, produceability, and life cycle costs?

_____   Are "design to cost" goals established and clear?

_____   Is a work breakdown structure available?

_____   Are technical requirements consistent with each other, correlatable from one level of detail to the next, and traceable throughout the work breakdown structure?

_____   Are technical performance measurement plans available?

_____   Are the interfaces between configuration items and to/from the system clear and consistent?

_____   Are engineering specialty disciplines such as test engineering, integrated logistic support, and reliability and maintainability engineering involved in all relevant aspects of the program?

_____   Are engineering decisions documented with justification, preferably in some form of engineering notebook?

_____   Are reusable designs and software considered when designing the system?

_____   Is the system designed for easy modifications as necessary? Are government requested changes handled promptly?

_____   Are engineering management activities compatible with related program management activities such as schedule tracking, contract administration, and production management?

12.2 DOD-HDBK-287A

DOD-HDBK-287A, *A Tailoring Guide for DOD-STD-2167A*, was developed under an Air Force contract to provide guidance for using DOD-STD-2167 on software development contracts. The guidance in DOD-HDBK-287A provides valuable insight into the government's thought process while writing DOD-STD-2167A. Perhaps the single most interesting part of DOD-HDBK-287A is a set of detailed tailoring guidelines for selecting which deliverables are required for individual contracts given factors such as life cycle considerations (e.g., Multiple contractor/agency involvement, projected software life cycle), managerial considerations (e.g., software development schedule, contracting agency manning and expertise), and system considerations (e.g., software magnitude, software complexity). It has been my personal experience that the informal tailoring guidance presented in the previous few chapters is more appropriate for the vast majority of software contracts. If, however, you are looking for a formal model which will tell you the specific data item deliverables to require for a specific contract, you may want to refer to this handbook.

12.3 MIL-STD-483A

MIL-STD-483A, *Configuration Management Practices for Systems, Equipment, Munitions, and Computer Programs*, provides specific guidance for setting up a configuration management program. This document is particularly valuable if you are not using a computer program to assist with tracking of configuration status. MIL-STD-483A includes requirements for

- generation of a configuration management plan,

- configuration identification,

- configuration control and audits,

- interface control,

- engineering release control,

- configuration management reports and records.

To a large extent, you are already familiar with most of the content of MIL-STD-483A simply by having read this far in this text. You understand the importance of configuration management, and the procedures for configuration control (Secs. 7.1 and 8.4). You should be comfortable with the concept of baseline management (Sec. 2.5) and major reviews/audits (Chap. 11). As a software engineer, you will be interested in the following information contained in MIL-STD-483A appendices:

- interface control,

- document and item identification numbering and marking,

- criteria for selecting configuration items.

Each of these areas will be discussed individually in the subsections which follow.

12.3.1 Interface Control

One of the most important areas for configuration management is at the interfaces between configuration items. Section 7.1 briefly mentioned the existence of a group called the *Interface Control Working Group* which must approve any changes to the external interface of a configuration item prior to submission of the change to the CCB. This requirement is especially obvious when, as is often the case, different companies are responsible for developing each configuration item.

The Interface Control Working Group, or ICWG, serves as the official project communication channel linking program participants to resolve interface problems. Interfaces are defined using a combination of *Interface Control Drawings* and *Programming and Timing Interfaces*. For the software, the interface is fully defined within the Interface Requirements Specification and Interface Design Document, which are discussed in depth in later chapters. The hardware folks, however, will be preparing their

Interface Control Drawings to DOD-STD-100 specifications. It is critical that an individual (preferred) or group of individuals with combined hardware and software backgrounds look at the hardware Interface Control Drawings and the software interface related documents to ensure that the two are compatible.

12.3.2   Document and Item Identification Numbering and Marking

MIL-STD-483A requires that all configuration items be marked with the following information prior to delivery:

- specification or standard number,

- software inventory number,

- serial number,

- drawing number for design graphics,

- change identification numbers, including: Specification Change Notice, Notice of Revision, Engineering Change Proposal, Request for Deviation/Waiver,

- program management code (when identified).

12.3.3 Criteria for Selecting Configuration Items

Selection of configuration items (Computer Software Configuration Items and Hardware Configuration Items) can have a profound effect on the success or failure of your project. Designating an area as a configuration item (as opposed to incorporating it in an already existing configuration item) has the following effects:

- Many documents must be prepared for *each* configuration item.

- Careful configuration management, including government approval of changes to the configuration item is required.

- Increased detail in providing requirements traceability will be necessary.

- Many reviews/audits are conducted for *each* configuration item.

- Engineering Change Proposals are submitted for each configuration item effected by a proposed change.

One of the most common, and costly, blunders in typical government software development projects is to split the segment into *far* to many Computer Software Configuration Items. This has the effect of increasing the documentation, review time, overall development time and cost, and management effort. Conversely, an extremely large program *must* be broken into smaller CSCIs to be effectively managed. In general, a software function should be designated as a Computer Software Configuration Item if it

- runs on a different *computer*,

- is being developed by a different contractor,

- is run at a different time (e.g., a data analysis program which is run after the main software has finished running).

You *may* want to designate software as a configuration item if it will run as a *independent* program or process and

- it is very complex,

- the interfaces to/from the program are complex or involve moving a large quantity of data,

- the requirements for the program are more fluid than other programs and you expect to see changes during development,

- the program is high risk from a technical, schedule, or cost perspective.

Personally I *do not* recommend designating *parts* of a program or process as individual configuration items.   For government projects consisting of 100K to 500K lines of code, the program should be set up with one, or at most two, Computer Software Configuration Items.

12.4 DOD-STD-480A

DOD-STD-480A, *Configuration Control – Engineering Changes, Deviations and Waivers*, describes configuration control requirements and provides instructions for preparing and submitting engineering change proposals and related forms.   DOD-STD-480A provides guidance which is much more tailored to the actual process of submitting engineering change proposals than MIL-STD-483A discussed.   DOD-STD-480A requires that engineering change proposals receive complete analysis of their impact if implemented, including a description of all known interface effects and information concerning changes required in the functional, allocated, or product baseline documents.   Many contracts use MIL-STD-481A, discussed next, instead of DOD-STD-480A because MIL-STD-481A does not require as extensive an analysis by the contractor as part of the engineering change proposal package (the government is responsible for performing the analysis).

Recall from Sec. 7.1 that configuration changes are broken down into Class I and Class II changes, and that these are further broken into emergency, urgent and routine changes.   DOD-STD-480A provides additional guidance in deciding if a change should be classified as Class I or Class II and how it should be prioritized.   DOD-STD-480A also provides more detailed guidance about requests for deviation and requests for waiver (as discussed in Sec. 7.1).   Finally, detailed instructions for completing the engineering change proposal is included.   *Teamplan* includes tools for automated preparation and tracking of engineering change proposals in accordance with this standard.

12.5 MIL-STD-481A

MIL-STD-481A, *Configuration Control – Engineering Changes, Deviations and Waivers (Short Form)*, is used on contracts in which the individual contractors submitting the engineering change proposals may not be aware of the system wide impacts of their proposed engineering change. MIL-STD-481A is also occasionally used on small contracts to avoid the expense and delay associated with preparing complex engineering change proposals to DOD-STD-480A requirements. When MIL-STD-481A is called for on a contract, the government is responsible for assuming the major responsibility for determining the possible effects of the engineering change on higher level or associated items.

12.6 DODD 3405.1 and DODD 3405.2

DODD 3405.1, *Computer Programming Language Policy*, is the most current statement of the government's policy with regard to selection of computer programming languages. This directive supersedes DODI 5000.31, *Interim List of DOD Approved Higher Order Languages*, which many contracts still mistakenly cite. The directive states that the order of preference for software is

1.   off-the-shelf applications packages,

2.   Ada-based software and tools,

3.   software coded using an approved language.

Approved languages are: Ada, C, Atlas, COBOL, CMS-2M, CMS-2Y, Fortran, Jovial (J73), Minimal Basic, Pascal, and SPL/1.

DODD 3405.2, *Use of Ada in Weapon Systems*, requires the use of Ada for all weapon systems. Software is considered to be used in weapon systems if it is part of the weapon systems, used for training or testing of the weapon system, or used for research and development of weapon systems. The directive does list three exceptions to the requirement to use Ada.

- If the program was already in full scale development when the directive was issued (30 March 1987) then Ada is not required. This will probably not apply to projects you will be working on.

- Ada is preferred, but not required, for writing test drivers for hardware unit testing.

- Ada is preferred, but not required, for commercially available off-the-shelf software which will be purchased.

In general, it is possible to get a waiver to write *some* of the code in another language (normally C) when Ada is simply not well suited for the particular function being performed. This waiver is typically used for routines performing bit level manipulations and hardware input and output.

12.7 MIL-STD-881A

MIL-STD-881A, *Work Breakdown Structures for Defense Materiel Items*, is used to provide guidance for the preparation of work breakdown structures. Unfortunately, this standard is of more value to the government program office than to contractors. MIL-STD-881A provides guidance *for government* program managers in the preparation of a very *top level* work breakdown structure.   The work breakdown structure consists of three levels.   The specific guidance in the standard assumes that the top level is a type of platform (aircraft, ships, etc.), the second level is a specific class of platform (plane, ship, etc.), and the third level is major systems within the platform class (airframe, propulsion unit, communications, etc.) At this top level, the projects you are working on will be somewhere *below* the third (bottom) level of the work breakdown structure! For "lesser systems/projects," the standard allows the three levels to be redefined such that the segment we are working on is level 1, level 2 consists of major aggregates of the segment (e.g., hardware, software, installation, training, support, maintenance), level 3 for software will be individual CSCIs. On most contracts you can safely ignore MIL-STD-881A and set up your internal work breakdown structure in any format you desire. All of the elements in your work breakdown structure will be below the reporting level of MIL-STD-881A anyway. Just be sure that your project tracking and accounting system can present results broken down by CSCI for use by the government program manager.

12.8 FM 770-78

Army Field Manual FM 770-78, *System Engineering*, is surprisingly valuable considering that it was released in 1979. This document describes the *system engineering process* as it applies to government procurements. The discussion is by no means specific to either the Army in particular or the military in general. In many ways, FM 770-78 is similar to a publication by the Defense System Management College called *Systems Engineering Management Guide*. On the whole, it is recommended that you refer to the Defense System Management Guide publication prior to looking to FM 770-78, primarily because *System Engineering Management Guide* is both more comprehensive and more up-to-date.

13 Data Item Descriptions

This chapter begins a series of chapters providing detailed guidance in the preparation of all documents which are required by DOD-STD-2167A. This chapter will cover the following:

- Present an overview of Data Item Description (DID) requirements

- Describe the government's outline used for DID descriptions

- Describe the format you must use to deliver all DIDs

- Explain some options you have for alternate presentation styles in preparing your DIDs

- Describe the way multiple paragraphs and sub-paragraphs are handled for all DIDs

- Show the proper format for DID title pages

- Explain how Appendices are used in DIDs

At this point it is worth stressing that the following chapters (describing each individual DID and each review/audit) are not meant to be read for casual, background information. Starting with Chap. 14, the remaining chapters are meant to serve as a reference to be used when tasked to prepare each of the specific DIDs.

13.1 Overview

All deliverables required on a government contract will be described by a Data Item Description or DID. The DID describes the exact format that the deliverable must be submitted in, and specifies the content of the deliverable in detail. At first, the government's rigid requirements for format and content of deliverables may seem like an annoyance. In fact, however, the DIDs make tremendous sense for both the government and the contractor. The government receives documentation which can be easily read. The content and format for all similar documents will be exactly the same from project to project and contractor to contractor. The contractor receives a checklist of contents and an easy to follow guide for preparing the document. In addition, the rigid format and content requirements of government DIDs are very conducive to automatic production.

Figure 13.1 shows the DIDs which will be discussed, broken out into management DIDs, engineering DIDs, test DIDs, and operational DIDs. The specific chapter number which discusses each DID is shown in the brackets.

13.2 DID Format

DIDs are identified by the characters *DI* followed by the DID identification. For example, the DID which describes the System/Segment specification is called DI-CMAN-80008A. The "DI" tells us this is a DID. The "CMAN" tells us that this DID falls in the configuration management area (older DIDs use different conventions here), the 80008 is the number of the DID, and the "A" tells us that this is the first major revision of this DID.

All DIDs contain the following paragraphs which are of particular interest:

- *Description/Purpose*: a brief description of the purpose of the DID and how it will be used,

- *Application/Interrelationship*: top-level guidance on what the DID as a whole should cover, how it should be submitted, and what requirements it meets,

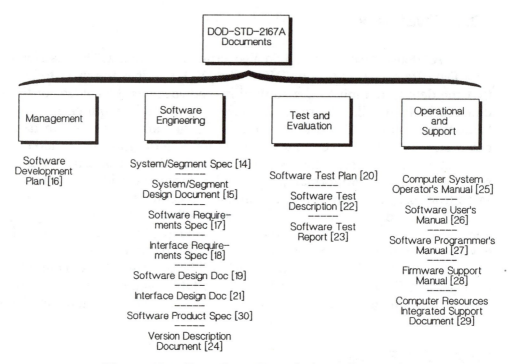

Figure 13.1 Data Item Descriptions discussed.

- *Preparation Instructions*: detailed instructions for writing the body of the DID.

13.3 Delivery Format

By default, DIDs are submitted on bound 8½ by 11 inch paper. Binding is often accomplished using comb binders, but other usually acceptable means include three ring notebooks or heavy duty staples. Significantly, *all* new DIDs encourage automated production of the deliverable and allow delivery on electronic media with government approval. If electronic media is selected, the government and contractor must agree on a precise format. Electronic delivery is normally in the best interest of both the government and the contractor.

The DID's table of contents is numbered using lower-case roman numerals starting with "i", while the body of the document is numbered using arabic numerals. The document control number should appear at the top outside edge of each page. All paragraphs must be numbered in strict accordance with the numbering scheme in the DID. Paragraphs which are not relevant are still included, containing the words "Not applicable."

13.4 Alternate Presentation Styles

By default, most DID paragraph descriptions are written as if you were meeting the requirement using a textual description. For many of the software requirements, however, more visual-oriented means are preferred. For example, a design is often much more clear when represented using an appropriate graphical representation or compilable Program Design Language (PDL) rather than a narrative description. For all DIDs, you may substitute charts, tables, matrices, or other presentation styles when the information required by the paragraphs and subparagraphs of the DID can be made more clear. The paragraph or subparagraph in the body of the DID would then reference the figure. If the figure does not meet all of the requirements of the DID for a given paragraph, the text can reference the figure and then add the missing information in narrative format. More than one figure can be used to meet the requirements of a single DID paragraph, and one figure can be referenced from multiple paragraphs. Figures should be placed in the document as soon after their reference as possible. If a large number of figures are used, perhaps to represent the software design, they may be placed at the end of the DID in an appendix. Figures, tables, and so on should also be on 8½ by 11 inch paper. Foldout figures are to be avoided whenever possible. The only exception which is normally acceptable is a single foldout to represent the "big picture" which the rest of the figures expand on.

13.5 Multiple (Sub)paragraphs

The DIDs include detailed guidance for the numbering of paragraphs and subparagraphs. Many of the DIDs have a set of paragraphs for *each* item being discussed. For example, if a CSCI is decomposed into CSC_1, CSC_2, and CSC_3 your paragraph numbers may be:

> 3.1 CSC_1
>> 3.1.1 Requirements

3.2 CSC_2
       3.2.1 Requirements

3.3 CSC_3
       3.3.1 Requirements

The DIDs would show this as 3.X for the paragraph numbers, and 3.X.1 for the subparagraphs.

When describing the DID, a square bracket is used to represent a paragraph title which will change based on the item being discussed. For example, paragraph 3.X in this example would be represented as

     3.X   [CSC Name]

You should also remember that you are *always* allowed to add more levels of paragraph numbering under that described in the DID, as long as the added numbers do not overlap the required paragraph numbers from the DID (i.e., as long as the numbers you want to use aren't used already). The only caveat to this is that no paragraph number is allowed to exceed seven levels of indentation.

13.6 Title Page

The title page for all DIDs is as follows:

Document Control Number and Date
Volume X of Y, if applicable

Revision number and date, if applicable

Title of DID
for the
System, Segment, or CSCI name (as appropriate)

Contract No. [contract number]
CDRL Sequence No. [CDRL number]

Prepared for:
Customer name and department code

Prepared by:
Contractor name and address

13.7 Appendices

Appendices are used to provide bulky information which would reduce the readability of the document if included in the main body. The appendix is then referenced in the main body of the document to refer the reader to the appropriate appendix. Appendices are lettered Appendix-A, Appendix-B, Appendix-C, and so on, and pages are numbered A-1, A-2, A-3, and so on. Paragraphs within an appendix are numbered using a multiple of 10, i.e., 10.1, 10.2, 10.3 for Appendix A; 20.1, 20.2, 20.3 for Appendix B, and so on.

14 Preparing the System/Segment Specification

This chapter describes specific procedures for preparing the *System/Segment Specification*, which is Data Item Deliverable (DID) number DI-CMAN-80008A. We will

- Discuss the purpose of this DID

- Present a sample schedule for preparing this DID

- Show a complete outline for the document

- Provide detailed instructions and hints for writing each paragraph of the DID

- Describe how the Government will judge the acceptability of the final DID as submitted

14.1 Purpose

The System/Segment Specification defines the requirements for an entire system or a segment of a system. The most important thing in the System/Segment Specification is the list of top-level requirements which will the developed system will be required to meet. Each of these requirements can be identified in the finished document by the use of the word *shall*, although you must be careful of phrases such as, "The final system shall meet all performance requirements shown in Table 3" to be sure that no requirements are overlooked. When defining requirements in the System/Segment Specification, it is *very* important to remember that *each requirement must not only be met but must also be verified through formal testing.* One of the most common mistakes made when writing a System/Segment Specification is to impose a requirement (through the use of the word shall) which is difficult or impossible to verify through testing. After approval, the System/Segment Specification becomes the functional baseline for the system or segment. The System/Segment Specification is also used to provide an overview of the system or segment for training personnel, support personnel, or users of the system.

The System/Segment Specification is often prepared by the government (perhaps with contractor assistance) *prior* to writing the Request For Proposal. If you win a contract based on a Request for Proposal, you will typically be required to take the government prepared System/Segment Specification and modify it as necessary to tailor it to your proposed solution.

14.2 Schedule

The System/Segment Specification is approved in preliminary form during the System Requirements Review, then approved again in final form during the System Design Review. As the system/segment design evolves during the development, the System/Segment Specification must be kept current using Specification Change Notices and revised editions of the document. Figure 14.1 shows a sample schedule for preparing and updating the System/Segment Specification during a typical project.

14.3 Outline

The following outline *must* be followed for the System/Segment Specification. Paragraph titles shown in italic will require significant input from software engineers. These paragraphs are discussed in depth in the next section.

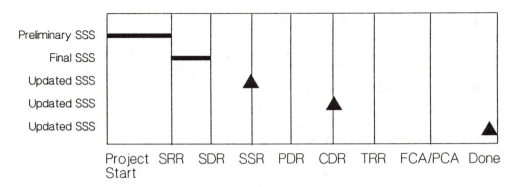

Figure 14.1 System/Segment Specification schedule.

1. Scope
1.1	**Identification**
1.2	**System overview**
1.3	**Document overview**

2. Applicable documents
2.1	**Government documents**
2.2	**Non-Government documents**

3. System requirements
3.1	***Definition***
3.2	***Characteristics***
3.2.1	*Performance characteristics*
3.2.1.X	*[System state name]*
3.2.1.X.Y	*[Mode name]*
3.2.1.X.Y.Z	*[Required capability]*
3.2.2	*System capability relationships*
3.2.3	*External interface requirements*
3.2.3.X	*[System name] external interface description*
3.2.4	Physical characteristics
3.2.4.1	Protective coatings
3.2.5	System quality factors
3.2.5.1	*Reliability*

3.2.5.2	Maintainability
3.2.5.3	Availability
3.2.5.4	*Additional quality factors*
3.2.6	Environmental conditions
3.2.7	Transportability
3.2.8	*Flexibility and expansion*
3.2.9	Portability
3.3	**Design and construction**
3.3.1	Materials
3.3.1.1	Toxic products and formulations
3.3.2	Electromagnetic radiation
3.3.3	Nameplates and product marking
3.3.4	Workmanship
3.3.5	Interchangeability
3.3.6	Safety
3.3.7	*Human engineering*
3.3.8	Nuclear control
3.3.9	System security
3.3.10	*Government furnished property usage*
3.3.11	Computer resource reserve capacity
3.4	**Documentation**
3.5	**Logistics**
3.6	**Personnel and training**
3.6.1	Personnel
3.6.2	*Training*
3.7	***Characteristics of subordinate elements***
3.7.X	***[Segment name and identifier]***
3.8	***Precedence***
3.9	**Qualification**
3.10	**Standard sample**
3.11	**Preproduction sample, periodic production sample, pilot, or pilot lot**

4. Quality assurance provisions

4.1	**Responsibility for inspection**
4.2	**Special tests and examinations**
4.3	**Requirements cross reference**

5.   Preparation for delivery

6.   Notes

6.1	**Intended use**
6.1.1	Missions
6.1.2	Threat

14.4 Detailed Instructions

This section presents specific instructions for meeting the requirements of each of the DID paragraphs with a significant software input (paragraphs shown here in italic). Other paragraphs will be completed by system or hardware engineers. Guidance for nonsoftware related paragraphs can be obtained by referring to the DID itself.

Paragraph 3.1: Definition

This paragraph presents a brief description of the system, including operational and logistical concepts. Significantly, the paragraph normally includes a system diagram which must be prepared as a joint effort of the software engineers and the hardware engineers. Figure 14.2 is a sample system diagram.

Paragraph 3.2: Characteristics

This paragraph may be left blank.

Paragraph 3.2.1: . Performance Characteristics

This paragraph is an introduction to a series of subparagraphs which define the performance characteristics of the system. This paragraph would normally include a list of the system states and a state transition diagram. In this context, states refer to *system* states, not detailed software states. States would normally be defined at this point in operational terms rather than actual internal states of the system. Figure 14.3 is a sample system level state transition diagram. Each of these system states can be further decomposed into modes. Once again, modes are defined in an operational sense. Modes are often represented either using mode transition charts

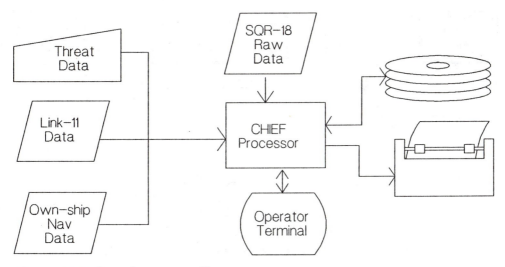

Figure 14.2 Sample system diagram.

(Fig. 14.4) or hierarchy charts (Fig. 14.5). This paragraph of the specification presents the state transition diagrams and mode transition (or mode hierarchy) charts for the system as an introduction to the paragraphs which follow.

Paragraph 3.2.1.X: [State name]

For each system state presented in paragraph 3.2.1, there will be a paragraph describing that state in detail. The paragraph will present a brief overview of the state and serve as an introduction to the detailed, lower level paragraphs. The portion of the mode transition charts or hierarchy charts falling beneath this system state is often shown here to summarize the paragraphs which will follow.

Paragraph 3.2.1.X.Y: [Mode name]

For each mode of each state, there will be a unique paragraph which identifies and describes the mode. Under this paragraph, you will have individual paragraphs for each required capability which must be demonstrated.

Figure 14.3 State transition diagram.

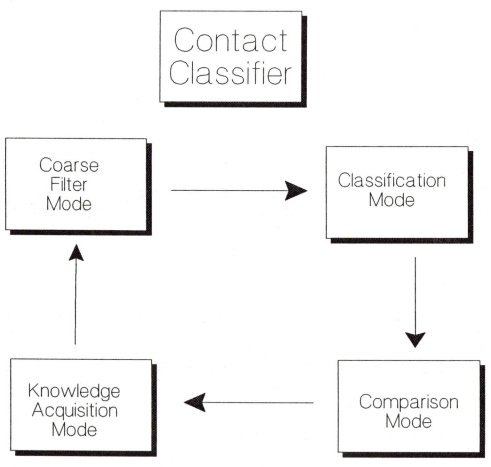

Figure 14.4 Mode transition
chart.

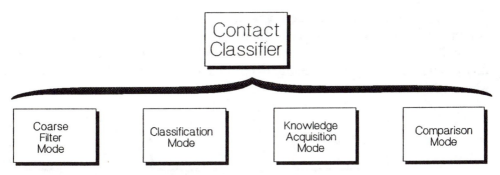

Figure 14.5 Mode hierarchy.

Paragraph 3.2.1.X.Y.Z: [Required Capability]

At this level specific requirements are identified. Requirements are identified for each *mode* under each *state* for the system. Requirements at this level will include detailed, specific parameters which must be met. Parameters must be expressed in measurable terms. Requirements can be expressed in narrative format or using requirements definition tables similar to Fig. 14.6. If a capability has been previously defined (for another mode), this paragraph references the other paragraph.

Type	Number	Name	Purpose and parameters
State	S1	Problem Init	
State	S2	Line Pre-process	
State	S3	Contact Classif.	
Mode	M3.1	Coarse Filter	
Mode	M3.2	Classification	
Mode	M3.3	Knowledge Acquis.	
Mode	M3.4	Comparison	
Req.	R3.4.1	Requirement A	Parameters for A
Req.	R3.4.2	Requirement B	Parameters for B
Req.	R3.4.3	Requirement C	See Requirement R3.2.6
State	S4	Display Results	
etc.			

Figure 14.6 Requirements definition table.

Figure 14.7 summarizes how these paragraphs fit together. The system exists in various states, which are then decomposed into modes, which then contain specific required capabilities. Note that the heart of this document is in these detailed paragraphs listing specific capabilities which must be delivered.

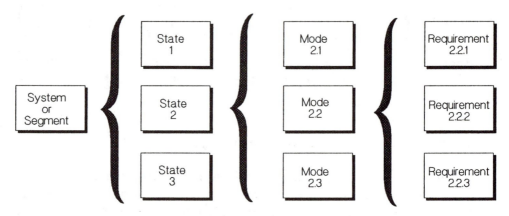

Figure. 14.7 System states, modes, and requirements.

Paragraph 3.2.2: System capability relationships

This paragraph summarizes the relationships between system capabilities and the states and modes of the system. It will often be sufficient to simply refer to the state transition diagrams, mode transition diagrams, and mode hierarchy.

Paragraph 3.2.3: External interface requirements

This system or segment will interface with the external systems listed in this paragraph. An external interface diagram similar to that shown in Fig. 14.8 is often sufficient.

Paragraph 3.2.3.X: [System name] external interface description

One of these paragraphs will be written for each external interface identified in paragraph 3.2.3. This paragraph describes the interface, including a

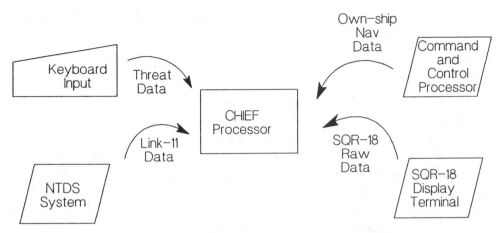

Figure. 14.8 External interface diagram.

statement of the purpose of the interface, the relationship between the interface and the states and modes of the system, data flows, and electrical characteristics when known. Detailed, quantitative descriptions of the interface (dimensions, tolerances, loads, speeds, protocols, etc.) are also included when known.

Paragraph 3.2.5.1: Reliability

This paragraph specifies reliability requirements in quantitative terms, and defines the conditions under which the reliability requirements are to be met. The paragraph may also include a reliability apportionment model to support the allocation of reliability values to various system requirements. In general, this paragraph is used for software to require that for a given environment the software operate without serious error for a specific percentage of the time. This percentage can then be used during testing to ensure that the software is sufficiently debugged prior to deliver to meet the customer's requirements for reliability.

Paragraph 3.2.5.4: Additional quality factors

This paragraph is often used for software to specify correctness requirements for the system. Numbers are expressed in probabilistic terms or as required maximum error values, as appropriate. An example for a complex command

and control decision aid might be a requirement that all results be accurate within plus or minus 5 percent.

Paragraph 3.2.8: Flexibility and expansion

This paragraph may be used to define specific areas of the software which the government anticipates will be expanded in the future. The software design and implementation must then allow for this planned expansion. For example, if the processing rate is currently 1000 updates per minute, the government may require that the software be capable of being expanded to accommodate 10,000 updates per minute. This may require a different input source and perhaps even a faster CPU, but the bulk of the software should be designed to handle this planned expansion.

Paragraph 3.3.7: Human engineering

This paragraph is primarily intended for hardware designers, but software related human engineering requirements are also appropriate. This paragraph typically identifies specific capabilities for which human engineering will be particularly critical. Requirements for prototyping of the software human interface would also be placed in this paragraph.

Paragraph 3.3.10: Government furnished property usage

This paragraph describes government furnished equipment, information, data, and so on which must be provided to the contractor. It is *very* important that *all* items required from the government be specifically called out in this paragraph. For software, this often includes:

- government furnished algorithms or code. This may apply when the existing software/algorithms were developed by a different company under contract to the government.

- government furnished data needed to properly test the system,

- government furnished equipment needed to test the system. This is particularly required for testing the system's interfaces to existing equipment.

Paragraph 3.6.2: Training

This paragraph describes the following training requirements, each of which will normally require extensive coordination with the software engineers:

- types of training and who is responsible for preparing and conducting the training,

- equipment that will be required to conduct training,

- training devices which must be developed to accomplish training.

Paragraph 3.7: Characteristics of subordinate elements

This paragraph only applies if this document is describing a system. This paragraph would then show how the system is decomposed into segments.

Paragraph 3.7.X: [Segment name and identifier]

If this document is describing a system, each segment under the system will have one of these paragraphs to describe the functions of the segment.

Paragraph 3.8: Precedence

This paragraph defines the relative priority of the various requirements described in this document. Priority can be described in general terms (A is more important than B) or in quantitative terms (A has a relative weight of .67, B has a relative weight of .39). The procedures describe in Sec. 3.4 of this text are one formal method of ranking requirements.

14.5 Evaluating the System/Segment Specification

The following checklist can be used when evaluating the System/Segment Specification:

_____ Is the required DID format followed exactly?

_____ Is the terminology consistent within the document?

_____ Is the document understandable?

_____ Are the performance characteristics quantitative and measurable? Can the final system be tested to verify _each_ of the capabilities required in this paragraphs?

_____ Do the states, and modes within states, make sense from an operation, development, and testing perspective?

_____ Are the required capabilities clear?

_____ If the final system meets all of the required capabilities defined in this document, will the system be useful to the end users?

_____ Are requirements for reliability specific and realistic?

_____ Is the government willing and able to supply all government furnished material identified in paragraph 3.3.10?

_____ Is the order of precedence for requirements in paragraph 3.8 sufficiently detailed and clear to be useful when making trade-off decisions and design-to-cost analysis?

15 Preparing the System/Segment Design Document

This chapter describes specific procedures for preparing the *System/Segment Design Document*, which is Data Item Description (DID) number DI-CMAN-80534. We will:

- Discuss the purpose of this DID

- Present a sample schedule for preparing this DID

- Show a complete outline for the document

- Provide detailed instructions and hints for writing each paragraph of the DID

- Describe how the Government will judge the acceptability of the final DID as submitted

15.1 Purpose

The System/Segment Design Document describes the design of a system or segment, including its operational and support environments. It describes how the system or segment will be decomposed into HWCIs, CSCIs, and manual operations. Requirements contained in the System/Segment Specification are allocated to specific CSCIs and HWCIs in the System/Segment Design Document. This top-level allocation of requirements then forms the basis for the design of the CSCIs and HWCIs.

15.2 Schedule

The System/Segment Design Document is approved in final form during the System Design Review. As the system/segment design evolves during the development, the System/Segment Design Document must be kept current, although it is not necessary to use the formal Specification Change Notices required for the System/Segment Specification.   When the system or segment is completed, an up-to-date version of the System/Segment Design Document must be submitted along with the source code. Figure 15.1 shows a sample schedule for preparing and updating the System/Segment Design Document during a typical project.

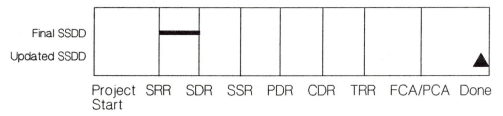

Figure 15.1 SSDD schedule.

15.3 Outline

The following outline *must* be followed for the System/Segment Design Document. Paragraph titles shown in italic will require significant input from software engineers. These paragraphs are discussed in depth in the next section.

1.   Scope
        1.1   Identification
        1.2   System overview
        1.3   Document overview

2.   Referenced documents

3. Operational concepts

3.1	**Mission**
3.1.1	User needs
3.1.2	Primary mission(s)
3.1.3	Secondary mission(s)
3.2	**Operational environment**
3.3	**Support environment**
3.3.1	Support concept
3.3.2	Support facilities
3.3.3	Supply
3.3.4	Government agencies
3.4	***System architecture***
3.5	**Operational scenarios**

4. System design

4.1	**HWCI identification**
4.1.X	[HWCI name and identifier]
4.2	***CSCI identification***
4.2.X	*[CSCI name and identifier]*
4.3	**Manual operations identifier**
4.3.X	[Manual operation name and identifier]
4.4	***Internal interfaces***
4.4.1	HWCI to HWCI interfaces
4.4.2	*HWCI to CSCI interfaces*
4.4.3	*CSCI to CSCI interfaces*

5. Processing resources

5.X	***[Processing resource name and identifier]***

6. Quality factor compliance

7. *Requirements traceability*

8. Notes

15.4 Detailed Instructions

This section presents specific instructions for meeting the requirements of each of the DID paragraphs with a significant software input (paragraphs shown in italic). Other paragraphs will be completed by system or hardware engineers. Guidance for nonsoftware related paragraphs can be obtained by referring to the DID itself.

Paragraph 3.4: System architecture

This paragraph presents an overview of the internal structure of the system. The segments, HWCIs, and CSCIs are identified (often using a figure similar to Fig. 15.2) and their purpose is summarized. The relationships among the segments, HWCIs, and CSCIs must be described either verbally or as in this figure. This paragraph must also identify and state the purpose of each external interface of the system. This can often be accomplished simply with a reference to paragraph 3.2.3 of the System/Segment Specification.

Paragraph 4.2: CSCI identification

This paragraph is a top level introduction to the various CSCIs in the system. Each CSCI is discussed in more detail in the subparagraphs which follow.

Paragraph 4.2.X: [CSCI name and identifier]

For each CSCI identified in paragraph 4.2, there will be a subparagraph describing the purpose of the CSCI. The identifier referred to in the subparagraph title is a project unique number assigned to this CSCI for configuration control purposes. This sub-paragraph identifies each requirement from the System/Segment Specification which this particular CSCI must meet. The interfaces, if any, from this CSCI to other systems is also discussed here. Each of these external interfaces must be defined in detail (e.g., bits per second, word length, message format, frequency of messages, priority rules, protocol). Design constraints such as maximum response time are also defined in this paragraph. Notice that these interfaces are *external* interfaces. Interfaces to other configuration items within this system (internal interfaces) are covered later in this document.

It is important to remember that the CSCIs are configuration management and testing entities designed to allow requirements from the System/Segment Specification to be allocated. They do not necessarily correspond to any particular software entity (program, module, package, etc.). However, the design documents are normally more clear if CSCIs *do* correspond to complete programs (or processes). When you are decomposing your requirements into CSCIs, try to envision how many independent programs you expect to be included in the final system. This will often be the number of CSCIs you will propose in your System/Segment Design Document.

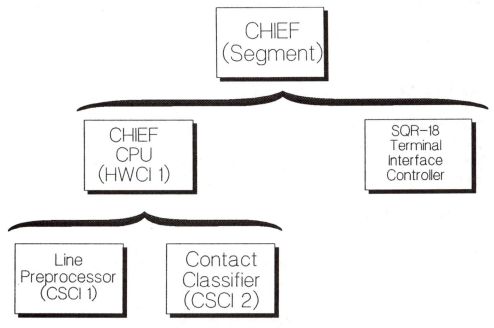

Figure 15.2 System architecture.

Paragraph 4.4: Internal interfaces

This paragraph presents an overview of the internal interfaces within the system, often with the use of a system internal interface diagram (Fig. 15.3). The relationship of the interfaces to the configuration items for the system must be described (or shown in the diagram). Subparagraphs then describe each interface individually.

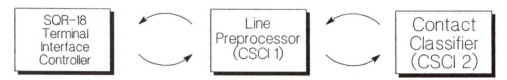

Figure 15.3 Internal interfaces.

Paragraph 4.4.2: HWCI to CSCI interfaces

This subparagraph identifies each signal transmitted between a CSCI and an HWCI, the source of the signal, and the destination of the signal. Each of these interfaces is assigned a project unique identifier and an interface name.

Paragraph 4.4.3: CSCI to CSCI interfaces

Similarly, this subparagraph identifies each signal transmitted between CSCIs, including the source and destination of the signal. Each of these interfaces is assigned a project unique identifier and an interface name.

Paragraph 5.X: [Processing resource name and identifier]

This paragraph is used to identify CPUs which will be running CSCIs. There will be one unique paragraph for each different CPU configuration. For each configuration, this paragraph specifies the hardware, programming, design, coding, and utilization characteristics of the processing resource. For each processing resource, the following must be defined:

- *Memory size*:   internal memory in absolute terms, spare memory required when complete (e.g., 50% reserve), or both

- *Word size*: in bits

- *Processing speed*: in absolute terms, spare required, or both

- *Character set standard*: normally ASCII

- *Instruction set architecture*

- *Interrupt capabilities*

- *Direct Memory Access (DMA) capabilities*

- *Channel requirements*: absolute, spare, or both

- *Auxiliary storage*: absolute, spare, or both

- *Growth capabilities*: required growth capability in any area

- *Diagnostic capabilities*:   required internal diagnostics. Especially used for hardware built in test (BIT)

- *Additional computer hardware capabilities*: other required capabilities, including fault tolerance, preprocessing, floating point, array processing, and so on.

This paragraph should also include a description of how the processing resources in the system will be allocated to the identified CSCIs.

Paragraph 7: Requirements traceability

This section must show traceability between the requirements identified in the System/Segment Specification and the requirements allocated to CSCIs within the System/Segment Design Document. For each requirement in the System/Segment Specification, this paragraph should show how identified requirements within one or more CSCI meets the requirement. For each requirement in the System/Segment Design Document, this paragraph should show which requirements from the System/Segment Specification are being met. Figure 15.4 shows a sample requirements traceability matrix which can be used to meet this requirement.

Requirement		CSCI	
Name	Number	Name	Number
Requirement A Requirement B Requirement C etc.	R3.4.1 R3.4.2 R3.4.3	Contact Classifier Contact Classifier Contact Classifier	C.2 C.2 C.2

Figure 15.4 Requirements traceability matrix.

15.5 Evaluating the System/Segment Design Document

The following checklist can be used when evaluating the System/Segment Specification:

_____ Is the required DID format followed exactly?

_____ Is the terminology consistent within the document?

_____ Is the document understandable?

_____ Do the paragraphs describing the mission, operational environment, and support environment show an adequate understanding of the operational concepts for the system or segment?

_____ Is the decomposition of the system or segment into HWCIs, CSCIs, and manual operations valid? Are the functions of each configuration item clear?

_____ Can each configuration item be developed and tested independently?

_____ Does each CSCI run on a single processing resource, or at least on one of a homogenous group (they are each the same) of processing resources?

_____ Are external interfaces consistent with the System/Segment Specification?

_____ Are internal interfaces clear and simple? Confusing interfaces are often a sign of an improper decomposition into CSCIs.

_____ Are the processing resource definitions sufficiently clear to allow design work to proceed? Do they describe an environment which will be able to accomplish the required tasks? Will the required processing resources be obtainable?

_____ If more than one CSCI will be simultaneously operating on a single CPU, are issues such as scheduling, interrupt handling, allocation of resources, and resource contention clear?

_____ If more than one CPU will be operating using a common bus, are issues such as bus arbitration and interrupt processing addressed and clear?

_____ Are all requirements in the System/Segment Specification clearly traceable to one or more requirements in the System/Segment Design Document?

_____ Are the performance characteristics quantitative and measurable? Can the final system be tested to verify _each_ of the capabilities required in this paragraph?

_____ Do the states, and modes within states, make sense from an operational, development, and testing perspective?

16 Preparing the Software Development Plan

This chapter describes specific procedures for preparing the *Software Development Plan*, which is Data Item Description (DID) number DI-MCCR-80030A. We will

- Discuss the purpose of this DID

- Present a sample schedule for preparing this DID

- Show a complete outline for the document

- Provide detailed instructions and hints for writing each paragraph of the DID

- Describe how the Government will judge the acceptability of the final DID as submitted

16.1 Purpose

The Software Development plan describes a contractor's procedures, management organization, and work plan for the software development effort.

234

16.2 Schedule

The Software Development Plan is approved in final form during the System Design Review although the document should be prepared as part of the proposal process. In fact, many companies submit their Software Development Plan as part of their proposal. No further formal deliveries of this document are typically required, but the document must be kept current throughout the development program. This is typically accomplished by updating the plan informally and informing the government of any changes in your monthly status reports.

On some projects, the government may require three deliveries of the Software Development Plan. These deliveries correspond to the concept-oriented plan, capability-oriented plan, and implementation-oriented plan which were discussed in Sec. 6.4. The concept-oriented plan is prepared prior to the System Requirements Review and is presented at this review. This plan is based on the overall requirements for the system or segment, and leaves several paragraphs of the DID to-be-determined. This plan is then revised for presentation at the System Design Review as the capability-oriented plan. At this point, the implementation schedule and plans for specific configuration items is known and planned for. Finally, as the detailed design is completed the capability-oriented plan is revised to show the schedule for implementing specific program modules. After the detailed design for the last CSCI is completed the implementation-oriented plan can be complete. The capability-oriented plan is typically presented at the Critical Design Review for the System or Segment. Figure 16.1 summarizes the schedule for preparing and submitting the Software Development Plan(s). If a single submission is called for, this submission will correspond to the capability-oriented plan shown in this figure.

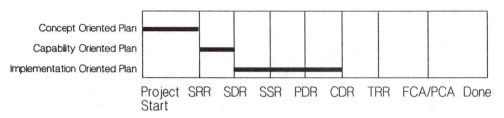

Figure 16.1 SDP schedule.

16.3 Outline

The following outline *must* be followed for the Software Development Plan.
All of the following paragraphs are discussed in the paragraphs that follow.

1.   Scope
      1.1   **Identification**
      1.2   **System overview**
      1.3   **Document overview**
      1.4   **Relationship to other plans**

2.   Referenced documents

3.   Software development management
      3.1   **Project organization and resources**
      3.1.1   Contractor facilities
      3.1.2   Government furnished equipment, software,
                     and services
      3.1.3   Organizational structure
      3.1.4   Personnel
      3.2   **Schedule and milestones**
      3.2.1   Activities
      3.2.2   Activity network
      3.2.3   Source identification
      3.3   **Risk management**
      3.4   **Security**
      3.5   **Interface with associate contractors**

6.1.1	Organizational structure – software product evaluations
6.1.2	Personnel – software product evaluations
6.2	**Software product evaluation procedures and tools**
6.2.1	Procedures
6.2.2	Tools
6.3	**Subcontractor products**
6.4	**Software product evaluation records**
6.5	**Activity-dependent product evaluations**
6.5.X	Software products evaluation – [activity name]

7.   Software configuration management

7.1	**Organization and resources – configuration management**
7.1.1	Organizational structure – configuration management
7.1.2	Personnel – configuration management
7.2	**Configuration identification**
7.2.1	Developmental configuration identification
7.2.2	Identification methods
7.3	**Configuration control**
7.3.1	Flow of configuration control
7.3.2	Reporting documentation
7.3.2.X	[Report name]
7.3.3	Review procedures
7.3.3.X	[Review board name] procedures
7.3.4	Storage, handling, and delivery of project media
7.3.5	Additional control
7.4	**Configuration status accounting**
7.5	**Configuration audits**
7.6	**Preparation for specification authentication**
7.7	**Configuration management major milestones**

8.   Other software development functions

8.X	**[Function name]**
8.X.1	Organizational structure – [function name]

8.X.2	Personnel – [function name]
8.X.3	Other resources – [function name]
8.X.4	Methods and procedures – [function name]

9.   Notes

16.4 Detailed Instructions

This section presents specific instructions for meeting the requirements of each of the DID paragraphs. For many paragraphs it is recommended that you leave the paragraph blank because all information for the paragraph is covered in lower level subparagraphs. For each of these, it would also be appropriate for the top-level paragraph to consist of a set of bullets presenting the titles of the lower level subparagraphs.

Paragraph 1: Scope

This paragraph may be left blank.

Paragraph 1.1: Identification

This paragraph says: "This plan applies to all CSCIs contained in the _____ [name] system, identification number _____ [number]."
          Simply fill in the appropriate system name and identification number. If you are only responsible for a subset of the system's CSCIs, modify the paragraph to identify which CSCIs this paragraph applies to.

Paragraph 1.2: System overview

Simply state: "See paragraph 1.2 of the _____ [name] System/Segment Specification, document number _____ [number]."

Paragraph 1.3: Document overview

This paragraph says: "This document summarizes the procedures, management approach, and contract work effort of the _____ [name] company's software development effort for the _____ [name] system."

Paragraph 1.4: Relationship to other plans

This paragraph will typically say "Not applicable."

Paragraph 2: Referenced documents

List all documents (including document number and title) referenced in this plan. Sources for documents not available through Government stocking activities must also be listed.

Paragraph 3: Software development management

This paragraph may be left blank.

Paragraph 3.1: Project organization and resources

This paragraph may be left blank.

Paragraph 3.1.1: Contractor facilities

This subparagraph describes the contractor's facilities used for this software engineering effort. The location of project specific resources (software engineering and test environments) and secure areas should be included. The contents of this paragraph will normally be the same from one contract to the next. For many companies, it is sufficient to state:

> All efforts associated with the _____ [name] project, including software engineering and testing, will be conducted at the _____ [facility name] facility located at _____ [street address] in the city of _____ [city]. This facility is approximately _____ [miles or minutes] from the government program office [or airport, if appropriate]. This site is cleared for classified work and storage up to the _____ [security level] level, and has _____ [number] square feet of SCI space.

Paragraph 3.1.2: Government furnished equipment, software, and services

Simply state: "See paragraph 3.3.10 of the _____ [name] System/Segment
Specification, document number _____ [number]."

Paragraph 3.1.3: Organizational structure

This is simply an organizational chart showing all organizational groups
participating in the software development effort. The chart *does not* identify
individuals, and lists only the major organizational entities. Groups such as
quality control, testing, and software library maintenance should be shown.
In general, the same organizational chart can be used from one project to
the next. Figure 16.2 is a sample chart.

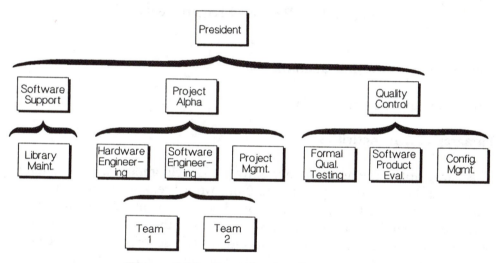

Figure 16.2 Organizational structure.

Paragraph 3.1.4: Personnel

This paragraph shows the resources required to perform the software
engineering effort. Resources should be broken down by labor category,
including listings for project management, software engineering, formal
software testing, software product evaluations (internal walk-throughs),

software configuration management, and any other functions identified in this plan. Although the DID only requires you to list a single number for each category showing the total, it is preferred to graphically show the personnel required versus time. A table similar to Fig. 16.3 meets the requirements of this paragraph.

Functional Area	Phase									
	1	2	3	4	5	6	7	8	9	10
Proj. Mgmt.	4	4	5	6	6	6	6	6	4	1
Software Eng.	18	24	28	34	44	45	45	45	35	24
Software Testing	4	4	4	6	12	12	15	15	15	15
Product Eval.	1	3	3	3	3	3	3	3	3	3
Config. Mgmt.	2	2	2	2	2	2	2	2	2	2

Figure 16.3 Personnel requirements.

Paragraph 3.2: Schedule and milestones

This paragraph may be left blank.

Paragraph 3.2.1: Activities

This paragraph is the heart of your Software Development Plan. It contains a list of all tasks to be accomplished (your work breakdown structure) and the schedule for the tasks. The work breakdown structure should include all tasks identified in Sec. 5.3 of this book. If other tasks are added, a description of these tasks should be included. The description should clearly specify a *product* which will be used to determine when the task is completed. Even a task to simply select the best of two alternatives has a product – the decision itself. For more guidance in developing a work breakdown structure, see my book *Structured Computer Project Management* (10). It is possible to show both the list of tasks and the schedule using a Gantt format (see Fig. 16.4). The DID also requires that areas of high risk be shown at this point. This can be shown directly on the Gantt chart using a column labeled "Risk" which contains a value of low, medium, or high. The project Gantt chart is often more clear if presented using a fold-out to show the entire chart on one page.

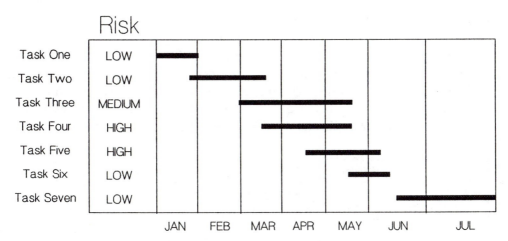

Figure 16.4 Task list and schedule.

Paragraph 3.2.2: Activity network

This paragraph shows the dependencies between your project tasks. Predecessor tasks must be identified and slack time must be calculated and shown. A network diagram similar to Fig. 16.5 can be used to show this information. My book *Structured Computer Project Management* also contains a detailed discussion of how to determine dependencies and calculate slack time.

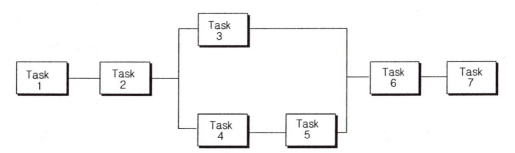

Figure 16.5 Sample network diagram.

Paragraph 3.2.3: Source identification

This paragraph shows where you intend to obtain all items (hardware, software, firmware) which you do not already have in-house. This paragraph typically applies to commercial hardware and software which you intend to purchase, and is simply a list of the vendors you will use to purchase the various items. A table similar to Fig. 16.6 can be used.

Item	Vendor	Address	Rcvd?
HP 9020F	HP	1234 Anyplace, SD, CA	Yes
Able Software	Able, Inc.	4321 Someplace, SD, CA	No
C Compiler	Borland	1234 Main St., Large, CA	No

Figure 16.6 Vendor Checklist

Paragraph 3.3: Risk management

Refer back to your Gantt chart (paragraph 3.2.1 and figure 16.4) and pull out each of the tasks which you ranked as high risk. Take the resulting list and estimate the technical risk, cost risk, schedule risk, and network risk. Network risk is the risk caused when problems with one task will adversely affect a large number of other tasks. You can do this ranking using high, medium, and low estimates for each category, or you can use the quantitative approach described in (10). These risk factors can be shown using a table similar to Fig. 16.7. For each of these tasks, you must then document

- How you will monitor the task to detect problems early. This typically includes monitoring expenditures versus progress for cost risk; scheduled progress versus actual progress for schedule risk; and perhaps technical performance measurement plans for technical risk.

- Actions you will take to attempt to avoid the problems. This typically includes prototyping; early development of high risk items; extra testing during development; and reduced risk design approaches.

Task Name	T. Risk	C. Risk	S. Risk	N. Risk	Overall
Task One	High	High	High	Medium	High
Task Two	Medium	Medium	Medium	Low	Medium
Task Three	Low	Medium	Medium	High	Medium
etc.					

Figure 16.7 Risk ranking table.

- Contingency plans, which may include parallel development of alternative solutions; fall-back design alternatives; or additional resources which can be applied to the project.

Paragraph 3.4: Security

This paragraph describes how you will implement the security requirements of the contract. You typically reference an appendix which describes your company's security procedures as they apply to this contract. The appendix is normally written by someone in your security department, and often does not change from one contract to the next.

Paragraph 3.5: Interface with associate contractors

Unless you are part of a joint venture, this paragraph will say, "Not applicable." If you *are* part of a joint venture team, this paragraph will describe your plans for coordinating the design and data management for the project.

Paragraph 3.6: Interface with software IV&V agent(s)

If the contract does not call for independent verification and validation of the software, this paragraph will say, "Not applicable," otherwise it will describe your plans for interfacing with the IV&V agent. This typically consists of a statement such as

Each software engineering and test document prepared during this contract will be provided to the software IV&V agent, _____, for review. As CSCIs are completed and ready for formal testing (following completion of the Test Readiness Review for the CSCI), the CSCI software will be delivered to _____ for independent testing. During this testing, we will be available to assist with software set-up and answer technical questions as necessary.

Paragraph 3.7: Subcontractor management

If no subcontractors will be used, this paragraph will say, "Not applicable," otherwise it will describe your plans for monitoring your subcontractors. This typically consists of a statement such as:

_____ [company name] will be working as a subcontractor on this contractor. _____ [company name] will be responsible for _____ [work areas] during the contract. They will accomplish this by performing the work shown in our work breakdown structure as tasks _____, _____, and _____ [WBS tasks]. Monthly reports will be provided from _____ [company name] to us describing:

- Progress to date on each task, planned progress to date, and estimated completion date.

- Expenditures to date for each task, planned expenditures to date for each task, and estimated costs to complete the task.

- Technical difficulties encountered in performing the tasks.

All contractual requirements, including quality control, configuration management, and software engineering, which are imposed on our company by the government will also be required of the _____ [name] company. _____ [name] will review all deliverables prior to submission to us. We will then review the materials for acceptability prior to incorporation in our products and delivery to the government.

Paragraph 3.8: Formal reviews

Start with a statement that "All formal reviews required by the contract will be conducted in accordance with MIL-STD-1521B procedures."   Then include the checklist in Sec. 11.2 of this text.

Paragraph 3.9: Software development libraries

This paragraph should be a standard paragraph describing the procedures and support tools you use to maintain your software development libraries.

Paragraph 3.10: Corrective action process

Use Sec. 9.13.2 of this text to write this paragraph.

Paragraph 3.11: Problem/change report

This paragraph describes the format to be used for problem/change reports. Figure 16.8 a sample report which meets this requirement.

Paragraph 4: Software engineering

This paragraph may be left blank.

Paragraph 4.1: Organizational and resources - software engineering

This paragraph may be left blank.

Paragraph 4.1.1: Organizational structure – software engineering

Unless you are dealing with external organizations as subcontractors, joint venture team members, or for independent verification and validation, this paragraph simply refers the reader back to paragraph 3.1.3 of this document. If you are dealing with external organizations, add these organizations to the figure from paragraph 3.1.3 and put the new figure here.

```
┌─────────────────────────────────────────────────────────────┐
│Project: _____    Problem #: _____               │
│Originator: _____          │
│           _____         │
│Status: _____                                            │
│                                                              │
│Problem Name: _____             │
│        Date: _____  Category: _____ Priority: ____    │
│        Items affected: _____          │
│                                                              │
│        Description:    _____          │
│                        _____          │
│                        _____          │
│                        _____          │
│                                                              │
│Analyst Name: _____        │
│        Org: _____         │
│        Date Assigned: _____ Completed: _____ Time: ____    │
│        Solution: _____         │
│                  _____         │
│                  _____         │
│        Impacts:  _____         │
│        Approval: _____         │
│                                                              │
│Corrector Name: _____         │
│        Org: _____         │
│        Date: _____ Version: _____ Time: _____                │
│        Solution: _____         │
│        Follow-up: _____         │
└─────────────────────────────────────────────────────────────┘
```

Figure 16.8 Problem/change report.

Paragraph 4.1.2: Personnel – software engineering

For each task identified in your work breakdown structure (paragraph 3.2.1), this paragraph identifies the staff required to perform the activities. Staff are identified by job title, not by individual name. An appendix should contain a description of the minimum qualifications for each job title (reference the appendix in this paragraph). If any task has special requirements (security level, extended hours, etc.), this will be shown here. It is also a good idea to include formal qualification testing, software product evaluation, and configuration management requirements on this one report.

Paragraph 4.1.3: Software engineering environment

This paragraph may be left blank.

Paragraph 4.1.3.1: Software items

This paragraph will normally refer back to the System/Segment Design Document, paragraph 5.X, for descriptions of the operating system and software development tools necessary to perform the work. For test drivers, test data generators, and so on, refer to the CSCI paragraph (4.2.X) in the System/Segment Design Document which describes the requirements for this category 3 CSCI software. This paragraph will also need to identify any classified processing or security issues associated with the software items.

Paragraph 4.1.3.2: Hardware and firmware items

Refer back to the System/Segment Design Document, paragraph 5.X, for descriptions of the hardware and firmware used for software engineering. This paragraph will then need to identify any classified processing or security issues associated with the hardware or firmware items.

Paragraph 4.1.3.3: Proprietary nature and Government rights

For each item in the software engineering environment, this paragraph identifies the proprietary nature and Government rights associated with each item of the software engineering environment. This should typically include a statement such as, "The rights to all commercial products (nondevelopmental items) used during this software development effort are restricted in accordance with the terms offered to our company by the holders of these rights." This covers your use of commercial hardware, operating systems, and so on. *If* you will be delivering hardware, software, data, or algorithms to the government which you have full rights to (probably because you developed the item previously), this paragraph *must* clearly spell out what these items are and what rights, if any, you are conveying to the government.

Paragraph 4.1.3.4: Installation, control, and maintenance

This paragraph describes your plans for installing and testing each item required for software engineering, along with plans for controlling and maintaining this equipment/software during use. If the environment is already installed and available, it is sufficient to state that the software environment "is currently installed and will be maintained in accordance with corporate policies and procedures."

Paragraph 4.2: Software standards and procedures

This paragraph may be left blank.

Paragraph 4.2.1: Software development techniques and methodologies

This paragraph describes the software development techniques and methodologies you plan to use to perform all phases of software development. It is important to note that all software design documents will be evaluated based on their compliance with the requirements of this technique. See Sec. 4.5 and 4.6 of this text for recommendations in this area.

Paragraph 4.2.2: Software development files

This paragraph defines your plans for the creation and maintenance of software development files, including their content and format. Refer to Sec. 9.13.3 of this text for help.

Paragraph 4.2.3: Design standards

This paragraph describes your design standards. If you are using a standard methodology this paragraph may simply reference that methodology as your design standard. If you are using an unusual methodology (perhaps one which was internally developed), this paragraph must describe the standards which are used to evaluate the correctness of designs produced using your methodology.

Paragraph 4.2.4: Coding standards

This paragraph references an appendix to this document which contains a copy of your internal coding standards. Appendix B of DOD-STD-2167A contains a list of items which must be covered by your coding standards.

Paragraph 4.3: Nondevelopmental software

This paragraph describes each nondevelopmental software item (such as commercially available, reusable, and Government furnished software) to be incorporated into the deliverable software. A rationale for the use of each item must be included. Refer to Sec. 12.6 of this text for justification for the use of off-the-shelf applications packages.

Paragraph 5: Formal qualification testing

This paragraph may be left blank.

Paragraph 5.1: Organization and resources – formal qualification testing

This paragraph may be left blank.

Paragraph 5.1.1: Organizational structure – formal qualification testing

This paragraph says, "See paragraph 3.1.3."

Paragraph 5.1.2: Personnel – formal qualification testing

This paragraph normally says, "See paragraph 4.1.2." If the contract calls for independent verification and validation, this paragraph says: "See paragraph 4.1.1."

Paragraph 5.2: Test approach/philosophy

This paragraph must state that

- the requirements allocated to each CSU will be tested individually, and test results will be recorded.,

- as CSUs are integrated, the requirements allocated to CSCs will be tested individually, and test results will be recorded,

- as CSCs are integrated, the requirements allocated to CSCIs will be tested individually, and the results will be recorded,

- as CSCIs are integrated, the system requirements will be tested individually and the results will be recorded.

You should also state that testing will be in accordance with requirements contained in DOD-STD-2167A, and the reviews will be in accordance with MIL-STD-1521B. You should include a statement that all problems identified during testing will be tracked to resolution, and that after resolution the component (CSU, CSC, CSCI, or system) will be analyzed to determine if new problems may have been introduced. Refer to Sec. 9.13.2 of this text for additional general guidance.

If testing of the system involves some special type of testing (real world testing, testing using recorded "live" data, special simulators, etc.), descriptions of this testing approach would be included in this paragraph.

Paragraph 5.3: Test planning assumptions and constraints

If any aspect of your testing is not 100 percent realistic, this paragraph must describe the specific assumptions made in your test planning. For example, a simulated environment is virtually *never* identical to a live environment. When using a simulated environment, this paragraph would describe the differences between your test environment and a live environment.

If you are relying on the government for *any* aspect of your testing (data, access to actual equipment, access to simulators, operational personnel, etc.) this paragraph should identify these items explicitly and state that adequate testing will not be feasible unless the items required are available when required. Be very explicit here about *exactly* what you require from the government.

Paragraph 6: Software product evaluations

This paragraph may be left blank.

Paragraph 6.1: Organization and resources – software product evaluations

This paragraph may be left blank.

Paragraph 6.1.1: Organizational structure – software product evaluations

This paragraph says, "See paragraph 3.1.3."

Paragraph 6.1.2: Personnel – software product evaluations

This paragraph says: "See paragraph 3.1.4."

Paragraph 6.2: Software product evaluation procedures and tools

This paragraph may be left blank.

Paragraph 6.2.1: Procedures

This paragraph is a standard paragraph (it does not change from contract to contract) which describes your procedures for performing software product evaluations. It is acceptable to simply state that all software products will be evaluated using the checklist contained in the chapters of this book describing each individual DID Chaps 13 to 30). A copy of this book may then be included with the Software Development Plan, or this text can be listed as a referenced document in Sec. 2 of your plan. If you decide to include an actual copy of this book, it must be a purchased copy (from Prentice-Hall), *not* photocopy.

Paragraph 6.2.2: Tools

This paragraph describes tools which will be used to assist with software product evaluations. If *Teamplan* is used during development, this paragraph may simply contain a reference to the Teamplan Owners Manual, which describes extensive software quality control tools and procedures built into the software engineering environment.

Paragraph 6.3: Subcontractor products

If you are not using subcontractors, this paragraph says, "Not applicable." If you are using subcontractors, this paragraph normally states that, "Subcontractors are required to follow procedures outlined in this plan for all software products developed under this contract. In addition, all subcontractor produced software products will be evaluated by us using procedures outlined in paragraph 6.2.1 of this document prior to final delivery to the government."

Paragraph 6.4: Software product evaluation records

This paragraph must describe the formats and contents of all reports you will use to track software product evaluations.

Paragraph 6.5: Activity-dependent product evaluations

This paragraph describes special evaluation procedures/requirements which are different than those referenced in paragraphs 6.2.1 and 6.2.2. This paragraph will typically be, "Not applicable" for most contracts. If this paragraph is, "Not applicable," there will be no lower level paragraphs (6.5.X). One example of an activity falling under this paragraph would be periodic quality control audits of the project.

Paragraph 6.5.X: Software products evaluation – [activity name]

This paragraph contains the special evaluation procedures/requirements for each special activity.

Paragraph 7: Software configuration management

This paragraph may be left blank.

Paragraph 7.1: Organization and resources – configuration management

This paragraph may be left blank.

Paragraph 7.1.1: Organizational structure – configuration management

This paragraph normally says, "See paragraph 3.1.3."

Paragraph 7.1.2: Personnel – configuration management

This paragraph normally says, "See paragraph 3.1.4."

Paragraph 7.2: Configuration identification

This paragraph may be left blank.

Paragraph 7.2.1: Developmental configuration identification

This paragraph normally says

> The developmental configuration identification for each Computer Software Configuration Item shall consist of the Software Design Document and Software Product Specification (including code). Configuration control shall be established in a phased manner as follows:
>
> - Following completion of the Preliminary Design Review, the Software Design Document defined allocation of CSCI requirements to CSCs and CSUs shall be placed under configuration control.
>
> - Following completion of the Critical Design Review, the final Software Design Document (including detailed design for the CSCI) shall be placed under configuration control.
>
> - Following completion of the Test Readiness Review, the Software Product Specification (including CSCI code) shall be placed under configuration control

Paragraph 7.2.2: Identification methods

If you are using *Teamplan,* this paragraph refers to the Teamplan Owner's Manual for the identification (naming, marking, numbering) of configuration items. If you are not using Teamplan, this paragraph describes your procedures for performing this activity. See Sec. 12.3.2 of this text for assistance.

Paragraph 7.3: Configuration control

This paragraph may be left blank.

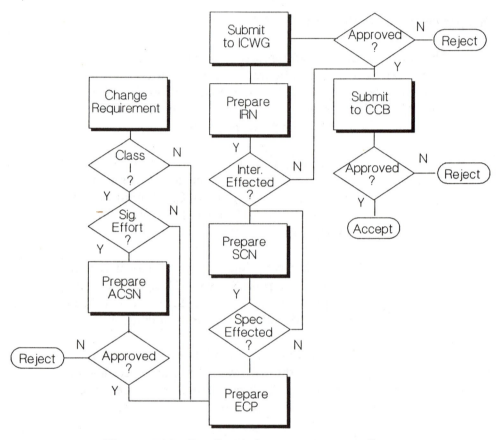

Figure 16.9 Configuration management flow.

Paragraph 7.3.1: Flow of configuration control

This paragraph consists of a flow chart similar to Fig. 16.9.

Paragraph 7.3.2: Reporting documentation

This paragraph lists all configuration control reports you will use. As a minimum, this list should include Engineering Change Proposals and Specification Change Notices. See Sec. 7.1 of this text for assistance.

Paragraph 7.3.2.X: [Report name]

For each report identified in 7.3.2, you will have one paragraph describing the report. When writing this section, you can use the descriptions of reports in Sec. 7.1.3 of this text.

Paragraph 7.3.3: Review procedures

This report lists the review boards which are used to review changes to the configuration. This paragraph will list any of your *internal* review boards used for configuration control. These boards will often parallel the government established review boards (Configuration Control Board and Interface Control Working Group). See Sec. 7.1 of this text for assistance.

Paragraph 7.3.3.X: [Review board name] procedures

For each board identified in 7.3.3, you will have one paragraph describing the review board procedures and purpose. Use Sec. 7.1 of this text for assistance.

Paragraph 7.3.4: Storage, handling, and delivery of project media

This paragraph normally states:

> All project media will be stored in Software Development Files under the control of the software librarian(s) (see organizational chart in paragraph 3.1.3). Media will be backed up regularly using standard corporate policies and procedures. Delivery of media will be in accordance with the CDRL requirement in the contract.

Paragraph 7.3.5: Additional control

This paragraph normally states, "Not applicable."

Paragraph 7.4: Configuration status accounting

This paragraph describes the content, format, and purpose of your configuration status accounting records and reports. Refer to Sec. 7.1.5 for further information.

Paragraph 7.5: Configuration audits

This paragraph describes your procedures for conducting configuration audits. Section 10.2 of this text contains information about configuration audits.

Paragraph 7.6: Preparation for specification authentication

This paragraph describes your procedures for submitting specifications to the government for review and authentication; incorporating changes to specifications; and updating the configuration status accounting reports to reflect approved baselines. Refer to Sec. 7.1 of this text for assistance.

Paragraph 7.7: Configuration management major milestones

This paragraph identifies major configuration management milestones. These milestones correspond directly to the reviews identified in MIL-STD-1521B. A figure such as Fig. 16.10 meets this requirement.

Paragraph 8: Other software development functions

This paragraph (and lower level paragraphs) is used to identify contractor functions not already covered. For most contracts, this paragraph will simply state "Not applicable." Lower level detailed paragraph are not included if no additional functions are identified.

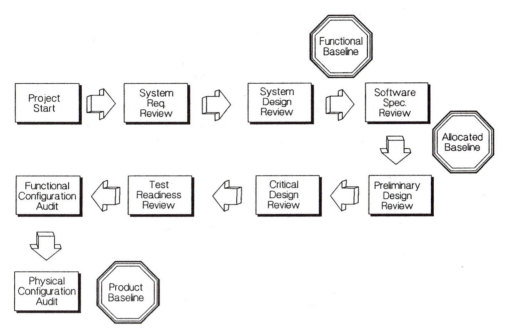

Figure 16.10 Configuration management milestones.

Paragraph 9: Notes

General information may be placed here. This paragraph must also contain an alphabetical listing of all acronyms and abbreviations used in the document along with their meaning.

16.5 Evaluating the Software Development Plan

The following checklist can be used when evaluating the Software Development Plan:

_____ Is the required DID format followed exactly?

_____ Is the terminology consistent within the document?

_____ Is the document understandable?

_____ Do contractor facilities and personnel have adequate facility clearances to do the work properly?

_____ In the organizational structure, is software quality control and testing handled by a separate group?; is software library management handled by a separate group or individual?; are there direct lines of communication from the project manager to the company senior management?

_____ Does the work breakdown structure (paragraph 3.2.1) address all tasks covered in section 5.3 of this book?

_____ Are high risk tasks highlighted?

_____ Is the proposed schedule in accordance with DOD-STD-2167A (as discussed in chapter 9 of this book)?

_____ Is risk management adequately addressed?

_____ Is the corrective action process, including problem/change reporting and tracking, clear?

_____ Are adequate personnel (in terms of both number and qualifications) available to do all aspects of the work?

_____ Is the selected software development methodology (paragraph 4.2.1) suitable for the project? Is the government sufficiently familiar with the technique to review the contractor's deliverables?

_____ Is configuration management adequately addressed?

17 Preparing the Software Requirements Specification

This chapter describes specific procedures for preparing the *Software Requirements Specification*, which is Data Item Description (DID) number DI-MCCR-80025A. We will

- Discuss the purpose of this DID

- Present a sample schedule for preparing this DID

- Show a complete outline for the document

- Provide detailed instructions and hints for writing each paragraph of the DID

- Describe how the Government will judge the acceptability of the final DID as submitted

17.1 Purpose

One Software Requirements Specification is prepared for each CSCI in the system. This document specifies the requirements allocated to this CSCI. It will be used to determine whether the completed CSCI meets these requirements, and will serve as the basis for the detailed design of the CSCI itself.

17.2 Schedule

The Software Requirements Specification is submitted in preliminary form at the System Design Review and is approved in final form during the Software Specification Review. As the CSCI design evolves during the development, the Software Requirements Specification must be kept current using Specification Change Notices and revised editions of the document. Figure 17.1 shows a sample schedule for preparing and updating the Software Requirements Specification during a typical project.

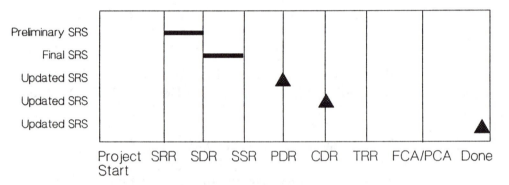

Figure 17.1 SRS schedule.

17.3 Outline

The following outline *must* be followed for the Software Requirements Specification.

1. **Scope**
   - **1.1** **Identification**
   - **1.2** **CSCI overview**
   - **1.3** **Document overview**

2. **Applicable documents**
   - **2.1** **Government documents**
   - **2.2** **Non-Government documents**

3.   Engineering requirements

3.1	**CSCI external interface requirements**
3.2	**CSCI capability requirements**
3.2.X	[Capability name and identifier]
3.3	**CSCI internal interfaces**
3.4	**CSCI data element requirements**
3.5	**Adaptation requirements**
3.5.1	Installation-dependent data
3.5.2	Operational parameters
3.6	**Sizing and timing requirements**
3.7	**Safety requirements**
3.8	**Security requirements**
3.9	**Design constraints**
3.10	**Software quality factors**
3.11	**Human performance/human engineering requirements**
3.12	**Requirements traceability**

4.   Qualification requirements

4.1	**Qualification methods**
4.2	**Special qualification requirements**

5.   Preparation for delivery

6.   Notes

17.4 Detailed Instructions

This section presents specific instructions for meeting the requirements of each of the DID paragraphs. For some paragraphs I recommend that you leave the paragraph blank because all information for the paragraph is covered in lower level subparagraphs. For each of these, it would also be appropriate for the top-level paragraph to consist of a set of bullets presenting the titles of the lower level subparagraphs.

Paragraph 1: Scope

This paragraph may be left blank.

Paragraph 1.1: Identification

This paragraph contains the approved name and identification number for the CSCI which is covered by this document.

Paragraph 1.2: CSCI overview

This paragraph typically references the appropriate paragraph (4.2.X) from the System/Segment Design Document which describes this CSCI.

Paragraph 1.3: Document overview

This paragraph states, "This document specifies the engineering and qualification requirements for the _____ [name] CSCI. It will be used as a basis for detailed CSCI design and testing."

Paragraph 2: Applicable documents

This paragraph may be left blank.

Paragraph 2.1: Government documents

List government documents referenced in this document. The DID contains specific information about the order referenced documents must be listed and some standard verbiage about obtaining documents.

Paragraph 2.2: Non-Government documents

List non-government documents referenced in this document. Documents which are not stocked by federal stocking activities must include a source. The DID contains specific information about the order referenced documents must be listed and some standard verbiage about obtaining documents.

Paragraph 3: Engineering requirements

This paragraph may be left blank.

Paragraph 3.1: CSCI external interface requirements

This paragraph shows all external interfaces from this CSCI to HWCIs, other CSCIs, or other systems. A diagram similar to Fig. 17.2 should be included, along with a brief description of each interface. Each interface should also include a reference to an Interface Requirements Specification (new interfaces) or a document describing the interface (existing interfaces).

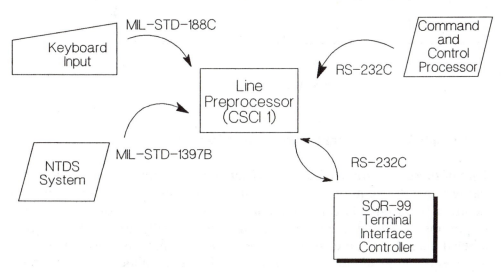

Figure 17.2 CSCI external interfaces.

Paragraph 3.2: CSCI capability requirements

This paragraph lists all requirements from the System/Segment Specification which this CSCI must satisfy. This list should match those assigned to this CSCI in the System/Segment Design Document. If the system can exist in various modes and states (as identified in the System/Segment Specification), this paragraph will also tell which requirements apply during each of the modes/states. A table similar to Fig. 17.3 meets the requirements of this paragraph.

Type	Number	Name	Purpose and parameters
State	S1	Problem Init	
State	S2	Line Pre-process	
State	S3	Contact Classify	
Mode	M3.1	Coarse Filter	
Req.	R3.1.1	Requirement N	Description of requirement
Req.	R3.1.4	Requirement Q	Description of requirement
Req.	R3.1.5	Requirement R	Description of requirement
etc.			

Figure 17.3 CSCI requirements.

Paragraph 3.2.X: [Capability name and identifier]

One of these paragraphs must be written for each requirement identified in paragraph 3.2. Requirements (capabilities) may be decomposed into more detailed requirements called *derived* requirement. Each of these derived requirements would then be addressed individually in a sub-paragraph labeled 3.2.X.Y. Each of these derived requirements must also be assigned a project-unique identifier for tracking. For each allocated requirement (from the System/Segment Design Document) and derived requirement, you must identify the inputs, processing requirements, and outputs. Figure 7.4 shows a sample representation.

Paragraph 3.3: CSCI internal interfaces

This paragraph identifies interfaces between requirements identified in paragraph 3.2 (and derived requirements from 3.2.X). The control flows *and* data flows must be shown. Figure 17.5 shows a sample representation of the control flow, and Fig. 17.6 shows a sample representation of data flow.

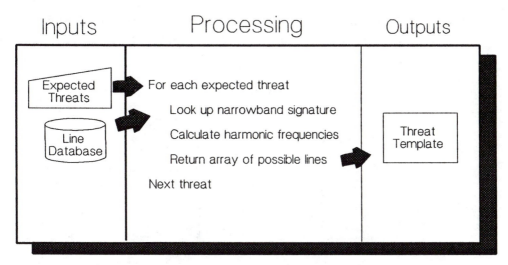

Requirement: Calculate Threat Template

Figure 17.4 Inputs-processing-outputs.

Paragraph 3.4: CSCI data element requirements

This paragraph identifies the data dictionary for the CSCI. For data elements internal to the CSCI, the data dictionary must contain (for each data element)

- a project-unique identifier,

- a brief description of the data element,

- units of measure for the data element,

- limit/range of values for the data element (or actual value for constants),

- accuracy required,

- if the data is used in the CSCI internal interfaces, identify the interface name, identifier, source requirement, and destination requirement.

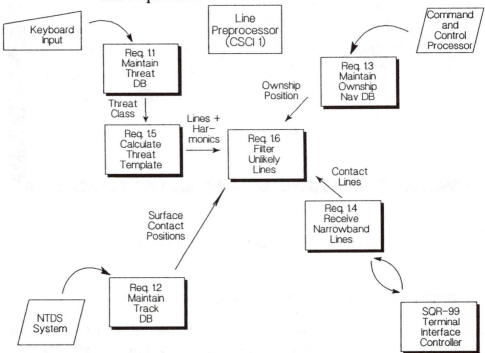

Fig. 17.6 Data Flow Representation

```
ChIEF
   ├─Keyboard Interrupt (I)
   │    ├─Maintain Threat DB (Req. 1.1)
   │    └─{Calculate Threat Template (Req. 1.5)
   ├─NTDS Interrupt (I)
   │    └─Maintain Track DB (Req. 1.2)
   ├─C²P Interrupt (I)
   │    └─Maintain Ownship Nav. DB (Req. 1.3)
   ├─ SQR-99 Processing
   │    └─Receive Narrowband Lines (Req. 1.4)
   └─ Filter Unlikely Lines (Req. 1.6
```

Figure 17. 5 HIPO-II control flow representation.

For data elements which are part of the CSCI's external interfaces

- project-unique identifier,

- interface name and identifier,

- source requirement from within this CSCI,

- name of the Interface Requirements Specification where this interface is defined.

A report similar to Fig. 17.7 meets the requirements of this paragraph.

Name	Identifier	Description	Units	Range	Interface
O.Lat	D1.1.3	Ownship lat	d.min	+-90	R1.3-R1.6
O.Long	D1.1.4	Ownship long	d.min	+-180	R1.3-R1.6
O.Speed	D1.1.5	Ownship speed	knots	0-50	R1.3-R1.6
O.Course	D1.1.6	Ownship course	deg	0-359	R1.3-R1.6
etc.					

Figure 17.7 Data element requirements.

Paragraph 3.5: Adaptation requirements

This paragraph may be left blank.

Paragraph 3.5.1: Installation-dependent data

If the report format recommended in paragraph 3.4 is followed, this paragraph simply references that paragraph.

Paragraph 3.5.2: Operational parameters

This paragraph describes parameters whose allowable range of values will vary based on operational needs.   These operational needs typically correspond to states (and perhaps modes) identified in the System/Segment Specification. A table similar to Fig. 17.8 may be used for this purpose.

Parameter	Number	State	Mode	Allowable Range
Param_1	P1.1.2	S1	All	0..10
Param_1	P1.1.2	S3	M3.1	0..10
Param_1	P1.1.2	S3	M3.2-3.4	0..20
Param_2	P1.1.3	All	All	0..100
etc.				

Figure 17.8 Operational parameters.

Paragraph 3.6: Sizing and timing requirements

This paragraph identifies the amount and location of on-line and off-line storage (memory and disk) required by this CSCI. If multiple CSCIs operate simultaneously on a single CPU, the percentage of CPU cycles allocated to this CSCI also should be stated here.

Paragraph 3.7: Safety requirements

This paragraph describes potential hazards to personnel, property, and the physical environment which the designers of the CSCI need to be aware of. It will often say, "Not applicable."

Paragraph 3.8: Security requirements

This paragraph identifies the level of security for this CSCI. If any aspect of the CSCI is classified, this paragraph should clarify if the data, algorithm, or entire program is classified.

Paragraph 3.9: Design constraints

This paragraph specifies miscellaneous design constraints. It typically says, "Not applicable."

Paragraph 3.10: Software quality factors

This paragraph typically refers to paragraph 3.2.5 of the System/Segment Specification.

Paragraph 3.11: Human performance/human engineering requirements

This paragraph typically refers to paragraph 3.3.7 of the System/Segment Specification.

Paragraph 3.12: Requirements traceability

This paragraph shows how each requirement from the System/Segment Design Document maps into requirements identified in this document. A report similar to Fig. 17.9 can be used.

Paragraph 4: Qualification requirements

This paragraph may be left blank.

Paragraph 4.1: Qualification methods

For each requirement, this paragraph tells whether the requirement will be tested (and verified) using demonstration; analysis; or inspection. Analysis includes statistical testing and interpretation of test results. Inspection involves visible inspection of CSCI code or documentation. A table similar to Figure 87 is typically used.

SSDD Requirement	Address by
R3.4.1	R3.4.1A, R3.4.1B
R3.4.2	R3.4.1A, R3.4.1C, R3.4.1D
R3.4.3	R3.4.1A, R3.4.1B
etc.	

Figure 17.9 Requirements traceability.

Requirement	Demonstrated	Analysis	Inspection
R3.4.1			
R3.4.1A			
R3.4.1B			
R3.4.1C			
R3.4.1D			
etc.			

Figure 17.10 Qualification method.

Paragraph 4.2: Special qualification requirements

If special testing is necessary to qualify this CSCI, this paragraph will contain a sub-paragraph for each test. The tests will be identified with

-       a project-unique identifier for the test,

-       the requirements which will be tested,

- a description of the test,

- the level of the test (CSU, CSC, CSCI, Segment, or System).

Paragraph 5: Preparation for delivery

This paragraph will typically reference paragraph 5 of the System/Segment Specification.

Paragraph 6: Notes

This paragraph may include any general information that is necessary, and must include a list of all acronyms and abbreviations which are used in this document (and their meaning).

17.5 Evaluating the Software Requirements Specification

The following checklist can be used when evaluating the Software Requirements Specification

_____ Is the required DID format followed exactly?

_____ Is the terminology consistent within the document?

_____ Is the document understandable?

_____ Are all requirements traceable to the System/Segment Specification and the System/Segment Design Document?

_____ Are data flows consistent with each other and consistent with Interface Requirements Specifications?

_____ Are all requirements testable?

_____ Were the analysis techniques used consistent with the requirements of paragraph 4.2.3 of the Software Development Plan?

_____ Are the sizing and timing requirements from paragraph 3.6 of this document realistic?

_____ Are the CSCI data flows clear? . . . consistent? . . . appropriate?

_____ Are the control flows clear? . . . consistent? . . . appropriate?

18 Preparing the Interface Requirements Specification

This chapter describes specific procedures for preparing the *Interface Requirements Specification*, which is Data Item Description (DID) number DI-MCCR-80026A. We will

- Discuss the purpose of this DID

- Present a sample schedule for preparing this DID

- Show a complete outline for the document

- Provide detailed instructions and hints for writing each paragraph of the DID

- Describe how the Government will judge the acceptability of the final DID as submitted

18.1 Purpose

The Interface Requirements Specification defines the requirements for all interfaces between one (or more) CSCIs and other configuration items or external systems. If the interfaces to/from one or more CSCIs are complex, each of those CSCIs should have their own Interface Requirements Specification. If the interfaces are not that complex, or if there are only two or three CSCIs in the segment, one Interface Requirement Specification may be used to describe all interfaces.

18.2 Schedule

The Interface Requirements Specification is submitted in preliminary form at the System Design Review and is approved in final form during the Software Specification Review. As the CSCI design evolves during the development, the Interface Requirements Specification must be kept current using Specification Change Notices and revised editions of the document. Figure 18.1 shows a sample schedule for preparing and updating the Interface Requirements Specification during a typical project.

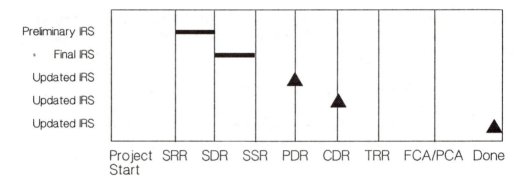

Figure 18.1 IRS schedule.

18.3 Outline

The following outline *must* be followed for the Interface Requirements Specification.

    1.   **Scope**
            1.1   **Identification**
            1.2   **System overview**
            1.3   **Document overview**

2.   Applicable documents

    2.1   **Government documents**

    2.2   **Non-Government documents**

3.   Interface specification

    3.1   **Interface diagrams**

    3.X   **[Interface name and identifier]**

    3.X.1   Interface requirements

    3.X.2   Data requirements

4.   Quality assurance

5.   Preparation for delivery

6.   Notes

18.4 Detailed Instructions

This section presents specific instructions for meeting the requirements of each of the DID paragraphs.

Paragraph 1: Scope

This paragraph may be left blank.

Paragraph 1.1: Identification

This paragraph contains the approved name and identification number for the interface which is covered by this document.

Paragraph 1.2: System overview

This paragraph briefly states the purpose of the system and describes the role, within the system of the interfaces which this document describes. The purpose of the system can be described by referencing (or copying) paragraph 1.2 from the System/Segment Design Document. The role of the interfaces can often be described by copying the appropriate portions from paragraphs 4.4.1, 4.4.2, or 4.4.3 of the System/Segment Design Document.

Paragraph 1.3: Document overview

This paragraph states, "This document specifies the requirements for one or more interfaces between the following CSCIs of the _____ [name] system (or segment) and other CSCIs and external systems

    _____ [CSCI 1]

    _____ [CSCI 2]

    _____ [etc.]

Paragraph 2: Applicable documents

This paragraph may be left blank.

Paragraph 2.1: Government documents

List government documents referenced in this document. The DID contains specific information about the order referenced documents must be listed and some standard verbiage about obtaining documents.

Paragraph 2.2: Non-Government documents

List non-Government documents referenced in this document. Documents which are not stocked by federal stocking activities must include a source. The DID contains specific information about the order referenced documents must be listed and some standard verbiage about obtaining documents.

Paragraph 3: Interface specification

This paragraph may be left blank.

Paragraph 3.1: Interface diagrams

This paragraph specifies the interfaces (by name and identifier) which are covered by this document. This is normally accomplished using one interface diagram (Fig. 18.2) per CSCI. These interface diagrams should be identical to the CSCI external interface diagram contained in paragraph 3.1 of the Software Requirements Specification for the CSCI.

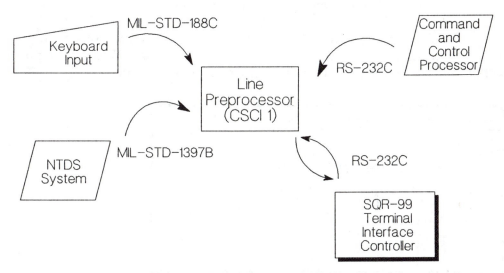

Figure 18.2 Interface diagrams.

Paragraph 3.X: [Interface name and identifier]

There will be one of these paragraphs for *each* interface identified in paragraph 3.1. Use extensive cross referencing to handle the common problem of redundancy in interface requirements. This paragraph states the interface name, identifier, and purpose (briefly).

Paragraph 3.X.1: Interface requirements

For each interface, this paragraph must specify

- whether the communicating CSCIs are executing concurrently or sequentially. If concurrently, the method which will be used for inter-CSCI synchronization (if required) must be described.

- the communication protocol to be used for the interface

- the priority level of the interface [typically 0 (high) through 9 (low) or High, Medium, and Low].

It is possible to use a single table (Fig. 18.3) which presents this information for *all* interfaces covered in this document. This paragraph would then reference the table for each interface paragraph.

Interface Name	Number	Execution	Protocol	Priority
Interface 1	I1.3	Conc.	802.3	High
Interface 2	I1.4	Rendev.	MIL-STD-1397	Med
Interface 3	I1.4	Sequen.	MIL-STD-180-100C	Low

Figure 18.3   Interface descriptions.

Paragraph 3.X.2:   Data requirements

This paragraph must identify each unique data element which will be transferred using this interface. The description of each data element must include:

- the name and identifier of the data element,

- a brief description of the data element,

- the CSCI, HWCI, or external system which is the source of the data element,

- the CSCI, HWCI, or external system which is the user of the data,

- the units of measure of the data,

- the limit/range values for the data (actual value for constants),

- the accuracy required for the data element,

- the precision or resolution required for the data element in terms of significant digits.

A table similar to Fig. 18.4 should be used to show this information. If the Software Requirement Specification includes a data dictionary containing this information (to meet the requirements of paragraph 3.4 of that document), this paragraph may simply list the data elements by name and identifier while referring the reader to the appropriate Software Requirements Specification for the details of the data element description.

Name	Ident.	Source	User	Units	Characteristics
O.lat	D1.1.3	C2P	CSCI 3	deg.m	Description
O.long	D1.1.4	C2P	CSCI 3	deg.m	Description
Data 3	D3.4.1	CSCI 1	CSCI 2	Knots	Description
etc.					

Figure 18.4 Message descriptions.

Paragraph 4: Quality assurance

This paragraph shall state, "NONE."

Paragraph 5: Preparation for delivery

This paragraph shall state, "NONE."

Paragraph 6: Notes

This paragraph may include any general information that is necessary, and must include a list of all acronyms and abbreviations which are used in this document (and their meaning).

18.5 Evaluating the Interface Requirements Specification

The following checklist can be used when evaluating the Software Requirements Specification:

_____ Is the required DID format followed exactly?

_____ Is the terminology consistent within the document?

_____ Is the document understandable?

_____ Are data flows consistent with each other and consistent with Software Requirements Specifications?

_____ Are all data flow requirements testable?

_____ Are data element definitions appropriate and consistent?

19 Preparing the Software Design Document

This chapter describes specific procedures for preparing the *Software Design Document,* which is Data Item Description (DID) number DI-MCCR-80012A. We will

- Discuss the purpose of this DID

- Present a sample schedule for preparing this DID

- Show a complete outline for the document

- Provide detailed instructions and hints for writing each paragraph of the DID

- Describe how the Government will judge the acceptability of the final DID as submitted

19.1 Purpose

One Software Design Document is prepared for each CSCI in the system. This document describes the complete design of the CSCI in terms of CSCs and CSUs. The requirements allocated to this CSCI are allocated within this document to the CSCs and CSUs which make up this CSCI.

19.2 Schedule

The Software Design Document is submitted in preliminary form at the Preliminary Design Review, and is approved in final form during the Critical Design Review. Figure 19.1 shows a sample schedule for preparing and updating the Software Design Document during a typical project.

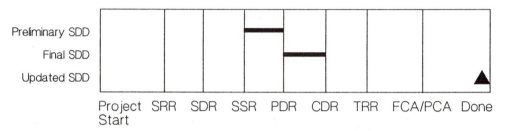

Figure 19.1 SDD schedule.

19.3 Outline

The following outline *must* be followed for the Software Design Document.

1.   Scope

        1.1   **Identification**
        1.2   **System overview**
        1.3   **Document overview**

2.   Referenced documents

3.   Preliminary design

        3.1   **CSCI overview**
        3.1.1   CSCI architecture
        3.1.2   System states and modes
        3.1.3   Memory and processing time allocation
        3.2   **CSCI design description**
        3.2.X   [CSC name and identifier]
        3.2.X.Y[Sub-level CSC name and identifier]

4.   Detailed design

4.X   **[CSC name and identifier]**
4.X.Y   [CSU name and identifier]
4.X.Y.1[CSU name] Design specification/constraints
4.X.Y.2[CSU name] Design

5.   CSCI data

6.   CSCI data files

6.1   **Data file to CSC/CSU cross reference**
6.X   **[Data file name and identifier]**

7.   Requirements traceability

8.   Notes

19.4 Detailed Instructions

This section presents specific instructions for meeting the requirements of
each of the DID paragraphs. For some paragraphs my recommendation is
to leave the paragraph blank because all information for the paragraph is
covered in lower level subparagraphs. For each of these, it would also be
appropriate for the top level paragraph to consist of a set of bullets
presenting the titles of the lower level subparagraphs.

Paragraph 1: Scope

This paragraph may be left blank.

Paragraph 1.1: Identification

This paragraph contains the approved name and identification number for
the CSCI which is covered by this document, and for the system which this
CSCI is part of. This paragraph also lists the Software Requirements
Specification and Interface Requirements Specification(s) which were used
as the basis for the design of the CSCI.

Paragraph 1.2: System overview

This paragraph references paragraph 1.2 of the Software Requirements Specification for this CSCI.

Paragraph 1.3: Document overview

This paragraph states:

> This document describes the complete design for the _____ [name] CSCI of the _____ [name] system, including the allocation of requirements to the CSCs and CSUs which make up this CSCI.

Paragraph 2: Referenced documents

This paragraph lists the documents (number and title) which are referenced in this document. The source for non-government documents must also be listed.

Paragraph 3: Preliminary design

This paragraph may be left blank.

Paragraph 3.1: CSCI overview

This paragraph describes the role of this CSCI within the system and states the purpose of each external interface of the CSCI, often with the aid of a system architecture diagram (Fig. 19.2). The technical information in this paragraph is basically a reorganization of information in paragraph 1.2 of the Software Requirements Specification and paragraph 3.1 of the Interface Requirements Specification.

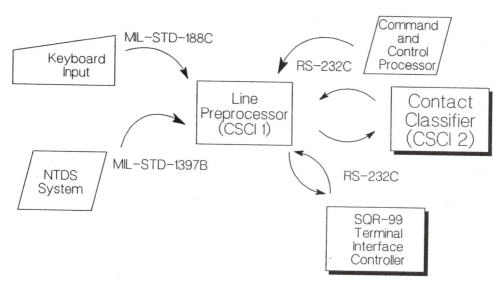

Figure 19.2 CSCI overview.

Paragraph 3.1.1: CSCI architecture

This paragraph shows the hierarchical decomposition of the CSCI requirements into CSCs. The sample figures will use a HIPO-II representation,
which is defined in appendix C. At the top level, my preference is put the
system states which this CSCI can operate in (taken from paragraph 3.2.1 of
the System/Segment Specification) (see Fig. 19.3). Note that the module
type column shows that the displayed elements are system *States*. Under
each system state, the state *modes* which this CSCI may operate in are
placed. Note that the HIPO-II representation for sequence, iteration,
concurrency, and alternation are used. Under the states and modes, the
CSCs which will be required to function within the states and modes are
shown. The CSCs are hierarchical decompositions of the requirements.
Note that some CSCs have the same name and project identifier. These are
examples of CSCs which are used in multiple system states/modes with
absolutely no change to the input, processing, or outputs. For each unique
CSC, the input data and output data must be defined. This data flow
information can then be used to generate a data flow diagram (Fig. 19.4) for
each system state/mode.

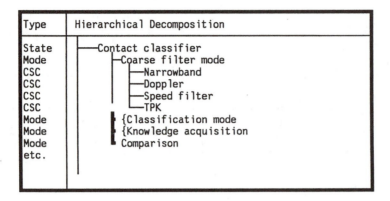

Type	Hierarchical Decomposition
State	──Contact classifier
Mode	──Coarse filter mode
CSC	──Narrowband
CSC	──Doppler
CSC	──Speed filter
CSC	──TPK
Mode	{Classification mode
Mode	{Knowledge acquisition
Mode	Comparison
etc.	

Figure 19.3 Software hierarchy.

Paragraph 3.1.2: System states and modes

This paragraph states, "See paragraph 3.1.1."

Paragraph 3.1.3: Memory and processing time allocation

This paragraph allocates memory and processing time to individual CSCs. A table similar to Fig. 19.5 is normally used.

Paragraph 3.2: CSCI design description

This paragraph lists all CSCs by name and project unique identifier. Each of these will be described in detail in the sub-paragraphs that follow. You should also include a sentence here stating that the CSC interfaces, control flows, and data flows are defined in paragraph 3.1.1 and are not repeated in the CSC descriptive paragraphs that follow.

Paragraph 3.2.X: [CSC name and identifier]

There will be one of these paragraphs for each unique top-level CSC identified in paragraph 3.1.1. A figure similar to Fig. 19.6 can be used to show where this CSC fits into the hierarchy. The processing requirements, the allocated and derived requirements, and any design constraints placed

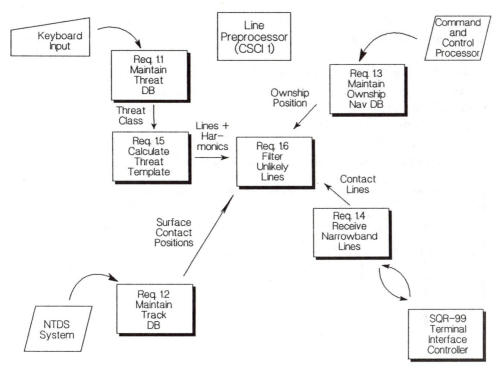

Figure 19.4 Sample data-flow diagram.

on this CSC are then defined. A format similar to Fig. 19.7 is acceptable.

Paragraph 3.2.X.Y: [Sub-level CSC name and identifier]

If the top-level CSC from paragraph 3.2.X contains lower level CSCs, this paragraph will be used to define them. The format of this paragraph is identical to the format of paragraph 3.2.X. If *this* CSC has lower level CSCs, this paragraph will have lower level paragraphs numbered 3.2.X.Y.Z. This process continues to a maximum of 5 levels of decomposition. You should not decompose your requirements below five levels in the hierarchy. Two levels is much more typical.

Paragraph 4: Detailed design

This paragraph describes the CSUs which will be incorporated into the CSCI design. Recall that CSCs are a tool for decomposing CSCI requirements

into pieces which a software engineering team can use for software design.
CSUs are the design elements which will eventually be implemented as
actual program modules. If you are working with Ada, CSUs will typically
be implemented as Ada packages. This paragraph takes the CSCI hierarchical decomposition and adds CSUs to the hierarchy (Fig. 19.8). Note that
some CSUs have the same name and project identifier. These will be
program elements which are used to meet multiple requirements. Each CSC
which has one or more CSUs under it (all low level CSCs) will then be
discussed individually in the paragraphs that follow.

CSC Name	CSC Number	Memory Budget	Allocated Processing Time
Narrowb	CSC 1	128 Kbytes	20 percent
Doppler	CSC 2	10 Kbytes	28 percent
Speed fil	CSC 3	10 Kbytes	1 percent
TPK	CSC 4	10 Kbytes	1 percent
etc.			

Figure 19.5 Processing time allocation.

Paragraph 4.X: [CSC name and identifier]

There will be one of these paragraphs for each CSC which has CSUs under
it. This paragraph shows this CSC and the CSUs which are under it (Fig.
19.9). Note that the figure shows the control flow between CSUs. Each
CSU is then discussed individually.

Paragraph 4.X.Y: [CSU name and identifier]

If this CSU has been previously described, this paragraph references the
appropriate paragraph and does not contain any subparagraphs. Otherwise,
this paragraph contains a brief narrative description of the CSU purpose.

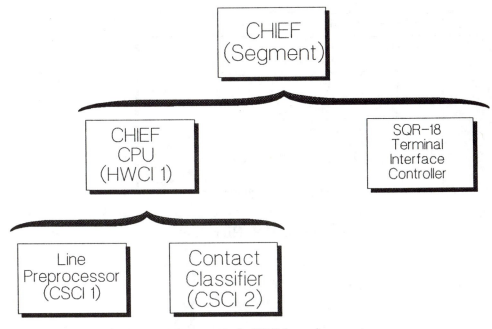

Figure 19.6 CSC location.

Processing Requirements	Allocated Requirements	Derived Requirements	Constraints
Description of CSC processing requirements	R1.3 R1.4	R1.3.A R1.3.D R1.4.A R1.4.B R1.4.M	List constraints on design

Figure 19.7 Requirements description.

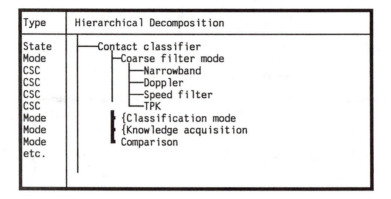

Type	Hierarchical Decomposition
State	┌──Contact classifier
Mode	┌─Coarse filter mode
CSC	├──Narrowband
CSC	├──Doppler
CSC	├──Speed filter
CSC	└──TPK
Mode	{Classification mode
Mode	{Knowledge acquisition
Mode	Comparison
etc.	

Figure 19.8 Hierarchy.

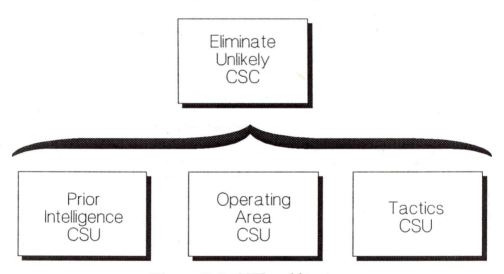

Figure 19.9 CSU architecture.

Paragraph 4.X.Y.1: [CSU name] Design specification/constraints

This paragraph describes the requirements (allocated and derived) which this CSU must meet, and the design constraints imposed on this CSU. If this CSU involves a man-machine interface then sample screens or prototyping should be used to document the interface.

Paragraph 4.X.Y.2: [CSU Name] Design

This paragraph gives the detailed design of the CSU. The following information must be included:

- *Programming language*: If the language is different than the language specified for this CSCI, include the rationale for its use.

- *Input-Output data elements:* This lists the data element by name and identifier. The data element descriptions are in Sec. 5. Input and output data elements should include not just pass parameters but *all* data elements which are referenced or modified. Specifically, this would include global data and off-line data.

- *Local data elements:* This is a local data definition table.

- *Interrupts, signals, and exceptions:* This is a list of all interrupts, signals, or exceptions which are handled by this CSU.

- *Algorithms:* This section describes all algorithms incorporated in this CSU. Algorithm descriptions are normally expressed in structured English.

- *Error handling:* Identify and describe any error detection and recovery features of the CSU. It is often best to have a single document describing your procedures for error identification and recovery, especially in the input-output area, and include this document as an appendix to all Software Design Documents.

- *Data conversion:* If any input or output variables must be converted in format, this conversion must be described. For example, the algorithm may require variables to use a particular unit of measure (perhaps standard) while the external interface definition requires that the variable be in metric units. As another example, perhaps the data is used externally in a compressed format but must be expanded internally for efficient processing.

- *Use of other elements:* This section defines other elements used by this CSU, including (but not restricted to) calls to external services (including other CSUs) and use of input/output buffers.

- *Logic flow:* This section defines the CSUs internal logic. This is typically accomplished using any combination desired of structured English, flow charts, state transition diagrams, Nassi-Schneiderman charts, and so on.

- *Local data files or database:* If this CSU maintains a local data file(s) or database (temporary files, for example), describe the structure of the file and access procedures.

- *Limitations:* This is a free text description of any limitations or unusual features that restrict the performance of the CSU.

Paragraph 5: CSCI data

This section defines all global data within the CSCI. Groupings of data into structures is also shown. The following information must be present for each data element:

- *Name*

- *Description*

- *Units of measure*

- *Limit/range*: for constants, provide the actual value

- *Accuracy required*

- *Precision/resolution*: in terms of significant digits

- *Update frequency*: for real time systems only

- *Legality checks*: if different than limit/range checks.

- *Data type*: integer, ASCII, and so on.

- *Data representation/format*

- *CSU(s) where set/calculated*

- *CSU(s) where used*

For data which is part of the CSCI external interface, identify the data element, the interface by name and identifier, and the Interface Design Document where the data description can be found.

Paragraph 6:   CSCI data files

This paragraph lists the names of each data file in this CSCI which is used by multiple CSUs.

Paragraph 6.1:   Data file to CSC/CSU cross reference

A table similar to Fig. 19.10 can be used here.

Paragraph 6.X: [Data file name and identifier]

For each data file identified in paragraph 6, a unique paragraph will describe the data file. This description includes the purpose of the data file, the maximum size of the file, the access method (sequential or random) and a file definition table (see Fig. 19.11).

Paragraph 7:   Requirements traceability

For each requirement identified in this CSCI's Software Requirements Specification and Interface Requirements Specification, this paragraph will show how the requirement is traceable down to individual requirements within the CSUs. Figure 19.12 is a sample format.

Data File Name	Number	Written by	Read by
Narrowb_Aux Speed_rules Current_dec etc.	F1 F2 F3	Knowledge Acquis.	Find Aux Find speed related Knowledge Acquis.

Figure 19.10 Cross reference.

File	Purpose	Max Size	Access	Structure
Narrow Aux	Store NB Line info	1 Mbyte	Random	Struct NB_Class[];
Speed R	Speed info for each class	25 Kbytes	Random	Struct SP_Class[];
Curr dec	Allow post operation analysis	10 Mbytes	sequential	Struct prob_class[];

Figure 19.11 File descriptors.

Paragraph 8: Notes

This paragraph may include any general information that is necessary, and must include a list of all acronyms and abbreviations which are used in this document (and their meaning).

```
┌─────────────────┬──────────────────────────────────────────────┐
│ SRS Requirement │ Addressed by                                 │
├─────────────────┼──────────────────────────────────────────────┤
│ R3.4.1          │ R3.4.1.9, R3.4.1.10, R3.4.1.11               │
│ R3.4.1A         │ R3.4.1.9, R3.4.1.12                          │
│ R3.4.1B         │ R3.4.1.1                                     │
│ R3.4.1C         │ R3.4.1.1, R3.4.1.2                           │
│ R3.4.1D         │ R3.4.1.5, R3.5.2.1                           │
│ etc.            │                                              │
│                 │                                              │
│                 │                                              │
│                 │                                              │
└─────────────────┴──────────────────────────────────────────────┘
```

Figure 19.12 Requirements traceability.

19.5 Evaluating the Software Design Document

The following checklist can be used when evaluating the Software Design Document.

_____ Is the required DID format followed exactly?

_____ Is the terminology consistent within the document?

_____ Is the document understandable?

_____ Are requirements traceable from the Software Requirements Specification and Interface Requirements Specification to individual CSCs?

_____ Are requirements traceable from individual CSCs to CSUs?

_____ Are the detailed design representations consistent with the design methodology approved in the Software Development Plan?

_____ Are all data flows consistent?

_____ Are data definitions and data use consistent?

_____ Are the memory and processing time allocations from paragraph 3.1.3 consistent with the hardware capabilities and other requirements for memory and processing time?

_____ Does the decomposition of requirements into CSCs enhance testability; modularity of design; reusability?

_____ Are the CSU detailed design specifications sufficiently clear to begin coding?

20 Preparing the Software Test Plan

This chapter describes specific procedures for preparing the *Software Test Plan*, which is Data Item Deliverable (DID) number DI-MCCR-80014A. We will

- Discuss the purpose of this DID

- Present a sample schedule for preparing this DID

- Show a complete outline for the document

- Provide detailed instructions and hints for writing each paragraph of the DID

- Describe how the Government will judge the acceptability of the final DID as submitted

20.1 Purpose

One Software Test Plan is typically prepared for the entire system or segment. This document describes the software test resources, test requirements, and test schedule for the formal qualification testing of one or more CSCIs.

20.2 Schedule

The Software Test Plan is approved in final form during the Preliminary Design Review. Figure 20.1 shows a sample schedule for preparing and updating the Software Test Plan during a typical project.

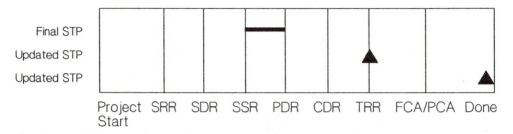

Figure STP schedule.

20.3 Outline

The following outline *must* be followed for the Software Test Plan:

1.   Scope

1.1	**Identification**
1.2	**System overview**
1.3	**Document overview**
1.4	**Relationship to other plans**

2.   Referenced documents

3.   Software test environment

3.1	**Software items**
3.2	**Hardware and firmware items**
3.3	**Proprietary nature, and Government rights**
3.4	**Installation, testing, and control**

4.   Formal qualification test identification

4.X	**[CSCI name and identifier]**

4.X.1	General test requirements
4.X.2	Test classes
4.X.3	Test levels
4.X.4	Test definitions
4.X.4.Y[Test name and identifier]	
4.X.5	Test schedule

5. Data recording, reduction, and analysis

6. Notes

20.4 Detailed Instructions

This section presents specific instructions for meeting the requirements of each of the DID paragraphs. For some paragraphs my recommendation is to leave the paragraph blank because all information for the paragraph is covered in lower level subparagraphs. For each of these, it would also be appropriate for the top-level paragraph to consist of a set of bullets presenting the titles of the lower level subparagraphs.

Paragraph 1: Scope

This paragraph may be left blank.

Paragraph 1.1: Identification

This paragraph normally states, "This document applies to all CSCIs of the _____ [name] system, identification number _____ [number]." If the document applies only to a subset of the CSCIs, then this paragraph identifies the specific CSCIs which are covered.

Paragraph 1.2: System overview

This paragraph references (or copies) paragraph 1.2 of the System Segment Design Document for a description of the purpose of the system. It then lists the CSCIs which are covered individually and provides a brief (one paragraph) description of each CSCI's purpose. The CSCI purposes can be paraphrased from paragraph 1.2 of each CSCI's Software Requirements Specification.

Paragraph 1.3: Document overview

This paragraph normally states: "This document describes the software test resources, test requirements, and test schedule for the formal qualification testing of all CSCIs in the _____ system.

Paragraph 1.4: Relationship to other plans

This paragraph typically states, "Not applicable."

Paragraph 2: Referenced documents

This paragraph lists the documents (number and title) which are referenced in this document. The source for non-Government documents must also be listed.

Paragraph 3: Software test environment

This paragraph may be left blank.

Paragraph 3.1: Software items

This paragraph lists which software items from paragraph 4.1.3.1 of the Software Development Plan will be used during formal qualification testing. The reader is referred to that paragraph for descriptions of the software items.

Paragraph 3.2: Hardware and firmware items

This paragraph lists which hardware and firmware items from paragraph 4.1.3.2 of the Software Development Plan will be used during formal qualification testing. The reader is referred to that paragraph for descriptions of the hardware and firmware items.

Paragraph 3.3: Proprietary nature, and Government rights

This paragraph states, "See paragraph 4.1.3.3 of the _____ [name] system Software Development Plan (document number _____ [number])."

Paragraph 3.4: Installation, testing, and control

This paragraph states, "See paragraph 4.1.3.4 of the _____ [name] system Software Development Plan (document number _____ [number])."

Paragraph 4: Formal qualification test identification

This paragraph lists the CSCIs which are covered by this test plan. Each CSCI will then be discussed individually in the paragraphs that follow.

Paragraph 4.X: [CSCI name and identifier]

This paragraph may be left blank.

Paragraph 4.X.1: General test requirements

This paragraph describes general requirements which apply to all of the formal qualification tests for this CSCI or to a group of formal qualification tests for this CSCI. Two examples from the DID are

> Each formal qualification test shall meet the following general test requirements:
>
> a.   CSCI size and execution time shall be measured.
>
> b.   The CSCI shall be tested using nominal, maximum, and erroneous input values.
>
> c.   The CSCI shall be tested for error detection and proper error recovery, including appropriate error messages.

Formal qualification tests to validate the radar tracking requirements shall meet the following test requirements:

    a.   The CSCI shall be tested using simulated test data for the specified combinations of environmental conditions.

    b.   The CSCI shall be tested using input data taken from the environment ("live data").

For general qualifications which will apply to all formal qualification tests, it is often best to put the general qualifications in an appendix. This paragraph for each CSCI would then simply reference the appendix.

Paragraph 4.X.2: Test classes

This paragraph describes the classes of formal tests that will be executed. Common examples are stress tests (operating with worst case loadings), timing tests (measuring response times in varying conditions), and erroneous input tests.

Paragraph 4.X.3: Test levels

This paragraph normally states:

Testing will be performed to verify CSCI performance at the following levels:

    a.   CSU, CSC, and CSCI level to verify compliance with CSCI requirements.

    b.   CSCI to CSCI integration level to verify CSCI compliance with external interface requirements to CSCIs.

c.   CSCI to HWCI integration level to verify CSCI compliance with external interface requirements to HWCIs.

d.   System level to verify CSCI requirements not evaluated at other levels.

Paragraph 4.X.4: Test definitions

This paragraph lists the individual formal qualification tests that will be conducted for this CSCI. The tests can be derived from paragraph 4 of this CSCI's Software Requirements Specification. Each test will then be described individually in the paragraphs that follow.

Paragraph 4.X.4.Y: [Test name and identifier]

For each formal qualification test, the following information must be provided:

a.   *Test objective*

b.   *Special requirements*: applies to tests which are taken from paragraph 4.2 of this CSCI's Software Requirements Specification

c.   *Test level*: CSU, CSC, CSCI, CSCI-CSCI, CSCI-HWCI, or system

d.   *Test type or class*: applies to tests which are taken from paragraph 4.3 of this CSCI's Software Requirements Specification

e.   *Qualification method*: take this from paragraph 4.1 of this CSCI's Software Requirements Specification

f.   *Software requirements cross reference*: cross-reference to CSCI engineering requirements in the Software Requirements Specification for this CSCI. Can be taken from paragraph 4.1 of this CSCI's Software Requirements Specification.

g.   *Interface requirements cross reference*: cross-reference to CSCI interface requirements in the Interface Requirements Specification for this interface. Can be taken from paragraph 3.X of this CSCI's Interface Requirements Specification.

h.   *Type of data to be recorded*

i.   *Assumptions and constraints*: should be based on paragraph 5.3 of the Software Development Plan.

Paragraph 4.X.5: Test schedule

This paragraph presents the test schedule for this CSCI. A Gantt chart is often used. For each individual test, you should explicitly show the start and stop time for the briefing, pretest activities (setup), test, debriefings, and data reduction and analysis.

Paragraph 5: Data recording, reduction, and analysis

This paragraph describes your plans for recording, reducing, and analyzing test data. If the testing simply involves verifying compliance with individual requirements, it is often sufficient to simply describe your test procedures. If the testing involves statistical testing or complex analysis of test data, you will need to describe the specific procedures which will be used.

Paragraph 6: Notes

This paragraph may include any general information that is necessary, and must include a list of all acronyms and abbreviations which are used in this document (and their meaning).

20.5 Evaluating the Software Test Plan

The following checklist can be used when evaluating the Software Test Plan:

_____ Is the required DID format followed exactly?

_____ Is the terminology consistent within the document?

_____ Is the document understandable?

_____ Are the proprietary nature and Government rights in paragraph 3.3 consistent with the Software Development Plan?

_____ Are all CSCIs covered by the Software Test Plan?

_____ Do tests identified in paragraph 4.X.4.Y cover *all* requirements from the Software Requirements Specification and Interface Requirements Specification for this CSCI?

_____ Are the qualification methods for each test appropriate? For Software Requirements Specification requirements, are the qualification methods in accordance with the Software Requirements Specification?

_____ Is the test schedule reasonable based on the development schedule for this CSCI and the system as a whole? Does the schedule match the schedule in the Software Development Plan?

_____ Are the procedures for tracking test completions and recording test data adequate?

21 Preparing the Interface Design Document

This chapter describes specific procedures for preparing the *Interface Design Document*, which is Data Item Description (DID) number DI-MCCR-80027A. We will

- Discuss the purpose of this DID

- Present a sample schedule for preparing this DID

- Show a complete outline for the document

- Provide detailed instructions and hints for writing each paragraph of the DID

- Describe how the Government will judge the acceptability of the final DID as submitted

21.1 Purpose

The Interface Design Document specifies the detailed design for one or more interfaces between one or more CSCIs and other CSCIs or HWCIs. If the interfaces for the system are relatively simple, one Interface Design Document is typically used. If the interfaces are complex, one Interface Design Document is typically written for each CSCI.

21.2 Schedule

The Interface Design Document is submitted in preliminary form at the Preliminary Design Review and is approved in final form during the Critical Design Review. Figure 21.1 shows a sample schedule for preparing and updating the Interface Design Document during a typical project.

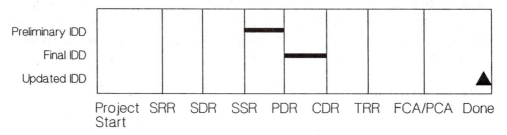

Figure 21.1 IDD schedule.

21.3 Outline

The following outline *must* be followed for the Interface Design Document:

1.   Scope
      1.1   **Identification**
      1.2   **System overview**
      1.3   **Document overview**

2.   Referenced documents

3.   Interface design
      3.1   **Interface diagrams**
      3.X   **[Interface name and identifier]**
      3.X.1   Data elements
      3.X.2   Message descriptions
      3.X.3   Interface priority
      3.X.4   Communications protocol
      3.X.4.Y[Protocol name]

4.   Notes

21.4 Detailed Instructions

This section presents specific instructions for meeting the requirements of each of the DID paragraphs. For some paragraphs my recommendation is to leave the paragraph blank because all information for the paragraph is covered in lower level subparagraphs. For each of these, it would also be appropriate for the top level paragraph to consist of a set of bullets presenting the titles of the lower level subparagraphs.

Paragraph 1: Scope

This paragraph may be left blank.

Paragraph 1.1: Identification

This paragraph contains the approved name and identification number for the system, CSCI(s), and interface(s) which are covered by this document.

Paragraph 1.2: System overview

This paragraph briefly states the purpose of the system and describes the role, within the system of the interfaces which this document describes. The purpose of the system can be described by referencing (or copying) paragraph 1.2 from the System/Segment Design Document. The role of the interfaces can often be described by copying the appropriate portions from paragraphs 4.4.1, 4.4.2, or 4.4.3 of the System/Segment Design Document.

Paragraph 1.3: Document overview

This paragraph states, "This document specifies the design for one or more interfaces between the following CSCIs of the ＿＿＿ [name] system (or segment) and other CSCIs and external systems:

＿＿＿ [CSCI 1]

＿＿＿ [CSCI 2]

_____ [etc.]

Paragraph 2: Referenced documents

This paragraph lists the documents (number and title) which are referenced in this document. The source for non-Government documents must also be listed.

Paragraph 3: Interface design

This paragraph may be left blank.

Paragraph 3.1: Interface diagrams

This paragraph specifies the interfaces (by name and identifier) which are covered by this document. This is normally accomplished using one interface diagram (Fig. 21.2) per CSCI. These interface diagrams should be identical to the CSCI external interface diagram contained in paragraph 3.1 of the Software Requirements Specification for the CSCI.

Paragraph 3.X: [Interface name and identifier]

There will be one of these paragraphs for *each* interface identified in paragraph 3.1. Use extensive cross referencing to handle the common problem of redundancy in interface designs. This paragraph states the interface name, identifier, and purpose (briefly).

Paragraph 3.X.1: Data elements

This paragraph describes each data element transmitted across the interface. The data element descriptions include:

- the name and identifier of the data element,

- a brief description of the data element,

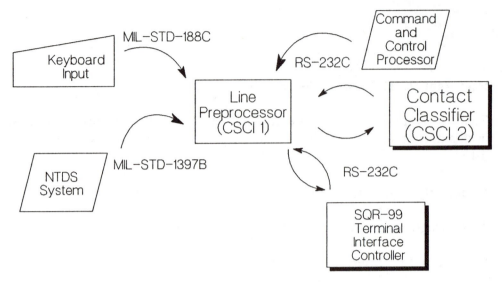

Figure 21.2 Interface diagram.

- the CSCI, HWCI, or external system which is the source of the data element,

- the CSCI, HWCI, or external system which is the user of the data,

- the units of measure of the data,

- the limit/range values for the data (actual value for constants),

- the accuracy required for the data element,

- the precision or resolution required for the data element in terms of significant digits,

- the frequency of transmission for the data element,

- legality checks performed on the data element,

- the data type,

- the data representation/format,

- the data element priority.

If the Software Requirement Specification includes a data dictionary containing this information (to meet the requirements of paragraph 3.4 of that document), this paragraph may simply list the data elements by name and identifier while referring the reader to the appropriate Software Requirements Specification for the details of the data element description.

Paragraph 3.X.2: Message descriptions

If data elements are grouped into messages, this paragraph describes the message formats. Unique message formats should be assigned a unique name and identifier. Message descriptions should include the data elements which are contained in each message. This is often shown using a table similar to Fig. 21.3. In addition, a table similar to Fig. 21.4 should be included to show which messages a specific data element may be found in.

Message Name	Identifier	Data Elements
Type_one Type_two etc.	M1.1 M1.2	D1.1.6, D1.1.9, D1.9.3 D1.1.9, D2.3.6, D3.7.9

Figure 21.3 Message descriptors.

Paragraph 3.X.3: Interface priority

A table similar to Fig. 21.5 is normally included as an appendix to this document. This paragraph then references that table.

Data Element	Message Name	Identifier
D1.1.6	Type One	M1.1
D1.1.9	Type One	M1.1
	Type Two	M1.2
D1.9.3	Type One	M1.1
etc.		

Figure 21.4 Cross reference.

Interface Name	Interface Number	Priority
Interface one	I1.3	High
Interface two	I1.4	Medium
Interface three	I1.5	Low

Figure 21.5 Interface priorities.

Paragraph 3.X.4: Communications protocol

This paragraph lists the protocols (if any) associated with this interface. Each protocol is then described in depth in the paragraphs which follow.

Paragraph 3.X.4.Y: [Protocol name]

This paragraph describes the technical details of a specific protocol. The following information is included (as applicable):

- fragmentation and reassembly of messages,

- message formatting,

- error control and recovery (including fault tolerance features),

- synchronization, including connection establishment, maintenance, termination, and timing,

- flow control, including sequence numbering, window size, and buffer allocation,

- data transfer rate, whether it is periodic or aperiodic, and minimum interval between transfers,

- routing, addressing, and naming conventions,

- transmission services, including priority and grade,

- status, identification, notification, and any other reporting features,

- security, including encryption, user authentication, compartmentalization, and auditing.

When possible, it is best to reference a military, government, or commercial standard as your answer to these questions. If the interface actually does use a custom protocol, it is common to have one subparagraph for each of the above topics to fully define the protocol.

Paragraph 4: Notes

This paragraph may include any general information that is necessary, and must include a list of all acronyms and abbreviations which are used in this document (and their meaning).

21.5 Evaluating the Interface Design Document

The following checklist can be used when evaluating the Interface Design Document:

_____ Is the required DID format followed exactly?

_____ Is the terminology consistent within the document?

_____ Is the document understandable?

_____ Are data element definitions appropriate and consistent?

_____ Are all CSCIs covered? Are all interfaces to/from each CSCI covered?

_____ Are data element definitions consistent with descriptions in the Software Design Documents for each CSCI?

_____ Are standard communication protocols used when possible? Are protocol definitions clear and unambiguous?

22 Preparing the Software Test Description

This chapter describes specific procedures for preparing the *Software Test Description*, which is Data Item Description (DID) number DI-MCCR-80015A. We will

- Discuss the purpose of this DID

- Present a sample schedule for preparing this DID

- Show a complete outline for the document

- Provide detailed instructions and hints for writing each paragraph of the DID

- Describe how the Government will judge the acceptability of the final DID as submitted

22.1 Purpose

One Software Test Description is typically prepared for each CSCI. This document describes the software test cases and procedures for the formal qualification testing of one CSCI.

22.2 Schedule

The Software Test Descriptions are approved in preliminary form during the Critical Design Reviews and in final form during the Test Readiness Review. Figure 22.1 shows a sample schedule for preparing and updating the Software Test Descriptions during a typical project.

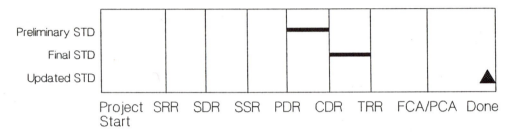

Figure 22.1 STD schedule.

22.3 Outline

The following outline *must* be followed for the Software Test Description:

1.   **Scope**
      1.1   **Identification**
      1.2   **System overview**
      1.3   **Document overview**

2.   **Referenced documents**

3.   **Formal qualification test preparations**
      3.X   **[Test name and identifier]**
      3.X.1   [Test name] schedule
      3.X.2   [Test name] pre-test procedures
      3.X.2.1   Hardware preparation
      3.X.2.2   Software preparation
      3.X.2.3   Other pre-test preparations

4.   **Formal qualification test descriptions**

4.X   **[Test name and identifier]**
4.X.Y   [Test case name and identifier]
4.X.Y.1[Test case name] requirements traceability
4.X.Y.2[Test case name] initialization
4.X.Y.3[Test case name] test inputs
4.X.Y.4[Test case name] expected test results
4.X.Y.5[Test case name] criteria for evaluating results
4.X.Y.6[Test case name] test procedure
4.X.Y.7[Test case name] assumptions and constraints

5.   Notes

22.4 Detailed Instructions

This section presents specific instructions for meeting the requirements of each of the DID paragraphs. For some paragraphs my recommendation is to leave the paragraph blank because all information for the paragraph is covered in lower level subparagraphs. For each of these, it would also be appropriate for the top level paragraph to consist of a set of bullets presenting the titles of the lower level subparagraphs.

Paragraph 1: Scope

This paragraph may be left blank.

Paragraph 1.1: Identification

This paragraph contains the name and identification number of the system and CSCI which is covered.

Paragraph 1.2: System overview

This paragraph references paragraph 1.2 of this CSCI's Software Requirements Specification.

Paragraph 1.3: Document overview

This paragraph normally states, "This document describes the software test cases and test procedures for the formal qualification testing of the _____ [name] CSCI of the _____ [name] system."

Paragraph 2: Referenced documents

This paragraph lists the documents (number and title) which are referenced in this document. The source for non-Government documents must also be listed.

Paragraph 3: Formal qualification test preparations

This paragraph lists the tests which are described in this document. Each of these tests will then be described in detail in the paragraphs that follow.

Paragraph 3.X: [Test name and identifier]

This paragraph may be left blank.

Paragraph 3.X.1: [Test name] schedule

This section references the test schedule for this specific test from your Software Test Plan (paragraph 4.X.5).

Paragraph 3.X.2: [Test name] pretest procedures

This paragraph may be left blank.

Paragraph 3.X.2.1: Hardware preparation

This paragraph describes the procedures necessary to prepare the hardware for the test, using references to hardware operating manuals where appropriate. The following should be covered (as appropriate):

- the specific hardware to be used,

- switch setting and cable connections,

- diagrams showing hardware, control and data paths,

- step-by-step instructions for setting up the hardware.

Paragraph 3.X.2.2: Software preparation

This paragraph describes the step-by-step procedures to load and run all software (including support software) required to execute the test.

Paragraph 3.X.2.3: Other pretest preparations

This paragraph describes any other pre-test preparations necessary to conduct the test.

Paragraph 4: Formal qualification test descriptions

This paragraph lists the test names discussed in this document, each of which will be covered in detail in the paragraphs that follow. This list should be identical to the list in paragraph 3.

Paragraph 4.X: [Test name and identifier]

To meet the requirements of a single test, it is normally necessary to perform multiple test cases. For example, to test the input range for a variable it will be necessary to have one test case with the minimum value and one test case with the maximum value. This paragraph lists the specific test cases which must be performed to satisfy the requirements of this test.

Paragraph 4.X.Y: [Test case name and identifier]

This paragraph briefly states the purpose of this particular test case and provides a brief description of the test case.

Paragraph 4.X.Y.1: [Test case name] requirements traceability

This paragraph describes the requirements from the Software Requirements Specification and Interface Requirements Specifications which are tested with this test case. A table similar to Fig. 22.2 is used for this purpose.

Test Case Name	Number	SRS Requirement	IRS Requirement
Test case 1	TC1	R1.3	R1.3.4
Test case 2	TC2	R2.9	R2.3.2
		R3.6	
		R4.9	
Test case 3	TC3		R1.1.1
etc.			

Figure 22.2 Requirement traceability.

Paragraph 4.X.Y.2: [Test case name] initialization

This paragraph describes pre-test preparations which must be made prior to running this test case. If the conditions are identical to those described in Sec. 3 of this document, it is sufficient to simply reference the appropriate paragraph. As appropriate, the following additional conditions may be specified: flags, initial breakpoints, pointers, control parameters, initial data, preset hardware conditions or electrical states, simulated environment setup, and special instructions.

Paragraph 4.X.Y.3: [Test case name] test inputs

This paragraph describes the inputs for this test case. The following information is provided (as applicable):

- name, purpose and range of values for each input data item,

- source of test input and method used to select the test input,

- whether the test input is real or simulated,

- time or event sequence of the test input (i.e., order of input).

Paragraph 4.X.Y.4: [Test case name] expected test results

This paragraph describes the expected intermediate and final results for the given input.

Paragraph 4.X.Y.5: [Test case name] criteria for evaluating results

This paragraph describes the expected intermediate and final results for the given input. For each test result, the following information is provided (as applicable):

- accuracy requirements for the result,

- allowable upper and lower bounds of the result,

- maximum and minimum number of test repetitions in order to obtain the test result,

- conditions under which the results are inconclusive and re-testing must be performed,

- severity of errors in the test result,

- additional criteria as appropriate.

A table similar to Fig 22.3 may be included in an appendix and referenced here.

Test Case Name	Number	Accuracy	Bounds	Min. Reps.	Max. Reps.	Comments
Test C 1	TC1	+-.10		3	5	
Test C 2	TC2		10-12	1	1	
Test C 3	TC3			1	2	
etc.						

Figure 22.3 Evaluation criteria.

Paragraph 4.X.Y.6: [Test case name] test procedure

This paragraph provides a set of detailed, numbered, sequential steps to be followed for this test case. The following information is typically included:

- test operator actions and equipment operation for each step,

- expected result for each step,

- evaluation criteria for each step (if applicable),

- action to be followed in the event of a program error,

- procedures to be used to analyze test results.

Paragraph 4.X.Y.7: [Test case name] assumptions and constraints

This paragraph describes any assumptions made and constraints imposed in the design of the test case. If waivers or exceptions to specified limits and parameters have been approved by the government, they are identified in this paragraph and their impact on the test case is described.

Paragraph 5: Notes

This paragraph may include any general information that is necessary, and must include a list of all acronyms and abbreviations which are used in this document (and their meaning).

22.5 Evaluating the Software Test Description

The following checklist can be used when evaluating the Software Test Description.

_____ Is the required DID format followed exactly?

_____ Is the terminology consistent within the document?

_____ Is the document understandable?

_____ Do the test names from paragraph 3 match the qualifications required by this CSCI's Software Requirements Specification (paragraph 4 of that document)?

_____ Do the test cases identified in paragraph 4.X verify the requirements being tested?

_____ Are the test case descriptions (paragraphs 4.X.Y.2 through 4.X.Y.6) sufficiently clear that a knowledgeable person _not familiar with this particular software_ would be able to perform the test and determine if the requirements have or have not been met?

23 Preparing the Software Test Report

This chapter describes specific procedures for preparing the *Software Test Report*, which is Data Item Description (DID) number DI-MCCR-80017A. We will

- Discuss the purpose of this DID

- Present a sample schedule for preparing this DID

- Show a complete outline for the document

- Provide detailed instructions and hints for writing each paragraph of the DID

- Describe how the Government will judge the acceptability of the final DID as submitted

23.1 Purpose

One Software Test Report is typically prepared for each CSCI. This document describes the software test results for the formal qualification testing of one CSCI. If *system* level testing will be required which is only performed after CSCI integration, a Software Test Report may be prepared for the system level testing. Note that paragraph 5.1 identifies remaining deficiencies and hence acts as an exception report to highlight problem areas.

23.2 Schedule

The Software Test Reports are approved during the Functional Configuration Audits. Figure 23.1 shows a sample schedule for preparing and updating the Software Test Reports during a typical project.

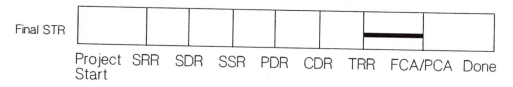

Figure 23.1 STR schedule.

23.3 Outline

The following outline *must* be followed for the Software Test Report:

1. **Scope**
    1.1   **Identification**
    1.2   **System overview**
    1.3   **Document overview**

2. **Referenced documents**

3. **Test overview**
    3.X   **[Formal qualification test name and identifier]**
    3.X.1   [Formal qualification test name] summary
    3.X.2   [Formal qualification test name] test record

4. **Test results**
    4.X   **[Formal qualification test name and identifier] test results**
    4.X.1   [Test case name and identifier]
    4.X.Y.1[Test case name] test results
    4.X.Y.2[Test case name] deviations from test procedures

5.   CSCI evaluation and recommendations
     5.1   CSCI evaluation
     5.2   Recommended improvements

6.   Notes

23.4 Detailed Instructions

This section presents specific instructions for meeting the requirements of each of the DID paragraphs. For some paragraphs my recommendation is to leave the paragraph blank because all information for the paragraph is covered in lower level subparagraphs. For each of these, it would also be appropriate for the top-level paragraph to consist of a set of bullets presenting the titles of the lower level subparagraphs.

Paragraph 1: Scope

This paragraph may be left blank.

Paragraph 1.1: Identification

This paragraph contains the name and identification number of the system and CSCI which is covered. If all formal qualification tests for this CSCI are covered in this report (the normal case), include a sentence stating this fact – otherwise list the specific formal qualification tests (by name and number) which are covered.

Paragraph 1.2: System overview

This paragraph references paragraph 1.2 of this CSCI's Software Requirements Specification.

Paragraph 1.3: Document overview

This paragraph normally states, "This document describes the software test results for the formal qualification testing of the _____ CSCI of the _____ system."

Paragraph 2: Referenced documents

This paragraph lists the documents (number and title) which are referenced in this document. The source for non-Government documents must also be listed.

Paragraph 3: Test overview

This paragraph lists the formal qualification tests covered in this document. Note that these are tests, *not* test *cases*. Each of these tests will then be discussed in detail in the paragraphs that follow.

Paragraph 3.X: [Formal qualification test name and identifier]

This paragraph may be left blank.

Paragraph 3.X.1: [Formal qualification test name] summary

This paragraph consists of a table similar to Fig. 23.2 which shows the results for each test case conducted as part of this formal qualification test.

Test Case	Success?	Failure/ Errors	Software Problem Reports Submitted	Remarks
	No	Step 6 Step 12	PR-011 PR-012	Not Critical
	Yes			
	No	Step 3	PR-086	Needs immediate attention

Figure 23.2 Test results.

Paragraph 3.X.2: [Formal qualification test name] test record

This paragraph documents the test procedures actually used. If a test log is used to record test procedures, this paragraph may reference the test log. The *Government Standards Toolbox* test log may be used for this purpose. Note that this information is for a formal qualification test, not a test *case*. As a minimum, the following information must be included:

- date(s), time(s), and location(s) of the test,

- hardware and software configuration used. For hardware, include the part number, model number, serial number, manufacturer, revision level (developmental hardware), and calibration date. For software, include the version number.

- date and time of each individual test activity, identity of individual(s) who performed the activity, and identities of witnesses,

- problems encountered and the specific step(s) of the test procedures where the problems were observed. If an individual step was repeated multiple times in an attempt to correct a problem, include the number of attempts, what was tried each time, and the results of each attempt.

- if testing was paused (perhaps to correct a problem), include the point at which the test was resumed.

Paragraph 4: Test results

This paragraph lists the formal qualification tests covered by this document. Each of these tests will then be discussed in detail in the paragraphs that follow. This paragraph should be identical to paragraph 3.

Paragraph 4.X: [Formal qualification test name and identifier] test results

This paragraph lists the test cases which make up this formal qualification test.

Paragraph 4.X.1:   [Test case name and identifier]

This paragraph may be left blank.

Paragraph 4.X.Y.1:   [Test case name] test results

This paragraph presents the detailed results for this particular test case. The results are recorded for *each* step identified in the test procedures. Any anomalies or discrepancies encountered during testing are described, including amplifying information (memory dumps, screen print outs, etc.) where appropriate. The assessment of the test conductor as to the cause of the problem and a possible means of correcting it should be included.

Paragraph 4.X.Y.2:   [Test case name] deviations from test procedures

If there were any deviations to the procedures identified in the Software Test Description (for this test case), this paragraph will describe the deviations, the rationale for allowing the deviation, and its impact on the validity of the test.

Paragraph 5:   CSCI evaluation and recommendations

This paragraph may be left blank.

Paragraph 5.1:   CSCI evaluation

This paragraph provides an overall analysis of the capabilities of the CSCI. Any remaining deficiencies, limitations, or constraints in the CSCI are identified.   Software problem/change reports should be referenced as appropriate. For each problem, the analysis should

- describe its impact on this CSCI's performance and the performance of the system,

- describe the CSCI and system impact in order to correct the problem,

- provide a recommended approach to correcting the problem.

Paragraph 5.2: Recommended improvements

This paragraph lists any recommended improvements in the design, operation, or testing of the CSCI. This paragraph is often viewed as an excellent vehicle for marketing, allowing you to describe improvements which are outside of the scope of the current work, thus resulting in follow-on work and additional funds.   On the other hand, it is important that you be cautious in making your recommendations to ensure that you do not appear unresponsive to the original requirements for this CSCI. If there are no recommended improvements, this paragraph states "None."

Paragraph 5: Notes

This paragraph may include any general information that is necessary, and must include a list of all acronyms and abbreviations which are used in this document (and their meaning).

23.5 Evaluating the Software Test Report

The following checklist can be used when evaluating the Software Test Report:

_____   Is the required DID format followed exactly?

_____   Is the terminology consistent within the document?

_____   Is the document understandable?

_____   Are all formal qualification tests identified in paragraph 3 of the Software Test Description covered?

_____   Are all test cases identified in paragraph 4 of the Software Test Description covered?

_____   Are all tests and test cases satisfactorily completed? Does the CSCI meet the requirements imposed on it in the Software Requirements Specification?

_____ When tests were repeated prior to success, is there evidence that the problem has in fact been corrected (or will the problem show up again)?

_____ Were the individuals performing the tests (paragraph 3.X.2) different than the individuals who developed the software?

_____ Were the deviations from test procedures (paragraph 4.X.Y.2) reasonable?

_____ Should the CSCI be accepted or should corrections and additional testing be required? The Software Test Report for a CSCI should not be accepted until the CSCI is judged to be satisfactory.

24 Preparing the Version Description Document

This chapter describes specific procedures for preparing the *Version Description Document,* which is Data Item Description (DID) number DI-MCCR-80013A. We will

- Discuss the purpose of this DID

- Present a sample schedule for preparing this DID

- Show a complete outline for the document

- Provide detailed instructions and hints for writing each paragraph of the DID

- Describe how the Government will judge the acceptability of the final DID as submitted

24.1 Purpose

One Version Description Document is typically prepared for each formal release of each CSCI. This document describes the version of the CSCI which is being delivered. It is the primary configuration control document for the delivered system, and is particularly important if different configurations of the software are delivered to different sites. If a system consists of many CSCIs which are delivered/updated together, the Version Description

Documents can be delivered in a single three-ring binder with one tab for each CSCI. This allows subsequent updates to individual CSCIs to be incorporated by inserting the latest Version Description Document in the binder.

24.2 Schedule

Every unique release of the software (including the initial release) must be described by a Version Description Document. If multiple forms of a CSCI are released at approximately the same time (perhaps to different sites), *each* must have a unique version number and a Version Description Document. The cost to prepare the Version Description Documents is nominal and is normally considered part of the coding costs (i.e., getting the code ready for delivery).

24.3 Outline

The following outline *must* be followed for the Version Description Document:

1. **Scope**
    1.1   Identification
    1.2   System overview
    1.3   Document overview

2. **Referenced documents**

3. **Version description**
    3.1   Inventory of materials released
    3.2   Inventory of CSCI contents
    3.3   Class I changes installed
    3.4   Class II changes installed
    3.5   Adaptation data
    3.6   Interface compatibility
    3.7   Biography of reference documents
    3.8   Summary of change
    3.9   Installation instructions

3.10   **Possible problems and known errors**

4.   Notes

24.4 Detailed Instructions

This section presents specific instructions for meeting the requirements of each of the DID paragraphs.

Paragraph 1: Scope

This paragraph may be left blank.

Paragraph 1.1: Identification

This paragraph contains the name and identification number of the system and CSCI which is covered.

Paragraph 1.2: System overview

This paragraph references paragraph 1.2 of this CSCI's Software Requirements Specification.

Paragraph 1.3: Document overview

This paragraph normally states, "This document describes version _____ [version number] of the _____ [name] CSCI of the _____ [name] system."

Paragraph 2: Referenced documents

This paragraph lists the documents (number and title) which are referenced in this document. The source for non-Government documents must also be listed.

Paragraph 3: Version description

This paragraph may be left blank.

Paragraph 3.1:   Inventory of materials released

This paragraph lists all physical media (disks, tapes, etc.) and documentation which make up this version. Documents must include the date and version number. All operation and support documents that are required to operate, load, or regenerate the CSCI (but which are not part of this delivery) are also listed.

Paragraph 3.2:   Inventory of CSCI contents

This paragraph lists all software files which are being delivered on the physical media.

Paragraph 3.3:   Class I changes installed

This paragraph lists all Class I changes incorporated in this CSCI since the previous version. The listing should include the Engineering Change Proposal number and date and the related Software Change Notice number and date. This paragraph does not apply for the initial release of the CSCI.

Paragraph 3.4:   Class II changes installed

This paragraph lists all Class II changes incorporated in this CSCI since the previous version. The listing should include the Engineering Change Proposal number and date and the related Software Change Notice number and date. This paragraph does not apply for the initial release of the CSCI.

Paragraph 3.5:   Adaptation data

Adaptation data are flags, variables, and so on, which tailor the CSCI to a particular configuration or site. For the initial release of a CSCI, this paragraph lists any unique-to-site data which is preset in the delivered software. For future versions, this paragraph lists any changes to this preset data.

Paragraph 3.6: Interface compatibility

For the initial release of a CSCI, this paragraph states "None." For subsequent releases, this paragraph lists any other systems or configuration items affected by the changes incorporated in this version.

Paragraph 3.7: Biography of reference documents

For the initial release of a CSCI, this paragraph lists all documents (by name, version number, and number) which describe the CSCI. This list typically consists of each of the DIDs required by DOD-STD-2167A which describe this CSCI or the system which this CSCI is part of. For subsequent versions of the CSCI, this paragraph lists any changes (updated versions, etc.) to this list of documents.

Paragraph 3.8: Summary of change

For each Class I or Class II change identified in paragraph 3.3 and 3.4, this paragraph contains a subparagraph summarizing the operational effect of the engineering change. This can be taken directly from the Engineering Change Proposal associated with this change.

Paragraph 3.9: Installation instructions

This paragraph provides the instructions for installing this CSCI version, including instructions for deletion of old versions, if applicable.

Paragraph 3.10: Possible problems and known errors

This paragraph identifies any possible problems or known errors with this CSCI version, and any steps being taken to resolve the problems or errors. Temporary work-arounds for known errors, if any, would also be included here.

Paragraph 4: Notes

This paragraph may include any general information that is necessary, and must include a list of all acronyms and abbreviations which are used in this document (and their meaning).

24.5 Evaluating the Version Description Document

The following checklist can be used when evaluating the Version Description Document:

_____ Is the required DID format followed exactly?

_____ Is the terminology consistent within the document?

_____ Is the document understandable?

_____ Is the inventory of materials released (paragraph 3.1) complete?

_____ Are all files on the delivered media listed in paragraph 3.2, along with a brief description (one line) of the file contents or purpose?

_____ Are all installed Class I and Class II changes incorporated since the last version included in paragraphs 3.3 and 3.4?

_____ Is the description of adaptation data in paragraph 3.5 accurate?

_____ Is the latest version of all documents in paragraph 3.7 listed? Are all documents which describe this CSCI listed?

_____ Are the installation instructions (paragraph 3.9) clear and unambiguous?

_____ For problems and known errors in paragraph 3.10, are work-arounds listed when known?

25 Preparing the Computer System Operator's Manual

This chapter describes specific procedures for preparing the *Computer System Operator's Manual,* which is Data Item Description (DID) number DI-MCCR-80018A. We will

- Discuss the purpose of this DID

- Present a sample schedule for preparing this DID

- Show a complete outline for the document

- Provide detailed instructions and hints for writing each paragraph of the DID

- Describe how the Government will judge the acceptability of the final DID as submitted

25.1 Purpose

One Computer System Operator's Manual (CSOM) is typically prepared for each unique computer system making up the system. A computer system may execute one or more CSCIs. Computer System Operator's Manuals are seldom written by the contractor unless the contract involved development of a unique computer (a rare event). Rather, the contractor is granted

340

permission by the government to use one or more hardware documents prepared by the computer manufacturer as the deliverable for this document.

25.2 Schedule

The Computer System Operator's Manual is delivered during the Physical Configuration Audit for the system. Figure 25.1 shows a sample schedule for preparing and updating the Computer System Operator's Manual during a typical project.

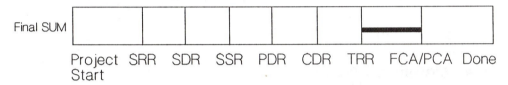

Figure 25.1 CSOM schedule.

25.3 Outline

The following outline *must* be followed for the Computer System Operator's Manual:

1.   Scope
- **1.1**   **Identification**
- **1.2**   **System overview**
- **1.3**   **Document overview**

2.   Referenced documents

3.   Computer system operation
- **3.1**   **Computer system preparation and shutdown**
- 3.1.1   Power on and off
- 3.1.2   Initiation
- 3.1.3   Shutdown
- **3.2**   **Operating procedures**
- 3.2.1   Input and output procedures

3.2.2	Monitoring procedures
3.2.3	Recovery procedures
3.2.4	Off-line routine procedures
3.2.5	Other procedures

4.   Diagnostic features

4.1	**Diagnostic features summary**
4.2	**Diagnostic procedures**
4.2.X	[Procedure name]
4.3	**Diagnostic tools**
4.3.X	[Diagnostic tool name]

5.   Notes

25.4 Detailed Instructions

For the Computer System Operator's Manual, your goal is to *write as little as possible*! You should attempt to tailor the contract requirements to allow you to make the maximum use possible of standard computer hardware documentation available from the computer manufacturer. In descending order of preference, you would like to

1.   deliver the manufacturer's documentation, without change, as this deliverable,

2.   follow the above outline for this deliverable, but for each paragraph simply reference the appropriate manual which is available from the manufacturer,

3.   follow the above outline for this deliverable, but for each paragraph simply reference the appropriate manufacturer's manual, chapter(s), and section(s) which meet the requirements of the paragraph.,

4.   follow the above outline for this deliverable, but meet the requirements for each paragraph by directly copying (with appropriate credit) from the appropriate manufacturer's manual, chapter(s), and section(s).

25.5 Evaluating the Computer System Operator's Manual

The following checklist can be used when evaluating the Computer System Operator's Manual

_____ Is all of the *information* required by the Data Item Deliverable present and clear?

_____ Can all of the information required by the Data Item Deliverable be easily found?

_____ Are the effects of any customization of hardware clear and well documented relative to the manufacturer's manuals?

_____ Was the deliverable produced in the most cost effective manner possible (through the use of tailoring)?

_____ Can the government obtain sufficient copies of the Computer System Operator's Manual (including commercial documentation which is referenced) for deployment of the system and for training of system operators?

26 Preparing the Software User's Manual

This chapter describes specific procedures for preparing the *Software User's Manual,* which is Data Item Description (DID) number DI-MCCR-80019A. We will

- Discuss the purpose of this DID

- Present a sample schedule for preparing this DID

- Show a complete outline for the document

- Provide detailed instructions and hints for writing each paragraph of the DID

- Describe how the Government will judge the acceptability of the final DID as submitted

26.1 Purpose

One Software User's Manual is typically prepared for each *program* which is delivered. A program may include one or more CSCIs. The Software User's Manual is identical in function to a user's manual for commercial software. It tells the user how to load, execute, and operate the software, including documentation about error messages which may appear. With this document more than any other, clarity and readability should take precedence over rigid format guidelines. If you are not comfortable with writing good user manuals, you may want to refer to Weiss (14), or a similar book on the topic. The description of the user manual contents you find in a commercial reference will appear in chapter three of this DID.

26.2 Schedule

The Software User's Manual is delivered during the Physical Configuration Audit. Figure 26.1 shows a sample schedule for preparing and updating the Software User's Manual during a typical project.

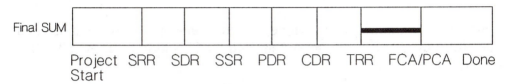

Figure 26.1 SUM schedule.

26.3 Outline

The following outline *must* be followed for the Software User's Manual:

    1.   **Scope**
        1.1   **Identification**
        1.2   **System overview**
        1.3   **Document overview**

    2.   **Referenced documents**

    3.   **Execution procedures**

    4.   **Error messages**

    5.   **Notes**

26.4 Detailed Instructions

This section presents specific instructions for meeting the requirements of each of the DID paragraphs.

Paragraph 1: Scope

This paragraph may be left blank.

Paragraph 1.1: Identification

This paragraph contains the name, version number, release number and identification number of the system and CSCI which is covered by this document.

Paragraph 1.2: System overview

This paragraph summarizes the purpose of the system and the CSCI(s) which are implemented in the program to which this document applies.

Paragraph 1.3: Document overview

This paragraph normally states, "This document provides the user instructions for operating the _____ [name] CSCI(s) of the _____ [name] system."

Paragraph 2: Referenced documents

This paragraph lists the documents (number and title) which are referenced in this document. The source for non-Government documents must also be listed.

Paragraph 3: Execution procedures

This paragraph describes how to use the software. Loading instructions may reference the Computer System Operator's Manual. You may set up lower level paragraphs under this one to match the format you use for writing your manual. The following information should be covered somewhere in this paragraph:

- initialization procedures,

- user inputs,

- inputs from external systems or devices (including format, frequency, range, units of measure, etc.),

- shut-down procedures,

- restart procedures,

- system Outputs.

If the software incorporates commercial software (e.g., data base management software), reference the manual for the software.

Paragraph 4: Error messages

Describe all error messages which may occur, their meaning, and the user action which is required.

Paragraph 5: Notes

This paragraph may include any general information that is necessary, and must include a list of all acronyms and abbreviations which are used in this document (and their meaning).

26.5   Evaluating the Computer System Operator's Manual

The following checklist can be used when evaluating the Software User's Manual:

_____ Is the manual clearly written?

_____ Is the manual geared to a non-technical reader?

_____ Is the tone of the writing conversational and informal?

_____ If the program incorporates a menu hierarchy, is the hierarchy shown in the manual as a figure?

_____ If the program uses data input forms or screens, are these screens reproduced in the manual?

_____ For *every* data entry field in the program, is the user informed of the meaning of the data being entered, the allowable range, the units of measure, and a source of the data (where not obvious)? If this information is provided on-line to the user, is the manual clear about how to access this on-line help facility?

_____ For each program operation, is the user informed of actions to take in the event of a mistake? Is the procedure for aborting an operation consistent?

_____ Are sample program outputs included?

_____ If the manual is longer than 30 pages, does it include an index (normally as an appendix)?

_____ For program operations which will take a significant amount of time, is the user informed of this fact? Is the user given some indication of the time which will be required, or a method of estimating the time required based on the parameters entered?

_____ Is the manual suitable both for the beginning user (as a tutorial) and for the advanced user (as a reference)?

_____ If commercial documentation is referenced, can the government purchase copies of the documentation for delivery with systems and for use during training? Can the government duplicate the commercial documentation?

27 Preparing the Software Programmer's Manual

This chapter describes specific procedures for preparing the *Software Programmer's Manual,* which is Data Item Description (DID) number DI-MCCR-80021A. We will

- Discuss the purpose of this DID

- Present a sample schedule for preparing this DID

- Show a complete outline for the document

- Provide detailed instructions and hints for writing each paragraph of the DID

- Describe how the Government will judge the acceptability of the final DID as submitted

27.1 Purpose

One Software Programmer's Manual is typically prepared for each unique computer system making up the system. A computer system may execute one or more CSCIs. This document describes the instruction set architecture of the computer hardware. Software Programmer's Manuals are seldom written by the contractor unless the contract involved development of a unique computer (a rare event). Rather, the contractor is granted permission by the government to use one or more documents prepared by the computer manufacturer as the deliverable for this document.

27.2 Schedule

The Software Programmer's Manual is delivered during the Physical Configuration Audit for the system. Figure 27.1 shows a sample schedule for preparing and updating the Software Programmer's Manual during a typical project.

Figure 27.1 SPM schedule.

27.3 Outline

The following outline *must* be followed for the Software Programmer's Manual:

1.   Scope
1.1   Identification
1.2   System overview
1.3   Document overview

2.   Referenced documents

3.   Software programming environment

4.   Programming information

5.   Notes

27.4 Detailed Instructions

The paragraph of this document describing the software programming environment describes the CPU, peripherals, memory, compilers, assembler, and linker. The requirements of this paragraph are typically met by the computer's hardware guide, compiler manual and assembler manual. The paragraph of this document presenting programming information describes the CPU instruction set and input/output programming. High level language instructions may be included. These requirements are normally met by the assembler manual and high level language manual (i.e., Fortran manual, C manual, etc.) for this system.

For the Software Programmer's Manual, your goal is to *write as little as possible*! You should attempt to tailor the contract requirements to allow you to make the maximum use possible of standard computer documentation available from the computer manufacturer. In descending order of preference, you would like to

1. deliver the manufacturer's documentation, without change, as this deliverable,

2. follow the outline for this deliverable, but for each paragraph simply reference the appropriate manual which is available from the manufacturer,

3. follow the outline for this deliverable, but for each paragraph simply reference the appropriate manufacturer's manual, chapter(s), and section(s) which meet the requirements of the paragraph,

4. follow the outline for this deliverable, but meet the requirements for each paragraph by directly copying (with appropriate credit) from the appropriate manufacturer's manual, chapter(s), and section(s).

27.5 Evaluating the Software Programmer's Manual

The following checklist can be used when evaluating the Software Programmer's Manual:

_____ Is all of the *information* required by the Data Item Deliverable present and clear?

_____ Can all of the information required by the Data Item Deliverable be easily found?

_____ Are the effects of any customization of hardware clear and well documented relative to the manufacturer's manuals?

_____ Was the deliverable produced in the most cost effective manner possible (through the use of tailoring)?

_____ Can the government obtain sufficient copies of the Software Programmer's Manual (including commercial documentation which is referenced) for deployment of the system and for training of system operators?

28 Preparing the Firmware Support Manual

This chapter describes specific procedures for preparing the *Firmware Support Manual,* which is Data Item Description (DID) number DI-MCCR-80022A. We will

- Discuss the purpose of this DID

- Present a sample schedule for preparing this DID

- Show a complete outline for the document

- Provide detailed instructions and hints for writing each paragraph of the DID

- Describe how the Government will judge the acceptability of the final DID as submitted

28.1 Purpose

One Firmware Support Manual is typically prepared for the entire system. This document describes the procedures necessary to load software or data into firmware (ROM, EPROM, etc.), including descriptions of support software and equipment.

28.2 Schedule

The Firmware Support Manual (FSM) is delivered during the Physical Configuration Audit for the system. Figure 28.1 shows a sample schedule for preparing and updating the Firmware Support Manual during a typical project.

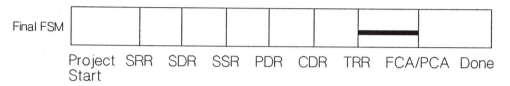

Figure 28.1 FSM schedule.

28.3 Outline

The following outline *must* be followed for the Firmware Support Manual:

1.   Scope
       1.1   **Identification**
       1.2   **System overview**
       1.3   **Document overview**

2.   Referenced documents

3.   Firmware device information
       3.1   **Device description**
       3.2   **Installation and repair procedures**
       3.3   **Security**
       3.4   **Limitations**

4.   Programming equipment and procedures
       4.1   **Programming hardware**
       4.2   **Programming software**
       4.3   **Loading procedures**

5.   Vendor information

6.   **Notes**

28.4 Detailed Instructions

For the Firmware Support Manual, your goal is to *write as little as possible*! You should attempt to tailor the contract requirements to allow you to make the maximum use possible of standard hardware and software documentation available from the computer manufacturer.   In descending order of preference, you would like to:

1.   deliver the manufacturer's documentation, without change, as this deliverable,

2.   follow the above outline for this deliverable, but for each paragraph simply reference the appropriate manual which is available from the manufacturer,

3.   follow the outline for this deliverable, but for each paragraph simply reference the appropriate manufacturer's manual, chapter(s), and section(s) which meet the requirements of the paragraph.

4.   follow the above outline for this deliverable, but meet the requirements for each paragraph by directly copying (with appropriate credit) from the appropriate manufacturer's manual, chapter(s), and section(s).

28.5 Evaluating the Firmware Support Manual

The following checklist can be used when evaluating the Firmware Support Manual:

_____   Is all of the *information* required by the Data Item Deliverable present and clear?

_____   Can all of the information required by the Data Item Deliverable be easily found?

_____ Was the deliverable produced in the most cost effective manner possible (through the use of tailoring)?

_____ Can the government obtain sufficient copies of the Firmware Support Manual (including commercial documentation which is referenced) for deployment of the system and for training of system operators?

29 Preparing the Computer Resources Integrated Support Document

This chapter describes specific procedures for preparing the *Computer Resources Integrated Support Document,* which is Data Item Description (DID) number DI-MCCR-80024A. We will

- Discuss the purpose of this DID

- Present a sample schedule for preparing this DID

- Show a complete outline for the document

- Provide detailed instructions and hints for writing each paragraph of the DID

- Describe how the Government will judge the acceptability of the final DID as submitted

29.1 Purpose

One Computer Resources Integrated Support Document (CRISD) is typically prepared for the entire system. The CRISD documents your plans for transitioning software support to the government.

29.2 Schedule

The Computer Resources Integrated Support Document is delivered during
the Physical Configuration Audit for the system. Figure 29.1 shows a sample
schedule for preparing and updating the Computer Resources Integrated
Support Document during a typical project.

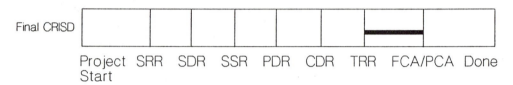

Final CRISD

Project   SRR   SDR   SSR   PDR   CDR   TRR   FCA/PCA   Done
Start

Figure 29.1 CRISD schedule.

29.3 Outline

The following outline *must* be followed for the Computer Resources
Integrated Support Document:

1.   Scope
          1.1   Identification
          1.2   System overview
          1.3   Document overview

2.   Referenced documents

3.   Support information
          3.1   Software support resources
          3.1.1   Software
          3.1.2   Hardware
          3.1.3   Facilities
          3.1.4   Personnel
          3.1.5   Other resources
          3.2   Operations
          3.2.1   Software modifications
          3.2.2   Software integration and testing
          3.2.3   Software generation

3.2.4	Simulation
3.2.5	Emulation
3.3	**Training**
3.4	**Anticipated areas of change**

4.   Transition planning

5.   Notes

29.4 Detailed Instructions

This section presents specific instructions for meeting the requirements of each of the DID paragraphs.

Paragraph 1: Scope

This paragraph may be left blank.

Paragraph 1.1: Identification

This paragraph contains the name and identification number of the system which is covered.

Paragraph 1.2: System overview

This paragraph references paragraph 1.2 of the System/Segment Specification.

Paragraph 1.3: Document overview

This paragraph normally states, "This document describes the plan for transitioning software support to the government."

Paragraph 2: Referenced documents

This paragraph lists the documents (number and title) which are referenced in this document. The source for non-Government documents must also be listed.

Paragraph 3: Support information

This paragraph may be left blank.

Paragraph 3.1: Software support resources

This paragraph uses a figure similar to Fig. 29.2 to illustrate the inter-relationships between software, hardware, facilities, personnel, and other resources to properly operate the system.

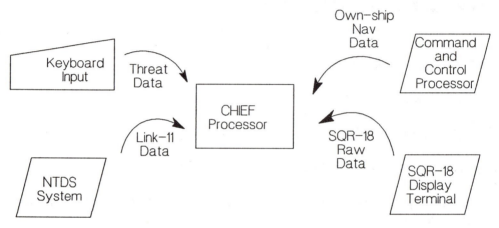

Figure 29.2 Software support resources.

Paragraph 3.1.1: Software

This paragraph identifies all software and software documentation necessary to properly support the delivered software.

Paragraph 3.1.2: Hardware

This paragraph identifies all hardware and hardware documentation necessary to properly support the delivered software. When appropriate, justification for the particular hardware configuration described should be included. A figure (similar to Fig. 29.3) showing how the hardware is interconnected may be included.

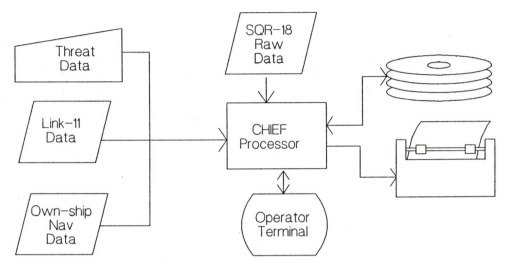

Figure 29.3 Hardware interconnections.

Paragraph 3.1.3: Facilities

This paragraph identifies all facilities necessary to properly support the delivered software.

Paragraph 3.1.4: Personnel

This paragraph references paragraph 3.6.1 of the System/Segment Specification.

Paragraph 3.1.5: Other resources

This paragraph identifies any other resources required for the software support environment.

Paragraph 3.2: Operations

This paragraph may be left blank.

Paragraph 3.2.1: Software modifications

This paragraph describes procedures which must be followed to modify the software, including modifications necessary to accommodate changes to commercially available computer resources. This paragraph typically refers to the Software Programmer's Manual for information about compiling revised code and to paragraph 3.2.3 of this document for information about compilation order.

Paragraph 3.2.2: Software integration and testing

This paragraph describes the procedures necessary to integrate and test all software modifications.

Paragraph 3.2.3: Software generation

This paragraph describes the procedures necessary to recompile the code, perhaps after making changes. If your development environment uses an automatic compilation routine such as *make*, it is normally sufficient to print the contents of the make file(s).

Paragraph 3.2.4: Simulation

This paragraph normally states, "Not applicable." If the software requires a simulation environment to support the software, the simulation environment should be described. This description should include all modes of simulation available and limitations imposed by the simulation methods.

Paragraph 3.2.5: Emulation

This paragraph normally states, "Not applicable." If the software emulates one or more operational modes, this paragraph will describe the modes emulated, the relation between the emulated modes and the simulated modes (if any), and limitations imposed by the emulation.

Paragraph 3.3: Training

This paragraph normally states, "Training will be conducted in accordance with paragraph 3.6.2 of the System/Segment Specification (document number _____ [number]).

Paragraph 3.4: Anticipated areas of change

This paragraph describes any parts of the software which you expect to change. Examples include outstanding Engineering Change Proposals and items discussed in paragraph 5.2 of each CSCI's Software Test Report.

Paragraph 4: Transition planning

This paragraph contains a complete transition plan for turning the software over to the government. The transition plan should include transition tasks and milestones, schedules, and procedures for installation and check-out of the deliverable software.

Paragraph 5: Notes

This paragraph may include any general information that is necessary, and must include a list of all acronyms and abbreviations which are used in this document (and their meaning).

29.5 Evaluating the Computer Resources Integrated Support Document

The following checklist can be used when evaluating the Computer Resources Integrated Support Document:

_____ Is the required DID format followed exactly?

_____ Is the terminology consistent within the document?

_____ Is the document understandable?

_____ Does the list of software and documentation in paragraph 3.1.1 seem complete? Are all of the listed items delivered under this contract?

_____ The procedures described in paragraph 3.2.1 and 3.2.3 should be followed to build executable code from source code. Does the resultant executable program(s) *exactly* match the executable program which was tested and delivered under the contract?

30 Preparing the Software Product Specification

This chapter describes specific procedures for preparing the *Software Product Specification,* which is Data Item Description (DID) number DI-MCCR-80029A. We will

- Discuss the purpose of this DID

- Present a sample schedule for preparing this DID

- Show a complete outline for the document

- Provide detailed instructions and hints for writing each paragraph of the DID

- Describe how the Government will judge the acceptability of the final DID as submitted

30.1 Purpose

One Software Product Specification is typically prepared for each CSCI. The Software Product Specification consists of the final Software Design Document and source code listings for the CSCI. The source code listings may normally be delivered in electronic format.

30.2 Schedule

The Software Product Specification is delivered during the Physical Configuration Audit for the system. The Software Product Specification normally does not involve any significant original writing, and costs for preparing the Software Product Specification are included in the costs for preparing the final software source code for delivery.

30.3 Outline

The following outline *must* be followed for the Software Product Specification:

1.   Scope
  1.1 **Identification**
  1.2 **System overview**
  1.3 **Document overview**

2.   Applicable documents
  2.1 **Government documents**
  2.2 **Non-Government documents**

3.   Requirements
  3.1 **Software design**
  3.2 **CSCI source code listings**
  3.3 **Compiler/assembler**
  3.4 **Measured resource utilization**

4.   Notes

30.4 Detailed Instructions

This section presents specific instructions for meeting the requirements of each of the DID paragraphs.

Paragraph 1: Scope

This paragraph may be left blank.

Paragraph 1.1: Identification

This paragraph contains the name and identification number of the system and CSCI which is covered.

Paragraph 1.2: System overview

This paragraph references paragraph 1.2 of this CSCI's Software Requirements Specification.

Paragraph 1.3: Document overview

This paragraph normally states, "This document describes the final software design and source code listings for the _____ [name] CSCI of the _____ [name] system."

Paragraph 2: Applicable documents

This paragraph may be left blank.

Paragraph 2.1: Government documents

List government documents referenced in this document. The DID contains specific information about the order referenced documents must be listed and some standard verbiage about obtaining documents.

Paragraph 2.2: Non-Government documents

List non-Government documents referenced in this document. Documents which are not stocked by federal stocking activities must include a source. The DID contains specific information about the order referenced documents must be listed and some standard verbiage about obtaining documents.

Paragraph 3:   Requirements

This paragraph may be left blank.

Paragraph 3.1:   Software design

This paragraph is simply a reference to the Software Design Document for this CSCI. The Software Design document must be kept current throughout the project, with modifications made normally made after each In Process Review or formal review/audit.

Paragraph 3.2:   CSCI source code listings

This paragraph is simply a reference to the source code listings for this CSCI. The source code listings themselves may be an appendix to this document (hard copy listings), an enclosure to this document (electronic deliveries), or in a different deliverable called out in the Contract Data Requirements List.

Paragraph 3.3:   Compiler/assembler

This paragraph gives the name and version number of the compiler, assembler, and linker used to translate the source code.

Paragraph 3.4:   Measured resource utilization

This paragraph gives the final program requirements for critical resources. It is normally sufficient to list the RAM requirements of each executable program and to reference the test results from the Software Test Report which verified that this CSCI did not exceed its allowable resource usage as defined in the Software Requirements Specification.

Paragraph 5:   Notes

This paragraph may include any general information that is necessary, and must include a list of all acronyms and abbreviations which are used in this document (and their meaning).

30.5 Evaluating the Software Product Specification

The following checklist can be used when evaluating the Software Product Specification

_____ Is the required DID format followed exactly?

_____ Is the terminology consistent within the document?

_____ Is the document understandable?

31 Conducting a System Requirements Review

This chapter describes specific procedures for conducting the *System Requirements Review,* which is described in MIL-STD-1521B, Appendix A. We will

- Discuss the purpose of this review

- List the software related documents to be reviewed

- List the significant issues to be discussed

- Present a sample agenda for the review

- Describe how the Government will judge the acceptability of the review

If the Government has done a considerable amount of work to refine the system requirements, it is common to combine the System Requirements Review with the System Design Review (or to skip the System Requirements Review entirely).

31.1 Purpose

The System Requirements Review is conducted to determine the acceptability of the detailed requirement definitions for the system. On most contracts, the Government prepares a set of requirements which are included in the Request for Proposal. These requirements are used by the contractor for costing during the proposal preparation stage. After contract award, the contractor builds on the proposal work to quantify exactly *what* will be delivered. Perhaps this is required because the Request for Proposal listed a range of acceptable values for a requirements, and it is now time to "sign up" to a specific value to be delivered. It is also possible that further analysis has demonstrated that one or more requirements can not be met given the current state-of-the-art. Perhaps the system can be greatly improved in several other areas by relaxing the requirements in one specific area. Whatever the reason, at this stage of a project the requirements are expected to change *somewhat*. The contractor is expected to match the government requirements to their proposed approach for solving the problem and arrive at a quantitative set of requirements which *they* are willing to commit to. This tailored set of requirements is approved during the Software Requirements Review.

Secondarily, the System Requirements Review is used by the government to verify that the contractor has a firm understanding of the operational problem which the system is designed to solve, and is on-track in the solution process. It is important that all parties realize that the primary purpose of the System Requirements Review is *not* to "test" the contractor's performance. Rather, the System Requirements Review should be viewed as an opportunity for the contractor to open a window into the system engineering process to allow the government to provide friendly guidance and clarification at an early stage in the engineering process.

31.2 Software Documents to be Reviewed

The primary document reviewed at the System Requirements Review is the preliminary System/Segment Specification (Type A specification). This is the document which defines the specific functional capability which the contractor will be delivering. The document should be complete at this point, although some modifications (refinements) to requirements are permitted prior to the final review at the System Design Review.

In addition, the contractor may have performed special purpose studies to help lay the foundation for a valid system design. The results of these special studies would be briefed during this review. Examples of typical studies which are sometimes required are

- *Functional Flow Analysis*: A set of flow charts or data flow diagrams to show the *current* flow of data, documents, or responsibility in the problem area which this system will address.

- *Cost Effectiveness Analysis*: A set of life cycle cost figures to justify modifications to one or more system requirements.

- *System Interface Studies*: One or more studies describing the characteristics of external systems which this system or segment must interface to (or work with).

- *Program Risk Analysis*: A top level analysis of which portions of the program in general, and the requirements in particular, are considered high risk.

In addition, a milestone schedule is typically presented at this point. This milestone schedule can normally be taken directly from the contract requirements for deliveries and reviews.

31.3 Software Related Issues to be Discussed

During the System Requirements Review, several software related issues should be addressed. Specifically,

- the computer hardware which will be used to run the system software should be identified, at least in a top-level fashion,

- the operating system to be used should be identified,

- candidate programming languages should be listed and a likely choice should be identified,

- trade-offs between system requirements should be explained,

- existing software design/code which is applicable to this project should be identified and described.

31.4 Sample Agenda

The requirements for the agenda format can be found in Data Item Deliverable (DID) description number DI-A-3029/S-105-1. This DID is titled *Agenda – Design Reviews, Configuration Audits and Demonstrations*. The sample agenda presented below meets the requirements of this DID.

System Requirements Review
Agenda

A.   Scope and purpose

        This review will cover the requirements analysis for the _____ system/segment.

B.   Time, date, location, and duration

        This review will commence at _____ (time), on _____ (date), at the facilities of _____ located at _____ . The review is expected to last _____ days.

C.   Previous reviews

        Not applicable.

D.   Objectives

The following items will be covered[1]:

1.	Meeting kickoff	[Introduce players and administrative details (schedule, washrooms, smoking policy, etc.)]

---

[1]Items in square brackets are notes of explanation and are not included in the published agenda.

2.   Milestone schedule

3.   Mission and threat   [Based on paragraphs
                                           6.1.1 and 6.1.2 of the
                                           System/Segment
                                           Specification.]

4.   System overview   [Based on paragraph 1.2
                                           of the System/Segment
                                           Specification.   Also
                                           includes   the   system
                                           diagram from paragraph
                                           3.1   of   the   Sys-
                                           tem/Segment Specifica-
                                           tion.]

5.   Functional Flow Analysis

6.   Performance characteristics   [Based on paragraph
                                           3.2.1 (and lower level
                                           subparagraphs) of the
                                           System/Segment
                                           Specification.]

7.   External interface requirements   [Based on paragraph
                                           3.2.3 of the System/Seg-
                                           ment Specification.]

8.   Computer resources   [Hardware, operating
                                           system, and language
                                           selections.   Existing
                                           design/code which will
                                           be reused is also covered
                                           here.]

9.   Physical characteristics   [Based on paragraph
                                           3.2.4   of   the   Sys-
                                           tem/Segment Specifica-
                                           tion.]

10.	System quality factors	[Based on paragraph 3.2.5 (and lower level sub-paragraphs) of the System/Segment Specification.]
11.	Environmental conditions	[Based on paragraph 3.2.6 of the System/Segment Specification.]
12.	Flexibility and expansion	[Based on paragraph 3.2.8 of the System/Segment Specification.]
13.	Safety	[Based on paragraph 2.3.6 of the System/Segment Specification.]
14.	Human engineering	[Based on paragraph 3.3.7 of the System/Segment Specification.]
15.	System security	[Based on paragraph 3.3.9 of the System/Segment Specification.]
16.	Risk factors	
17.	Government furnished property	[Based on paragraph 3.3.10 of the System/Segment Specification.]
18.	Precedence	[Based on paragraph 3.8 of the System/Segment Specification.]

E.   Responsibilities

_____ (contractor name) will supply all resources and materials necessary to perform the Review/Audit effectively and act as Co-chairperson. Minutes will be recorded as dictated by either Co-Chairperson and a list of action items will be recorded. Official minutes will be published and distributed.

_____ (government agency) will serve as Co-Chairperson, review the daily minutes to ensure that they reflect all significant contracting agency inputs, and will be responsible for establishing the adequacy of the review. In addition, _____ shall provide the name, organization, and security clearance of each Government representative prior to the review.

F.   Documents vailable for review

System/Segment Specification for the _____ system (or segment)

G.   Progress

Not applicable.

H.   Methods used

The presentation will consist of a mixture of viewgraphs, verbal presentations, and discussions.

I.   Facilities provided

The following office facilities will be available for use by the Government representatives during the review: [List facilities available].

J.   Other information

This review will be conducted at the _____ [classification] level.

31.5 Evaluating the Review

The following checklist may be used when evaluating the adequacy of the software portion of the System Requirements Review:

_____ Was the System/Segment Specification available prior to review?

_____ Was the agenda available prior to review?

_____ Were the physical facilities for the review adequate?

_____ Has the contractor shown a clear understanding of the problem which this system is designed to solve?

_____ Has the contractor demonstrated an understanding of the current methods used to solve this problem?

_____ Does the milestone schedule as presented match the deliverable requirements of the contract?

_____ Are the requirements which the system must meet clear?

_____ Do the requirements covered in the review satisfy the Government's requirements as described in the Request for Proposal? Are any deviations acceptable?

_____ Do the requirements covered in the review meet or exceed the system functionality promised in the contractor's proposal?

_____ Are trade-offs between requirements recognized and realistic?

_____ Has the contractor demonstrated an adequate understanding of areas of significant risk on this contract? Is preliminary risk avoidance planning demonstrated? Are contingency plans for high risk areas being considered?

_____ Is a comprehension of the cost versus benefit trade-offs in system design recognized?

_____ Does the contractor show satisfactory progress in selecting the computer hardware, operating system, and language?

_____ If the selected language is not Ada, is the choice justified adequately?

32 Conducting a System Design Review

This chapter describes specific procedures for conducting the *System Design Review,* which is described in MIL-STD-1521B, Appendix B. We will

- Discuss the purpose of this review

- List the software related documents to be reviewed

- List the significant issues to be discussed

- Present a sample agenda for the review

- Describe how the Government will judge the acceptability of the review

32.1 Purpose

The System Design Review finalizes the functional capabilities to be delivered, resulting in a functional baseline for the system. In addition, the functional requirements are allocated to individual configuration items. These configuration items consist of a combination of Hardware Configuration Items (HWCIs), Computer Software Configuration Items (CSCIs), and manual operations. The allocation of system requirements to individual configuration items is sometimes called the *system level* allocated baseline. We will see that the allocated baselines for individual CSCIs is not established until the Software Specification Review.

32.2 Software Documents to be Reviewed

The following software related documents are reviewed at the System Design Review:

- The final *System/Segment Specification*: changes from the preliminary version reviewed during the System Requirements Review should be minor. After approval, this document defines the formal functional baseline configuration for the system.

- The *System/Segment Design Document*: which defines the operational concepts for the system and shows how the requirements identified in the System/Segment Specification will be allocated to individual configuration items. This document defines the *system level* allocated baseline for the system.

- The *Software Development Plan*

- A preliminary version of the *Software Requirements Specification* and *Interface Requirements Specification* for each CSCI.

The Software Requirements Specification(s) and Interface Requirements Specification(s) are reviewed to assist the contractor by providing early guidance about Government desires prior to the finalization of these documents. The milestone schedule should be briefed, including information about actual progress to date versus planned progress to date.

It is also expected that by this point the contractor's system design will be quite advanced. The contractor is expected to brief major system design decisions, including justification for design choices. Examples of this type of design decision are:

- Centralized versus decentralized system

- Automated versus manual operations

- Use of existing equipment/software versus new development

- Cost versus performance

32.3 Software Related Issues to be Discussed

During the System Design Review, several software related issues should be addressed. Specifically.

- detailed descriptions of the computer hardware environment (developmental and operational) should be presented,

- programming language(s) should be identified,

- all critical algorithm requirements should be identified, and candidate algorithms should be described,

- technical program risks should be identified,

- interfaces between CSCIs should be covered in depth.

32.4 Sample Agenda

The requirements for the agenda format can be found in Data Item Deliverable (DID) description number DI-A-3029/S-105-1. This DID is titled *Agenda – Design Reviews, Configuration Audits and Demonstrations*. The sample agenda presented meets the requirements of this DID.

System Design Review
Agenda

A. Scope and purpose

This review will cover the requirements analysis, operational concept, and system level requirements allocation for the _____ system/segment.

B.   Time, date, location, and duration

        This review will commence at _____ (time), on _____ (date), at the facilities of _____ located at _____. The review is expected to last _____ days.

C.   Previous reviews

        The System Requirements Review for this system/segment was approved on _____.

D.   Objectives

The following items will be covered[1]:

1.   Meeting kickoff   [Introduce players and administrative details (schedule, washrooms, smoking policy, etc.)]

2.   Milestone schedule

3.   System overview   [Based on paragraph 1.2 of the System/SegmentSpecification. Also includes the system diagram from paragraph 3.1 of theSystem/Segment Specification.]

4.   Requirement modifications   [Covers changes to System/Segment Specification Requirements since the System Requirements Review.]

---

[1]Items in square brackets are notes of explanation and are not included in the published agenda.

5.	Operational concept	[Based on paragraph 3 (and lower level sub-paragraphs) from the System/Segment Design Document.]
6.	System design	[Based on paragraph 4 (and lower level sub-paragraphs) from the System/Segment Design Document.]
7.	External interfaces	[Covers all interfaces from this system/segment to/from external systems and between configuration items within this system/segment.]
8.	Configuration item number 1	[For *each* CSCI and HWCI, brief the requirements allocated to that configuration item, the algorithmic functions required to implement satisfy the requirements, the candidate algorithms, and the high risk requirements/algorithms.]
9.	Requirements traceability	[Based on paragraph 7 from the System/Segment Design Document.]
10.	Software schedule	[Based on paragraph 3.2 from the Software Development Plan.]
11.	Software engineering environment	[Based on paragraph 4.1.3 from the Software Development Plan.]

12.	Software methodologies	[Based on paragraph 4.2.1 from the Software Development Plan.]
13.	Test philosophy	[Should also cover test assumptions and constraints. Based on paragraphs 5.2 and 5.3 from the Software Development Plan.]
14.	Software configuration management	[Based on paragraph 7 (and lower level sub-paragraphs) from the Software Development Plan.]
15.	Processing resources	[Based on paragraph 5 (and lower level sub-paragraphs) from the System/Segment Design Document.]

E.   Responsibilities

_____ (contractor name) will supply all resources and materials necessary to perform the Review/Audit effectively and act as Co-Chairperson. Minutes will be recorded as dictated by either Co-Chairperson and a list of action items will be recorded. Official minutes will be published and distributed.

_____ (government agency) will serve as Co-Chairperson, review the daily minutes to ensure that they reflect all significant contracting agency inputs, and will be responsible for establishing the adequacy of the review. In addition, _____ shall provide the name, organization, and security clearance of each Government representative prior to the review.

F.   Documents available for review

• *System/Segment Specification* for the _____ system (or segment)

- *System/Segment Design Document* for the _____ system (or segment)

- *Software Development Plan* for the _____ system (or segment)

- Preliminary *Software Requirements Specification* for the _____ CSCI of the _____ system (or segment) [one for *each* CSCI]

- Preliminary *Interface Requirements Specification* for the _____ CSCI of the _____ system (or segment) [normally one for *each* CSCI]

G.   Progress

See monthly status report(s) for the months of _____, _____, etc.

H.   Methods used

The presentation will consist of a mixture of viewgraphs, verbal presentations, and discussions.

I.   Facilities provided

The following office facilities will be available for use by the government representatives during the review: [List facilities available].

J.   Other Information

This review will be conducted at the _____ [classification] level.

32.5 Evaluating the Review

The following checklist may be used when evaluating the adequacy of the software portion of the System Design Review:

_____ Was the System/Segment Specification available prior to review?

_____ Was the System/Segment Specification complete in final form (no "To Be Determined" items)?

_____ Was the System/Segment Design Document complete in final form?

_____ Was the Software Development Plan complete in final form?

_____ Was a preliminary version of the Software Requirements Specification available for _each_ CSCI?

_____ Was a preliminary version of the Interface Requirements Specification available covering all interfaces (normally one per CSCI)?

_____ Was the agenda available prior to review?

_____ Were the physical facilities for the review adequate?

_____ Does the milestone schedule as presented match the deliverable requirements of the contract?

_____ Are the requirements which the system must meet clear?

_____ Do the requirements covered in the review satisfy the Government's requirements as described in the Request for Proposal? . . . Are any deviations acceptable?

_____ Do the requirements covered in the review meet or exceed the system functionality promised in the contractor's proposal?

_____ Is the operational concept for the deployment of this system reasonable? Does it incorporate a reasonable transition plan for initial introduction of the new system? Is the system interoperable with existing equipment which will be used during the transition to the new system?

_____ Is the operational concept for the new system compatible with the organizational structure and "way of thinking" for personnel who will be using the system?

_____ Is the selected software development methodology satisfactory?

_____ Is the Software Development Plan clear and well thought out?

_____ For each CSCI, are the requirements clear? Are they compatible with the requirements in the System/Segment Specification?

_____ Are critical algorithmic functions identified and candidate algorithms clear?

_____ Are all interfaces between configuration items within this system clear?

_____ Are all interfaces between this system/segment and external systems clear?

_____ Has the contractor demonstrated an adequate understanding of areas of significant risk on this contract? Is risk avoidance planning demonstrated? Are contingency plans for high risk areas clear?

33 Conducting a Software Specification Review

This chapter describes specific procedures for conducting the *Software Specification Review,* which is described in MIL-STD-1521B, Appendix C. We will

- Discuss the purpose of this review

- List the software related documents to be reviewed

- List the significant issues to be discussed

- Present a sample agenda for the review

- Describe how the Government will judge the acceptability of the review

33.1 Purpose

By default, one Software Specification Review is conducted for each CSCI. In practice, it is normally advantageous to cover multiple CSCIs during a single review to reduce travel costs and meeting time.   The Software Specification Review is used to review and approve the final allocated baseline *for each CSCI.* Notice that this allocated baseline for each CSCI is different from the allocated baseline for the system (which was approved during the System Design Review). The functional requirements allocated to each CSCI (and approved during this review) will then be used during the CSCI software design.

33.2 Software Documents to be Reviewed

The following software related documents are reviewed at the Software Specification Review:

- the final version of the *Software Requirements Specification* for each CSCI being reviewed,

- the final version of the *Interface Requirements Specification* for each CSCI being reviewed.

33.3 Software Related Issues to be Discussed

During the Software Specification Review, the following software related issues should be addressed:

- any actions or procedures deviating from the Software Development Plan,

- any changes to the System/Segment Specification or System/Segment Design Document.

33.4 Sample Agenda

The requirements for the agenda format can be found in Data Item Deliverable (DID) description number DI-A-3029/S-105-1. This DID is titled *Agenda − Design Reviews, Configuration Audits and Demonstrations*. The sample agenda presented meets the requirements of this DID.

Software Specification Review
Agenda

A.   Scope and purpose

This review will cover the interface definitions and allocated requirements for the _____, _____, ... and _____ CSCIs of the _____ system/segment.

B.   Time, date, location, and duration

This review will commence at _____ (time), on _____ (date), at the facilities of _____ located at _____ . The review is expected to last _____ days.

C.   Previous reviews

The System Design Review for this system/segment was approved on _____ .

D.   Objectives

The following items will be covered[1]:

1.   Meeting kickoff   [Introduce players and administrative details (schedule, washrooms, smoking policy, etc.)]

2.   Milestone schedule   [Include progress to date. Development schedule for CSCIs being

---

[1]Items in square brackets are notes of explanation and are not included in the published agenda.

		reviewed should be covered in depth.]
3.	Requirement modifications	[Covers changes to System/Segment Specification and System/Segment Design Document requirements since the System Design Review.]
4.	System design	[Based on paragraph 4 (and lower level sub-paragraphs) from the System/Segment Design Document.]
5.	System interfaces	[Based on paragraph 3.1 from *all* of the Interface Requirements Specifications (combined into one presentation).]
6.	[CSCI number 1]	[For each CSCI being reviewed]
	• External interfaces	[From paragraph 3.1 of the Software Requirements Specification and paragraph 3.1 from the Interface Requirements Specification. Each interface should be fully defined in terms of requirements (paragraph 3.X.1 from the Interface Requirements Specification) and data (para-

graph 3.X.2 from the Interface Requirements Specification).]

- Capability requirements

[From paragraph 3.2 of the Software Requirements Specification. For each requirement identified (functional capability), the inputs, processing, and outputs should be defined.]

- Internal interfaces

[From paragraph 3.3 of the Software Requirements Specification.]

- CSCI data dictionary

[From paragraph 3.4 of the Software Requirements Specification.]

- Adaptation requirements

[From paragraph 3.5 of the Software Requirements Specification.]

- Sizing and timing

[From paragraph 3.6 of the Software Requirements Specification.]

- Design constraints

[From paragraph 3.9 of the Software Requirements Specification.]

- Human factors

[From paragraph 3.11 of the Software Requirements Specification. For man-machine interfaces, often includes a demonstration using

either dummy screens
or prototype software.]

E.   Responsibilities

_____ (contractor name) will supply all resources and materials necessary to perform the Review/Audit effectively and act as Co-chairperson. Minutes will be recorded as dictated by either Co-Chairperson and a list of action items will be recorded. Official minutes will be published and distributed.

_____ (government agency) will serve as Co-Chairperson, review the daily minutes to ensure that they reflect all significant contracting agency inputs, and will be responsible for establishing the adequacy of the review. In addition, _____ shall provide the name, organization, and security clearance of each Government representative prior to the review.

F.   Documents available for review

- *Software Requirements Specification* for the _____ CSCI of the _____ system (or segment) [one for *each* CSCI]

- *Interface Requirements Specification* for the _____ CSCI of the _____ system (or segment) [normally one for *each* CSCI]

G.   Progress

See monthly status report(s) for the months of _____, _____, etc.

H.   Methods used

The presentation will consist of a mixture of viewgraphs, verbal presentations, and discussions. Demonstrations of prototype user interfaces will be presented for the _____, _____, . . . and _____ CSCIs.

I.   Facilities provided

The following office facilities will be available for use by the government representatives during the review: [List facilities available].

J.   Other information

This review will be conducted at the _____ [classification] level.

33.5 Evaluating the Review

The following checklist may be used when evaluating the adequacy of the Software Specification Review:

_____   Was the Software Requirements Specification available prior to the review?

_____   Was the Interface Requirements Specification available prior to the review?

_____   Was the agenda available prior to review?

_____   Were the physical facilities for the review adequate?

_____   Does the milestone schedule as presented match the deliverable requirements of the contract?

_____   Are the requirements which the CSCI(s) must meet clear?

_____   Is the purpose of each CSCI crystal clear? If *you* don't see *exactly* how the CSCIs fit together to accomplish the required mission, you can be sure that at least some of the software engineers will not understand the requirements either!

_____ Are the Software Requirements Specifications and Interface Requirements Specifications adequate (see the evaluation guidelines for these documents in chapters 17 and 18).

34 Conducting a Preliminary Design Review

This chapter describes specific procedures for conducting the *Preliminary Design Review,* which is described in MIL-STD-1521B, Appendix D. We will

- Discuss the purpose of this review

- List the software related documents to be reviewed

- List the significant issues to be discussed

- Present a sample agenda for the review

- Describe how the Government will judge the acceptability of the review

34.1 Purpose

By default, one Preliminary Design Review is conducted for each CSCI. In practice, it is normally advantageous to cover multiple CSCIs during a single review to reduce travel costs and meeting time. The Preliminary Design Review is used to review and approve the top level design *for each CSCI*. The Software Test Plan, which describes CSCI level testing, is reviewed. If multiple Preliminary Design Reviews are held (e.g., one per CSCI), the Software Test Plan is normally reviewed at the *first* review. This will make sense when you remember that only one Software Test Plan is typically written for the entire system or segment. The technical, cost, and schedule related risks associated with each CSCI are also covered.

34.2 Software Documents to be Reviewed

The following software related documents are reviewed at the Preliminary Design Review:

- Preliminary *Software Design Document*: For each CSCI being reviewed, the following paragraphs (including lower level detail paragraphs) from the Software Design Document(s) should be completed: 1, 2, 3, 5, and 8. Paragraph 7 should be completed to the CSC level.

- Preliminary *Interface Design Document*: One Interface Design Document is normally prepared for each CSCI being reviewed. The document(s) should be complete, but some detail paragraph should include items which are "To Be Determined."

34.3 Software Related Issues to be Discussed

During the Preliminary Design Review, several software related issues should be addressed. Specifically

- any changes to the Software Requirements Specifications and Interface Requirements Specifications for each CSCI,

- software reliability,

- software maintainability,

- human factors,

- software test procedures.

34.4 Sample Agenda

The requirements for the agenda format can be found in Data Item Deliverable (DID) description number DI-A-3029/S-105-1. This DID is titled *Agenda – Design Reviews, Configuration Audits and Demonstrations*. The sample agenda presented below meets the requirements of this DID.

Preliminary Design Review
Agenda

A.   Scope and purpose

       This review will cover the interface definitions and allocated requirements for the _____, _____, . . . and _____ CSCIs of the _____ system/segment.

B.   Time, date, location, and duration

       This review will commence at _____ (time), on _____ (date), at the facilities of _____ located at _____ . The review is expected to last _____ days.

C.   Previous Reviews

       The Software Specification Review for this CSCI was approved on _____

D.   Objectives

The following items will be covered[1]:

    1.   Meeting kickoff   [Introduce players and
                                                                           administrative details

---

   [1]Items in square brackets are notes of explanation and are not included in the published agenda.

		(schedule, washrooms, smoking policy, etc.)]
2.	Milestone schedule	[Include progress to date. Development schedule for CSCIs being reviewed should be covered in depth.]
3.	Requirement modifications	[Covers changes to System/Segment Specification, System/Segment Design Document, Software Requirements Specification, and Interface Requirements Specification since the System Design Review.]
4.	System design	[Based on paragraph 4 (and lower level subparagraphs) from the System/Segment Design Document.]
5.	[CSCI number 1]	[The following items are covered for *each* CSCI being reviewed.]
	• Functional flow	[The decomposition of the CSCI into CSCs (paragraph 3.1.1 of the Software Design Document) and the functional flows between CSCs (paragraph 3.1.2 of the

Software Design Document).]

- Storage allocations

[Allocation of memory and processing time to CSCs (based on paragraph 3.1.3 of the Software Design Document).]

- System states and modes

[Based on paragraph 3.1.2 of the Software Design Document.]

- Security

[Describe classified algorithms, data, programs, and so on which will be used in the CSCI and how security requirements will be met (based on paragraph 3.8 of the Software Requirements Specification).]

- Requirements traceability

[Based on paragraph 7 of the Software Design Document.]

6. Software development facilities

[Describe software development facilities which will be used for each CSCI (based on paragraph 4.1.3 of the Software Development Plan).]

7. Support software

[Describe software which will be developed to assist with the develop-

		ment/testing of CSCIs but not required for the operational use of the software (based on paragraphs 4.1.3.1 and 6.2.2 of the Software Development Plan).]
8.	Existing documentation	[Describe existing documentation of commercially available computer resources which will be used for preparing support documentation (Software Programmer Manual, Firmware Support Manual, etc.)]
9.	Support resources	[Describe resources which will be necessary to support the software and firmware after delivery (based on paragraph 3.1.1 of the Computer Resources Integrated Support Document).]
10.	Software reliability	[Based on paragraph 3.10 of the Software Requirements Specification.]
11.	Software maintainability	[Show how the proposed CSCI top level designs promote software maintainability.]

12.	Human factors	[Demonstrate updated versions of all prototypes and present updated sample screens for all portions of the CSCI(s) which involves human interaction. Updated sample outputs should be included.]
13.	Test approach	[Based on paragraph 5.2 of the Software Development Plan. Include discussion of assumptions and constraints (based on paragraph 5.3 of the Software Development Plan).]
14.	Testing organizational structure	[Based on paragraph 5.1.1. of the Software Development Plan.]
15.	Software test environment	[Based on paragraph 3 of the Software Test Plan.]
16.	Test identification	[Based on paragraph 4 of the Software Test Plan.]

E.   Responsibilities

_____ (contractor name) will supply all resources and materials necessary to perform the Review/Audit effectively and act as Co-chairperson. Minutes will be recorded as dictated by either Co-Chairperson and a list of action items will be recorded. Official minutes will be published and distributed.

_____ (government agency) will serve as Co-Chairperson, review the daily minutes to ensure that they reflect all significant contracting agency inputs, and will be responsible for establishing the adequacy of the review. In addition, _____ shall provide the name, organization, and security clearance of each Government representative prior to the review.

F. Documents available for review

- Preliminary *Software Design Document* for the _____ CSCI of the _____ system (or segment) [one for *each* CSCI]

- Preliminary *Interface Design Document* for the _____ CSCI of the _____ system (or segment) [normally one for *each* CSCI]

G. Progress

See monthly status report(s) for the months of _____, _____, etc.

H. Methods used

The presentation will consist of a mixture of viewgraphs, verbal presentations, and discussions. Demonstrations of updated prototype user interfaces will be presented for the _____, _____, .. . and _____ CSCIs.

I. Facilities provided

The following office facilities will be available for use by the government representatives during the review: [List facilities available].

J. Other information

This review will be conducted at the _____ [classification] level.

34.5 Evaluating the Review

The following checklist may be used when evaluating the adequacy of the software portion of the Preliminary Design Review:

_____ Was the Software Design Document for each CSCI available prior to the review? Were paragraphs 1, 2, 3, 5, and 8 complete? Is the document satisfactory (see Chap. 19 for criteria)?

_____ Was the Interface Design Document for each CSCI available prior to the review? Were the documents complete (with some "To Be Determined" details? Is the document satisfactory (see Chap. 21 for criteria)?

_____ Was the Software Test Plan available prior to the review? Is the document satisfactory (see Chap. 20 for criteria)?

_____ Was the agenda available prior to review?

_____ Were the physical facilities for the review adequate?

_____ Does the milestone schedule as presented match the Software Development Plan?

_____ Do the internal and external CSCI interfaces meet the requirements of the Software Requirements Specifications and Interface Requirements Specifications?

_____ Does the top level CSCI design meet all of the requirements of the Software Requirements Specifications and Interface Requirements Specifications?

_____ Was the design methodology called for in paragraph 4.2.1 of the Software Development Plan used during top-level design?

_____ Are the prototype user interfaces and sample outputs satisfactory?

_____ Are the CPU and memory usage allocations satisfactory?

_____ Is the CSC and CSCI test approach satisfactory?

35 Conducting a Critical Design Review

This chapter describes specific procedures for conducting the *Critical Design Review*, which is described in MIL-STD-1521B, Appendix E. We will

- Discuss the purpose of this review

- List the software related documents to be reviewed

- List the significant issues to be discussed

- Present a sample agenda for the review

- Describe how the Government will judge the acceptability of the review

35.1 Purpose

By default, one Critical Design Review is conducted for each CSCI. In practice, it is normally advantageous to cover multiple CSCIs during a single review to reduce travel costs and meeting time. A single Critical Design Review is also conducted at the end to review the design of the entire system. For complex CSCIs, the CSCI may be incrementally approved during multiple Critical Design Reviews. The Critical Design Review is used to review and approve the detail design *for each CSCI* (and for the system during the final Critical Design Review).

The government recognizes that the software detail design is likely to change during the actual coding and testing of the CSCIs (after the Critical Design Review is completed). MIL-STD-1521B recommends that additional in-process reviews be schedule after the Critical Design Review to cover:

- responses to action items,

- modifications to the detailed design,

- updated sizing and timing estimates,

- updated software detailed design,

- problems encountered during unit or module testing.

On most programs, an in-process review should be held every two months during the period of time between completion of the Critical Design Review(s) and the start of the Test Readiness Review(s).

35.2 Software Documents to be Reviewed

The following software related documents are reviewed at the Critical Design Review:

- *Software Design Document*: One document for each CSCI being reviewed. The completed document is reviewed.

- *Interface Design Document*: One Interface Design Document is normally prepared for each CSCI being reviewed. The document(s) should be complete at this point (no "To be determined" information).

- Preliminary *Software Test Description*: One document for each CSCI being reviewed. The following document sections should be completed: 1, 2, 3, 5. In addition, all of Sec. 4

should be completed except paragraph 4.X.Y.6 (test case step-by-step procedures).

After approval, the Software Design Document for each CSCI becomes part of the *product baseline* for that CSCI. The product baseline is fully defined after the Software Product Specification is completed, which combines the Software Design Document with the software source code.

35.3 Software Related Issues to be Discussed

During the Critical Design Review, several software related issues should be addressed. Specifically,

- the assignment of CSCI requirements to specific Computer Software Units (CSUs) and the traceability of CSCI requirements to individual CSUs. Design details should include local data definitions, timing and sizing information, and data flows between CSUs and Computer Software Components (CSCs).

- the detailed design characteristics of all interfaces,

- the detailed characteristics of the CSCI data dictionary,

- detailed discussions of the software reliability prediction model which will be used during testing and refined predictions of software complexity metrics,

- demonstration of updated prototypes of human interface and sample outputs,

- detailed review of the Software Test Description for each CSCI.

35.4 Sample Agenda

The requirements for the agenda format can be found in Data Item Deliverable (DID) description number DI-A-3029/S-105-1. This DID is

titled *Agenda – Design Reviews, Configuration Audits and Demonstrations*.
The sample agenda presented below meets the requirements of this DID.

Critical Design Review
Agenda

A.   Scope and purpose

    This review will cover the detailed design for the _____,
_____, . . . and _____ CSCIs of the _____ system/segment.

B.   Time, date, location, and duration

    This review will commence at _____ (time), on _____ (date),
at the facilities of _____ located at _____.   The review is
expected to last _____ days.

C.   Previous reviews

    The Preliminary Design Review for these CSCIs was
approved on _____.

D.   Objectives

The following items will be covered[1]:

1.	Meeting kickoff	[Introduce players and administrative details (schedule, washrooms, smoking policy, etc.)]
2.	Milestone schedule	[Include progress to date. Development and

---

[1]Items in square brackets are notes of explanation and are not
included in the published agenda.

		test schedule for CSCIs being reviewed should be covered in depth.]
3.	Requirement modifications	[Covers changes to System/Segment Specification, System/Segment Design Document, and Software Requirements Specification since the Preliminary Design Review.]
4.	System design	[Based on paragraph 4 (and lower level subparagraphs) from the System/Segment Design Document. This is a quick review to show how the CSCI(s) being covered fits into the overall system.]
5.	[CSCI number 1]	[The following items are covered for *each* CSCI being reviewed.]
	• Functional flow	[The decomposition of the CSCI into CSCs (paragraph 3.1.1 of the Software Design Document) and the functional flows between CSCs (paragraph 3.1.2 of the Software Design Document).]
	• CSC detailed design	[The decomposition of the CSC into CSUs, and

the detailed design of the CSUs (paragraph 4.X of the Software Design Document).]

- Requirements traceability

[Based on paragraph 7 of the Software Design Document.]

- Software tests

[Covers tests (names and cases) to be conducted for this CSCI (paragraphs 3 and 4 of the Software Test Description for this CSCI). Also details requirements traceability for testing (paragraph 4.X.Y.1 of the Software Test Description).]

- Test preparations

[Covers test preparations for each test name (paragraph 3.X from the Software Test Description).]

- Test assumptions

[Covers important assumptions and constraints (from paragraph 4.X.Y.7 of the Software Test Description).]

E.   Responsibilities

_____ (contractor name) will supply all resources and materials necessary to perform the Review/Audit effectively and act as Co-Chairperson. Minutes will be recorded as dictated by either

Co-Chairperson and a list of action items will be recorded. Official minutes will be published and distributed.

_____ (government agency) will serve as Co-Chairperson, review the daily minutes to ensure that they reflect all significant contracting agency inputs, and will be responsible for establishing the adequacy of the review. In addition, _____ shall provide the name, organization, and security clearance of each government representative prior to the review.

F.   Documents available for review

- *Software Design Document* for the _____ CSCI of the _____ system (or segment) [one for *each* CSCI]

- *Interface Design Document* for the _____ CSCI of the _____ system (or segment) [normally one for *each* CSCI]

- *Software Test Description* for the _____ CSCI of the _____ system (or segment) [one for *each* CSCI]

G.   Progress

See monthly status report(s) for the months of _____, _____, etc.

H.   Methods used

The presentation will consist of a mixture of viewgraphs, verbal presentations, and discussions. Demonstrations of updated prototype user interfaces will be presented for the _____, _____, .. . and _____ CSCIs.

I.   Facilities provided

The following office facilities will be available for use by the government representatives during the review: [List facilities available].

J.   Other information

> This review will be conducted at the _____ [classification] level.

35.5 Evaluating the Review

The following checklist may be used when evaluating the adequacy of the software portion of the Critical Design Review:

_____   Was the Software Design Document for each CSCI available prior to the review? Is the document satisfactory (see Chap. 19 for criteria)?

_____   Was the Interface Design Document for each CSCI available prior to the review? Were the documents complete. Is the document satisfactory (see Chap. 21 for criteria)?

_____   Was the Software Test Description(s) available prior to the review? Is the document complete except for paragraphs 4.X.Y.6? Is the document satisfactory (see Chap. 22 for criteria)?

_____   Was the agenda available prior to review?

_____   Were the physical facilities for the review adequate?

_____   Does the milestone schedule as presented match the Software Development Plan.

_____   Do the internal and external CSCI interfaces meet the requirements of the Software Requirements Specifications and Interface Requirements Specifications?

_____   Does the detailed CSCI design meet all of the requirements of the Software Requirements Specifications and Interface Requirements Specifications?

_____ Was the design methodology called for in paragraph 4.2.1 of the Software Development Plan used during detail design?

_____ Are the prototype user interfaces and sample outputs satisfactory?

_____ Is the CSCI test approach satisfactory?

36 Conducting a Test Readiness Review

This chapter describes specific procedures for conducting the *Test Readiness Review*, which is described in MIL-STD-1521B, Appendix F. We will

- Discuss the purpose of this review

- List the software related documents to be reviewed

- List the significant issues to be discussed

- Present a sample agenda for the review

- Describe how the Government will judge the acceptability of the review

36.1 Purpose

By default, one Test Readiness Review is conducted for each CSCI. In practice, it is normally advantageous to cover multiple CSCIs during a single review to reduce travel costs and meeting time. A single Test Readiness Review may also be conducted at the end prior to formal testing of the entire system. The Test Readiness Review is used to verify that the CSCI (or system) is ready for formal qualification testing.

36.2 Software Documents to be Reviewed

The following software related document is reviewed at the Test Readiness Review:

- *Software Test Description*: One document for each CSCI being reviewed. The review will focus on newly completed paragraphs 4.X.Y.6 from this document.

- Preliminary *Software Test Reports*: One document for each CSCI being reviewed. The Software Test Reports should describe testing of CSCIs *to the CSC level*.

36.3 Software Related Issues to be Discussed

During the Test Readiness Review, several software related issues should be addressed. Specifically

- requirements modifications,

- design changes,

- test plan/description changes,

- software test procedures,

- CSC and CSU test procedures (from the Software Test Description) and test results (from the Software Test Report),

- software test resources available for formal qualification testing,

- software problems (summary of software problem status),

- test schedules.

36.4 Sample Agenda

The requirements for the agenda format can be found in Data Item Deliverable (DID) description number DI-A-3029/S-105-1. This DID is titled *Agenda – Design Reviews, Configuration Audits and Demonstrations*. The sample agenda presented below meets the requirements of this DID.

Test Readiness Review
Agenda

A.   Scope and purpose

       This review will cover the test readiness for the _____, _____, . . . and _____ CSCIs of the _____ system/segment.

B.   Time, date, location, and duration

       This review will commence at _____ (time), on _____ (date), at the facilities of _____ located at _____ . The review is expected to last _____ days.

C.   Previous reviews

       The Critical Design Review for these CSCIs was approved on _____ .

D.   Objectives

The following items will be covered[1]:

1.	Meeting kickoff	[Introduce players and administrative details (schedule, washrooms, smoking policy, etc.)]

---

[1]Items in square brackets are notes of explanation and are not included in the published agenda.

2.   Milestone schedule   [Include progress to date. Test schedule for CSCIs being reviewed should be covered in depth.]

3.   Requirement modifications   [Covers changes to System/Segment Specification, System/Segment Design Document, and Software Requirements Specification requirements since the Critical Design Review.]

4.   System design   [Covers changes to CSCI detailed design since the Critical Design Review.]

5.   Test plans and descriptions   [Covers changes to test plans and test descriptions since the Critical Design Review.]

6.   [CSCI number 1]   [The following items are covered for *each* CSCI being reviewed.]

•   CSC/CSU results   [Covers CSC/CSU test procedures (section 4 of the Software Test Description) and test results (Software Test Report).]

•   CSCI test procedures   [Covers CSCI and system test procedures

(Sec. 4 of the Software
Test Description).]

7.   Software Test Resources   [Covers test resources
                                               available for formal
                                               qualification testing.]

8.   Software problems   [Summarizes status of
                                               all software problems.]

E.   Responsibilities

        _____ (contractor name) will supply all resources and
materials necessary to perform the Review/Audit effectively and act
as Co-Chairperson. Minutes will be recorded as dictated by either
Co-Chairperson and a list of action items will be recorded. Official
minutes will be published and distributed.

        _____ (government agency) will serve as Co-Chairperson,
review the daily minutes to ensure that they reflect all significant
contracting agency inputs, and will be responsible for establishing the
adequacy of the review. In addition, _____ shall provide the name,
organization, and security clearance of each Government representative prior to the review.

F.   Documents available for review

        • *Software Test Description* for the _____ CSCI of the
          _____ system (or segment) [one for *each* CSCI]

        • Preliminary *Software Test Report* for the _____ CSCI
          of the _____ system (or segment) [one for each CSCI]

G.   Progress

        See monthly status report(s) for the months of _____, _____,
etc.

H.   Methods used

The presentation will consist of a mixture of viewgraphs, verbal presentations, and discussions.

I.   Facilities provided

The following office facilities will be available for use by the government representatives during the review: [List facilities available].

J.   Other information

This review will be conducted at the _____ [classification] level.

36.5 Evaluating the Review

The following checklist may be used when evaluating the adequacy of the software portion of the Test Readiness Review:

_____   Was the Software Test Description(s) available prior to the review? Is the document satisfactory (see Chap. 22 for criteria)?

_____   Was the Software Test Report(s) available prior to the review covering test results of the CSCI to the CSC level? Is the document satisfactory (see Chap. 23 for criteria)?

_____   Was the agenda available prior to review?

_____   Were the physical facilities for the review adequate?

_____   Does the milestone schedule as presented match the Software Development Plan?

_____   Are the CSCI test procedures satisfactory?

_____   Are the CSCI test facilities adequate?

_____ Is CSC and CSU testing completed?

_____ Are all significant software problems resolved?

_____ Does the CSCI appear to be complete (i.e. ready for delivery)?

37 Conducting a Functional Configuration Audit and Physical Configuration Audit

This chapter describes specific procedures for conducting the *Functional Configuration Audit* and *Physical Configuration Audit,* which are described in MIL-STD-1521B, Appendices G and H. Earlier meetings were termed "reviews" because they review work in process and facilitate a dialogue between the Government and the engineers. These meetings are termed "audits" because they involve inspection of the finished product to ensure that the final system functions properly and should be accepted. Although these audits can be conducted separately (and often are for hardware items), they are almost always combined for Computer Software Configuration Items (CSCIs). We will

- Discuss the purpose of these audits

- List the software related documents to be reviewed

- List the significant issues to be discussed

- Present a sample agenda for the audit

- Describe how the Government will judge the acceptability of the audit

37.1 Purpose

The Functional Configuration Audit reviews the as-built system to ensure that it functions properly and meets the requirements of the contract and the approved design. The Physical Configuration Audit reviews the documentation which is ready for delivery to ensure that it is accurate (up-to-date) and complete. By default, one combined Functional Configuration Audit and Physical Configuration Audit is conducted for each CSCI. In practice, it is normally advantageous to cover multiple CSCIs during a single audit to reduce travel costs and meeting time. A single combined audit may also be conducted at the end to measure the acceptability of the system after CSCI integration. The combined audit is used to verify that the CSCI (or system) is acceptable for delivery.

37.2 Software Documents to be Reviewed

The following software related documents are reviewed at the combined audit:

- *Software Test Reports*: One document for each CSCI being reviewed. The Software Test Reports should include final test results which verify that the CSCI meets all of the requirements imposed by the Software Requirements Specification and Interface Requirements Specification.

- *Version Description Document*: One document for each CSCI being reviewed. If multiple versions of the CSCI will be simultaneously approved (perhaps different versions for different sites), there should be one Version Description Document for each version of the software.

- *Computer Software Operator's Manual*: One for each computer system. A computer system may run multiple CSCIs.

- *Software User's Manual*: One for each computer program. A computer program may include more than one CSCI.

- *Firmware Support Manual*

- *Computer Resources Integrated Support Document*

- *Software Product Specification*: One for each CSCI.

37.3 Software Related Issues to be Discussed

During the combined Functional Configuration Audit and Physical Configuration Audit, several software related issues should be addressed. Specifically,

- an overview of the test results is presented for each CSCI being audited. This overview must include, as a minimum, any requirements that were not met (including a proposed solution), any Engineering Change Proposals incorporated into the CSCI and tested, and general problems encountered during testing.

- the status of all Engineering Change Proposals for this CSCI. For Engineering Change Proposals which have been approved, it must be verified that the change has been incorporated in the CSCI.

- any updates to previously delivered documents must be described.

37.4 Sample Agenda

The requirements for the agenda format can be found in Data Item Deliverable (DID) description number DI-A-3029/S-105-1. This DID is titled *Agenda – Design Reviews, Configuration Audits and Demonstrations*. The sample agenda presented below meets the requirements of this DID.

Functional Configuration Audit and
Physical Configuration Audit
Agenda

A.   Scope and purpose

This review will cover the functional and physical readiness for delivery of the _____, _____, . . . and _____ CSCIs of the _____ system/segment.

B.   Time, date, location, and duration

This review will commence at _____ (time), on _____ (date), at the facilities of _____ located at _____ . The review is expected to last _____ days.

C.   Previous reviews

The Test Readiness Review for these CSCIs was approved on _____ .

D.   Objectives

The following items will be covered[1]:

1.   Meeting kickoff   [Introduce players and administrative details (schedule, washrooms, smoking policy, etc.)]

---

[1]Items in square brackets are notes of explanation and are not included in the published agenda.

2.	Document modifications	[Covers changes to all documents which were previously delivered.]
3.	[CSCI number 1]	[The following items are covered for *each* CSCI being reviewed.]
	• CSCI test results	[Covers CSCI/CSC/-CSU test procedures (Secs. 4 and 3 of the Software Test Description) and test results (Software Test Report).]
	• ECP status	[Covers status of all Engineering Change Proposals.]
	• Data base characteristics	[Reviews final data dictionary, storage allocation data and timing.]

E. Responsibilities

_____ (contractor name) will supply all resources and materials necessary to perform the Review/Audit effectively and act as Co-chairperson. Minutes will be recorded as dictated by either Co-Chairperson and a list of action items will be recorded. Official minutes will be published and distributed.

_____ (government agency) will serve as Co-Chairperson, review the daily minutes to ensure that they reflect all significant contracting agency inputs, and will be responsible for establishing the adequacy of the review. In addition, _____ shall provide the name, organization, and security clearance of each government representative prior to the review.

F.   Documents available for review

- *Software Test Report* for the _____ CSCI [one per CSCI being audited].

- *Version Description Document* for the _____ version of the _____ CSCI [one per CSCI version].

- *Computer Software Operator's Manual* for the _____ computer system [one for each computer system].

- *Software User's Manual for* the _____ Computer Program [one for each computer program being delivered.]

- *Firmware Support Manual for* the _____ System/Segment

- *Computer Resources Integrated Support Document for* the _____ System/Segment

- *Software Product Specification for* the _____ CSCI [one per CSCI being audited].

G.   Progress

See monthly status report(s) for the months of _____, _____, etc.

H.   Methods used

The presentation will consist of a mixture of viewgraphs, verbal presentations, and discussions.

I.   Facilities provided

The following office facilities will be available for use by the government representatives during the review: [List facilities available].

J.   Other information

This review will be conducted at the _____ [classification] level.

37.5 Evaluating the Review

The following checklist may be used when evaluating the adequacy of the software portion of the Functional Configuration Audit and Physical Configuration Audit:

_____   Was the Software Test Report(s) complete and available for review? Was the document satisfactory (see Chap. 23)?

_____   Was the Version Description Document(s) complete and available for review? Was the document satisfactory (see Chap. 24)?

_____   Was the Computer System Operator's Manual complete and available for review? Was the document satisfactory (see Chap. 25)?

_____   Was the Software User's Manual(s) complete and available for review? Was the document satisfactory (see Chap. 26)?

_____   Was the Firmware Support Manual complete and available for review? Was the document satisfactory (see Chap. 28)?

_____   Was the Computer Resources Integrated Support Document complete and available for review? Was the document satisfactory (see Chap. 29)?

_____   Was the Software Product Specification(s) complete and available for review? Was the document satisfactory (see Chap. 30)?

_____   Was the agenda available prior to the review?

_____ Were the physical facilities for the review adequate?

_____ Is all CSCI testing complete?

_____ Are the CSCI test results satisfactory?

_____ Are all significant software problems resolved?

_____ Are all outstanding Engineering Change Proposals resolved?

_____ Does the CSCI appear to be complete (i.e. ready for delivery)?

_____ Are all previously delivered documents updated properly?

_____ Are all outstanding action items from previous reviews completed?

_____ Do the software listings match the design documents?

_____ Do the software listings comply with the approved coding standards (paragraph 4.2.4 of the Software Development Plan).

A HyperText Standards On-Line

HyperText Standards On-Line (HTSO) is an IBM-PC based program which includes the complete text (including appendices) of 41 government documents which are applicable to software development. These documents include DOD-STD-2167A (and all of its DIDs), MIL-STD-1521B, and DOD-STD-2168. HTSO also includes routines to search the document text for keywords (or combinations of keywords) and locate specific paragraphs within the documents containing those keywords. The individual paragraphs can then be read on the screen or printed out. HTSO includes an on-line look-up capability to allow any acronym in the 41 documents to be expanded. HTSO also includes the complete text of all 41 documents in Word Perfect 5.0 format. This program is especially valuable when researching requirements to locate all applicable references in all standards. Each relevant paragraph can then be easily and quickly read.

HTSO is available for $492 (plus $6 shipping and handling) from William H. Roetzheim & Associates, 13518 Jamul Drive, Jamul, CA 92035. You may also order by calling (619) 669-6970. All orders are shipped COD or prepaid. A 30-day money-back guarantee is offered.

B Teamplan System

The *Teamplan System* is an integrated software development environment tailored to DOD-STD-2167A. The integrated environment includes:

- *Teamplan,* a project management program tailored to software development in general and DOD-STD-2167A in particular. *Teamplan* supports management of very large projects using an easy to learn graphical user interface (running under Microsoft Windows^{tm}). Network based support for groupware concepts simplify project planning, tracking, and controlling.

- *Magnum,* an automated software development environment which supports a wide range of development languages and compilers. *Magnum* combines many features commonly found in CASE tools with features found in advanced programmer's editor products. Configuration management tools, both for documentation and code, are incorporated in *Magnum.*

- *Integrity,* which provides automated support for unit and integration testing along with requirement traceability throughout testing. *Integrity* automates the production of DOD-STD-2167A test related documents.

All tools run using a graphical user interface and a mouse, with the user interface so intuitive that for each tool you are guaranteed to be able to install and learn the tool in 15 minutes or your money back!

Additional information on any of these tools is available by writing to William H. Roetzheim & Associates, 13518 Jamul Drive, Jamul, CA 92035. To order, or to request additional information, call (619) 669-6970.

C Overview of HIPO-II

This appendix presents a brief summary of HIPO-II notation. HIPO-II is well suited for use on many contracts developing software to DOD-STD-2167A because of its strong emphasis on hierarchical representations. HIPO-II is oriented toward traditional programming, and has limited utility if you are using an object-oriented approach to program design. Hierarchical notation is shown in the format that would be used if the design was prepared manually without using the CASE features of *Structured Designer's Toolbox* (described in the previous chapter). For a detailed description of HIPO-II, refer to Roetzheim. (12)

Data Hierarchy

General Structure

Data structures are represented hierarchically.

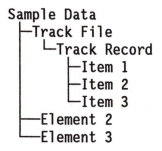

```
Sample Data
   ├─Track File
   │   └─Track Record
   │       ├─Item 1
   │       ├─Item 2
   │       └─Item 3
   ├─Element 2
   └─Element 3
```

Data Types

Data types are written in parenthesis next to each data element. Some typical types are File (F), Record (R), Structure (S), Bit (B), Character (C), Unsigned Character (UC), Integer (I), Unsigned Integer (UI), Long Integer (L), Unsigned Long Integer (UL), Floating point number (F), Double precision floating point number (D).

```
Sample Data
  ├─Track File (DF)
  │   └─Track Record (R)
  │       ├─Item 1 (C)
  │       ├─Item 2 (I)
  │       └─Item 3 (F)
  ├──Element 2 (S)
  └──Element 3 (C)
```

Arrays

If the data element is actually an array of the appropriate type, the size of the array is shown next to the data element.

```
Sample Data
  ├─Track File (DF)
  │   └─Track Record (R)
  │       ├─Item 1 (C) [30]
  │       ├─Item 2 (I)
  │       └─Item 3 (F) [10]
  ├──Element 2 (S)
  └──Element 3 (C)
```

Quantity

For data elements representing aggregates of data (e.g. file, record, structure), the estimated quantity of aggregate elements is shown next to the data element. Whether the number represents an array size or aggregate quantity is based on the data element type.

```
Sample Data
  ├─Track File (DF)
  │  └─Track Record (R) [1000]
  │        ├─Item 1 (C) [30]
  │        ├─Item 2 (I)
  │        └─Item 3 (F) [10]
  ├─Element 2 (S) [100]
  └─Element 3 (C)
```

Matrices

Matrices are represented by showing both matrix dimensions separated by a comma.

```
Sample Data
  ├─Track File (DF)
  │  └─Track Record (R) [1000]
  │        ├─Item 1 (C) [30]
  │        ├─Item 2 (I)
  │        └─Item 3 (F) [10,10]
  ├─Element 2 (S) [100]
  └─Element 3 (C)
```

Program Hierarchy

General Structure

Program structures are represented hierarchically.

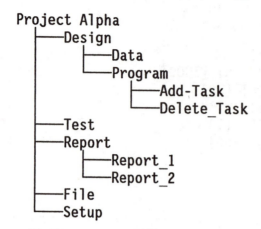

```
Project Alpha
    ├──Design
    │      ├──Data
    │      └──Program
    │             ├──Add-Task
    │             └──Delete_Task
    ├──Test
    ├──Report
    │      ├──Report_1
    │      └──Report_2
    ├──File
    └──Setup
```

Module Types

Module types are written in parenthesis next to each program module. Some typical types are Menu choice (M), Interrupt (I), Key-activated (K), Processing (P), Common (C), and Library (L). The concept and function-oriented design normally will contain only Menu, Interrupt, and Key modules. The implementation-oriented design will add the Processing, Common, and Library modules.

```
Project Alpha
    ├──Design (M)
    │      ├──Data (M)
    │      └──Program (M)
    │             ├──Add-Task (M)
    │             └──Delete_Task (M)
    ├──Test (M)
    ├──Report (M)
    │      ├──Report_1 (M)
    │      └──Report_2 (M)
    ├──File (M)
    └──Setup (M)
```

Sequence

Sequential control flow is shown by a single line (the default). Program logic executes from top to bottom of the program hierarchy.

```
Module A
      ├─Module A.1
      ├─Module A.2
      └─Module A.3
```

Iteration

Program loops are shown using a double line.

```
Module A
      ╞ Module A.1
      ╞ Module A.2
      ╘ Module A.3
```

Alternation

Conditional execution is shown using a brace to connect the program module to the hierarchy.

```
Module A
      ╞ {Module A.1
      ╞ {Module A.2
      ╘ {Module A.3
```

Concurrency

Concurrent execution is shown using an epsilon to connect the program module to the hierarchy. Note that a module may be both conditional and concurrent.

```
Module A
    ├ εModule A.1
    ├ εModule A.2
    └ εModule A.3
```

Recursion

Recursion is shown by putting a module under itself. The lower level copy of the module is of type Common.

```
Module A
    ├ εModule A.1
    ├ εModule A.2
    └ εModule A.3 (P)
         └─Module A.3 (C)
```

Input-Process-Output

Module detailed descriptions involve completing a module header which contains

- the module coding/design history,

- the usage of the module (if applicable),

- input parameters (including global variables),

- processing in pseudocode form,

- output parameters (including global variables),

- a brief description of the module,

- return value(s).

As the module descriptions are completed, a "Y" is written next to the module name on the program hierarchy. As the design progresses into coding, the module descriptions are used as the headers for the actual code.

Sample Outputs

Menu, Key, and Interrupt modules may have sample outputs included in the design. Sample outputs may be screens, reports, or overlays. Overlays are a window that is output on top of the current screen. If a program module has a sample output defined, the output number is written next to the module name on the program hierarchy. The output number is then used to reference a document containing all output definitions.

D Abbreviations and Acronyms

This appendix presents a complete list of all acronyms used in the 41 most important Government software development standards, handbooks, instructions, and data item descriptions (DIDs). This appendix is included here as a handy reference.

ACI	Allocated Configuration Identification
ACO	Administrative Contracting Officer
ACSN	Advance Change Study Notice
ADA	Ada computer language
AF	Air Force
AFB	Air Force Base
AFLC	Air Force Logistics Command
AFLCM	Air Force Logistics Command Manual
AFM	Air Force Manual
AFPI	Air Force Part Identification
AFR	Air Force Regulation
AFSC	Air Force Systems Command
AFSCM	Air Force Systems Command Manual
AFSCR	Air Force Systems Command Regulation
AFTO	Air Force Technical Order
AMC	Acquisition Method Coding
AMSC	Air Force Material Support Command
AMSDL	Acquisition Management Systems and Data Requirements Control List
ATE	Automatic Test Equipment
ATTN	Attention

BITE	Built In Test Equipment
BPI	Bits Per Inch
CAO	Contract Administrative Office
CAS	Contract Administrative Services
CCB	Configuration Control Board
CCO	Contract Change Order
CCP	Contract Change Proposal
CD	Classification of Defects
CDR	Critical Design Review
CDRL	Contract Data Requirements List
CEM	Communication-Electronic-Meteorological
CFE	Contract Furnished Equipment
CI	Configuration Item
CID	Critical Item Development specification
CIDS	Critical Item Development Specification
CII	Configuration Item Identification
CL	Classification
CLIN	Contract Line Item Number
CM	Configuration Management
CMAN	Configuration Management
CMOS	Complementary Metal Oxide Semi-conductor
CPC	Computer Program Component
CPCI	Computer Program Configuration Item
CPU	Central Processing Unit
CRISD	Computer Resource Integrated Support Document
CRLCMP	Computer Resources Life Cycle Management Plan
CSC	Computer Software Component
CSCI	Computer Software Configuration Item
CSDM	Computer System Diagnostic Manual
CSOM	Computer System Operator's Manual
CSU	Computer Software Unit
CWBS	Contract Work Breakdown Structure
DBDD	Data Base Design Document
DC	District of Columbia
DCP	Decision Coordinating Paper
DD	Department of Defense
DI	Data Item
DID	Data Item Description
DIDS	Data Item Descriptions

DMA	Direct Memory Access
DOD	Department of Defense
DODD	Department of Defense Directive
DODI	Department of Defense Instruction
DODISS	Department of Defense Index of Specifications and Standards
DSA	Defense System Acquisition
DSARC	Defense Systems Acquisition Review Council
DT	Development Test
ECO	Engineering Change Order
ECP	Engineering Change Proposal
EDP	Electronic Data Processing
EM	ElectroMagnetic
EMC	ElectroMagnetic Compatibility
EMI	ElectroMagnetic Interference
EPROM	Electrically Programmable Read Only Memory
EQ	Equipment
ESD	Electronic Systems Division
FAR	Federal Acquisition Regulations
FCA	Functional Configuration Audit
FCI	Functional Configuration Identification
FQR	Formal Qualification Review
FQT	Formal Qualification Test
FSD	Full Scale Development
FSM	Firmware Support Manual
FSN	Federal Stock Number
GFE	Government Furnished Equipment
GFI	Government Furnished Information
GFP	Government Furnished Property
GFS	Government Furnished Software
GPO	Government Printing Office
HDB	Handbook
HDBK	Handbook
HFE	Human Factors Engineering
HOL	High Order Language
HQ	HeadQuarters
HW	Hardware
HWCI	Hardware Configuration Item
ICD	Interface Control Drawing
ICWG	Interface Control Working Group
IDD	Interface Design Document

IFB	Invitation For Bid
ILS	Integrated Logistics Support
IPS	Integrated Program Summary
IRS	Interface Requirements Specification
JMSNS	Justification of Major System New Starts
LLCSC	Lower-Level Computer Software Component
LR	Limited Rights
LRU	Line Replaceable Units
LSA	Logistic Support Analysis
LSI	Large Scale Integration
MANTECH	Manufacturing Technology
MCCR	Mission Critical Computer Resources
MCCS	Mission Critical Computer System
MDS	Mission, Design, Series
MEA	Maintenance Engineering Analysis
MIL	Military
MIPR	Military Inter-department Procurement Request
MOS	Metal Oxide Semiconductor
MRB	Material Review Board
MSI	Medium Scale Integration
MTTR	Mean Time To Repair
MTU	Mobile Training Unit
NDS	Non-Developmental Software
NPFC	Naval Publications and Forms Center
NSN	National Stock Number
OCD	Operational Concept Document
OJCS	Organization of the Joint Chiefs of Staff
OPCODE	Operational Code
OPCODES	Operational Codes
ORLA	Optimum Repair-Level Analysis
OSD	Office of the Secretary of Defense
OT	Operational Test
PCA	Physical Configuration Audit
PCO	Procuring Contract Officer
PDL	Program Design Language
PDM	Program Decision Memorandum
PDR	Preliminary Design Review
PERT	Program Evaluation and Review Technique
PID	Prime Item Development Specification

PIDS   Prime Item Development Specifications
PM   Project Management
POM   Program Objectives Memorandum
PROM   Programable Read Only Memory
PROMS   Programmable Read Only Memories
PRR   Production Readiness Review
PTDP   Preliminary Technical Development Plan
QAR   Quality Assurance Representative
QPL   Qualified Products List
RAM   Random Access Memory
RDT   Research, Development, Test
RFP   Request For Proposal
RLA   Repair Level Analysis
ROM   Read Only Memory
ROMS   Read Only Memories
RR   Restricted Rights
SAD   System Allocation Document
SAM   Software Acquisition Manager
SCCB   Software Configuration Control Board
SCMP   Software Configuration Management Plan
SCN   Specification Change Notice
SCP   Systems Concept Paper
SCPR   Software Product Change Request
SDD   Software Design Document
SDDD   Software Detailed Design Document
SDDM   Secretary of Defense Decision Memorandum
SDF   Software Development File
SDI   Strategic Defense Initiative
SDL   Software Development Library
SDP   Software Development Plan
SDPE   Special Design Protective Equipment
SDR   System Design Review
SDS   Software Development Standard
SE   System Engineering
SECDEF   Secretary of Defense
SEMP   System Engineering Management Plan
SERD   System Engineering Requirements Document
SOW   Statement of Work
SPCR   Software Problem Change Report
SPM   Software Programmer

SPO	System Program Office
SPS	Software Product Specification
SQEP	Software Quality Evaluation Plan
SQPP	Software Quality Program Plan
SQS	Software Quality Standards
SRA	Software Requirements Analysis
SRR	System Requirements Review
SRS	Software Requirements Specification
SSA	Software Support Agency
SSDD	System/Segment Design Document
SSPM	Software Standards and Procedures Manual
SSR	Software Specification Review
SSS	System/Segment Specification
STD	Software Test Document
STLDD	Software Top-Level Design Document
STP	Software Test Plan
STPR	Software Test Procedure
STR	Software Test Report
SUM	Software Users Manual
SW	Software
TBD	To Be Determined
TCP	Task Change Proposal
TCTO	Time Compliance Technical Order
TEMP	Test and Evaluation Master Plan
TIM	Technical Interchange Meeting
TLCSC	Top-Level Computer Software Component
TLCSCI	Top-Level Computer Software Configuration Item
TPM	Technical Performance Measurement
TRR	Test Readiness Review
UHF	Ultra High Frequency
UR	Unlimited Rights
US	United States
USAF	United States Air Force
VDD	Version Description Document
VE	Value Engineering
VECPS	Value Engineering Change Proposal
WBS	Work Breakdown Structure

E Definitions

This appendix presents selected definitions from the various government standards which are used when developing software. At the end of each definition we state the specific standard from which the definition was extracted.

Advance Change Study Notice

Prior to the preparation of a formal routine ECP or CCP/TCP, the contractor notifies via an Advance Change Study Notice (ACSN) the contracting agency of his intent to submit a proposal. The ACSN contains information establishing the need for a change and enables effective initial evaluation of a suggested change prior to preparation of a formal proposal. The ACSN states the problem, provides a solution, any known alternative solutions and a cost estimate. It may also be prepared by the contracting agency to request the contractor to prepare a proposal based on its content. Emergency, urgent, compatibility and record type ECPs do not require an ACSN prior to submittal. Use of ACSNs are subject to agreement between the contractor and the contracting agency. [MIL-STD-483A]

Advanced development

Includes all projects which have moved into the development of hardware for experimental or operational test. [DODI 3200.6]

Allocated baseline

The initial approved allocated configuration. [MIL-STD-481A]

Allocated configuration identification

Current, approved performance oriented specifications governing the development of configuration items that are part of a higher level CI, in which each specification (a) defines the functional characteristics that are allocated from those of the higher level CI, (b) establishes the tests required to demonstrate achievement of its allocated functional characteristics, (c) delineates necessary interface requirements with other associated configuration items, and (d) establishes design constraints, if any, such as component standardization, use of inventory items, and integrated logistic support requirements. [DODD 5010.19]

Authentication

Determination by the government that specification content is acceptable. [DOD-STD-2167A]

Baseline

A configuration identification document or a set of such documents (regardless of media) formally designated and fixed at a specific time during a configuration item's life cycle. Baselines, plus approved changes from those baselines, constitute the current configuration identification. [DOD-HDBK-287]

Baseline management

Baseline management is the application of technical and administrative direction to designate the documents which formally identify and establish the initial configuration identification at specific times during the life cycle, i.e., Functional, Allocated, and Product baselines. [DOD-HDBK-287]

Certification

A process, which may be incremental, by which a contractor provides objective evidence to the contracting agency that an item satisfied its specified requirements. [DOD-STD-2168]

Code identification number

A five digit number listed in Cataloging Handbook H4-1, Federal Supply Code for Manufacturers, which is assigned to activities that manufacture or develop items for the federal government. When used with an ECP number, the code identification number designates the contractor or government agency from whose series the ECP number is assigned. When used with a drawing number or part number, the code identification number designates the design activity from whose series the drawing or part number is assigned. [MIL-STD-481A]

Computer data definition

A statement of the characteristics of the basic elements of information operated upon by hardware in responding to computer instructions. These characteristics may include, but are not limited to, type, range, structure, and value. [DOD-STD-2167A]

Computer hardware

Devices capable of accepting and storing computer data, executing a systematic sequence of operations on computer data, or producing control outputs. Such devices can perform substantial interpretation, computation, communication, control, or other logical functions. [DOD-STD-2167A]

Computer resources

The totality of computer hardware, software, personnel, documentation, supplies, and services applied to a given effort. [DOD-STD-2167A]

Computer software (or software)

A combination of associated computer instructions and computer data definitions required to enable the computer to perform computational or control functions. [DOD-STD-2167A]

Computer Software Component (CSC)

A distinct part of a computer software configuration item (CSCI). CSCs may be further decomposed into other CSCs and Computer Software Units (CSUs). [DOD-STD-2167A]

Computer Software Configuration Item (CSCI)

A configuration item for computer software. [DOD-STD-2167A]

Computer software documentation

Technical data or information, including computer listings and printouts, which documents the requirements, design, or details of computer software, explains the capabilities and limitations of the software, or provides operating instructions for using or supporting computer software during the software's operational life. [DOD-STD-2167A]

Computer Software Unit (CSU)

An element specified in the design of a Computer Software Component (CSC) that is separately testable. [DOD-STD-2167A]

Configuration

The functional and/or physical characteristics of hardware/software as set forth in technical documentation and achieved in a product. [DODD 5010.19]

Configuration control

The systematic evaluation, coordination, approval or disapproval, and implementation of all approved changes in the configuration of an item after formal establishment of its configuration identification. [MIL-STD-481A]

Configuration Identification

The current approved or conditionally approved technical documentation for a configuration item as set forth in specifications, drawings, and associated lists, and documents referenced therein. [DOD-HDBK-287]

Configuration Item

Hardware or software, or an aggregate of both, which is designated by the contracting agency for configuration management. [DOD-HDBK-287]

Configuration item development record

The configuration item development record provides status information on the development progress of a configuration item as reflected by configuration audits and design reviews. [MIL-STD-483A]

Configuration item identification number

A CII number is a permanent number assigned by the design activity to identify a configuration item. The number is a common identification for all units in a configuration item type, model, series, and serves as a permanent address for all actions and documentation applicable to the type, model, and series. The CII number is seven-digits with alpha-numeric characters. [MIL-STD-483A]

Configuration item specification addendum

A configuration item specification addendum is accomplished by writing a new specification (addendum) by direct reference to an existing specification and recording in the new specification reference to each paragraph in the existing specification. A specification created in this manner is a new and complete specification with a new specification number. [MIL-STD-483A]

Configuration Management

A discipline applying technical and administrative direction and surveillance to (a) identify and document the functional and physical characteristics of a configuration item, (b) control changes to those characteristics, and (c) record and report change processing and implementation status. [MIL-STD-481A]

Configuration management plan

The configuration management plan defines the implementation (including policies and methods) of configuration management on a particular program/project. It may or may not impose contractor requirements depending on whether it is incorporated on the contract. [DOD-HDBK-287]

Configuration status accounting

The recording and reporting of the information that is needed to manage configuration effectively, including a listing of the approved configuration identification, the status of proposed changes to configuration, and the implementation status of approved changes.

Contract

The legal agreement between Department of Defense (DOD) and industry, or a similar internal agreement wholly within the Government, for the development, production, maintenance, or modification of an item(s). [DOD-HDBK-287]

Contract administration office

The office which performs assigned functions related to the administration of contracts. [MIL-STD-481A]

Contract change proposal

A formal priced document also referred to as "Task Change Proposal (TCP)" used to propose changes to the scope of work of the contract. It is differentiated from an ECP by the fact it does not affect specification or drawing requirements. It may be used to propose changes to contractual plans, the SOW, CDRL, etc. [MIL-STD-483A]

Contracting agency

Contracting agency refers to the "contracting office" as defined in the Federal Acquisition Regulation Subpart 2.1, or its designated representative. [DOD-STD-2167A]

Contractor

An individual, partnership, company, corporation, or association having a contract with the contracting agency for the design, development, design and manufacture, manufacture, maintenance, modification, or supply of configuration items under the terms of a contract. A government agency performing any or all of the above actions is considered to be a contractor for configuration management purposes. [DOD-HDBK-287]

Conversion

The process of changing existing software to enable it to operate with similar functional capabilities in a different environment; for example, converting a program from FORTRAN to Ada, converting a program that runs on one computer to run on another computer. [DOD-HDBK-287]

Cost

The term "cost" means cost to the Government. [DOD-HDBK-287]

Critical design review

This review shall be conducted for each configuration item when detail design is essentially complete. The purpose of this review will be to (1) determine that the detail design of the configuration item under review satisfies the performance and engineering specialty requirements of the HWCI development specifications, (2) establish the detail design compatibility among the configuration item and other items of equipment, facilities, computer software and personnel, (3) assess configuration item risk areas (on a technical, cost, and schedule basis), (4) assess the results of the producibility analysis conducted on system hardware, and (5) review the preliminary hardware specifications. For CSCIs, this review will focus on the determination of the acceptability of the detailed design, performance, and test characteristics of the design solution, and on the adequacy of the operation and support documents. [MIL-STD-1521B]

Critical item

An item within a configuration item which, because of special engineering or logistic considerations, requires an approved specification to establish technical or inventory control at the component level. [DOD-HDBK-287]

Data (technical data and information)

The means for communication of concepts, plans, descriptions, requirements, and instructions relating to technical projects, materiel, systems, and services. These may include specifications, standards, engineering drawings, associated lists, manuals, and reports, including scientific and technical reports; they may be in the form of documents, displays, sound records, punched cards, and digital or analog data. [MIL-STD-481A]

Deficiencies

Deficiencies consist of two types: (a) conditions or characteristics in any hardware/software which are not in compliance with specified configuration, or (b) inadequate (or erroneous) configuration identification which has resulted, or may result, in configuration items that do not fulfill approved operational requirements. [MIL-STD-481A]

Developmental configuration

The contractor's software and associated technical documentation that defines the evolving configuration of a CSCI during development. It is under the development contractor's configuration control and describes the software design and implementation. The Developmental Configuration for a CSCI consists of a Software Design Document and source code listings. Any item of the Developmental Configuration may be stored on electronic media. [DOD-STD-2167A]

Deviation

A specific written authorization, granted prior to the manufacture of an item, to depart from a particular performance or design requirement of a specification, drawing or other document, for a specific number of units or a specific period of time. A deviation differs from an engineering change in that an approved engineering change requires corresponding revision of the documentation defining the affected item, whereas a deviation does not contemplate revision of the applicable specification or drawing. [MIL-STD-481A]

Engineering change

An alteration in the configuration of a configuration item delivered, to be delivered, or under development, after formal establishment of its configuration identification. [DOD-HDBK-287]

Engineering Change Proposal

A term which includes both a proposed engineering change and the documentation by which the change is described and suggested. [MIL-STD-481A]

Engineering development

Includes those development programs being engineered for service use but which have not yet been approved for procurement or operation. [MIL-STD-481A]

Engineering management

The management of the engineering and technical effort required to transform a military requirement into an operational system. It includes the system engineering required to define the system performance parameters and preferred system configuration to satisfy the requirement, the planning and control of technical program tasks, integration of the engineering specialties, and the management of a totally integrated effort of design engineering, specialty engineering, test engineering, logistics, engineering, and production engineering to meet cost, technical performance and schedule objectives. [MIL-STD-499A]

Engineering release record

The engineering release record comprises the official data file which records and interrelates engineering data, and changes thereto, which technically describe and are to be or have been used to build/operate/maintain configuration items. [MIL-STD-483A]

Engineering specialty integration

The timely and appropriate intermeshing of engineering efforts and disciplines such as reliability, maintainability, logistics engineering, human factors, safety, value engineering, standardization, transportability, etc., to insure their influence on system design. [MIL-STD-499A]

Evaluation

The process of determining whether an item or activity meets specified criteria. [DOD-STD-2167A]

Facility

Any fixed installation which is an intimate part of a system. This includes real property installed equipment.

Firmware

The combination of a hardware device and computer instructions or computer data that reside as read-only software on the hardware device. The software cannot be readily modified under program control. [DOD-STD-2167A]

Form, fit, and function

That configuration comprising the physical and functional characteristics of the item as an entity but not including any characteristics of the elements making up the item. [MIL-STD-481A]

Formal Qualification Review

The test, inspection, or analytical process by which a group of configuration items comprising the system are verified to have met specific contracting agency contractual performance requirements (specifications or equivalent). This review does not apply to hardware or software requirements verified at FCA for the individual configuration item. [MIL-STD-1521B]

Formal Qualification Testing

A process that allows the contracting agency to determine whether a configuration item complies with the allocated requirements for that item. [DOD-STD-2167A]

Formal test

A test conducted in accordance with test plans and procedures approved by the contracting agency and witnessed by an authorized contracting agency representative to show that the software satisfies a specified requirement. [DOD-HDBK-287]

Functional area

A distinct group of system performance requirements which, together with all other such groupings, forms the next lower level breakdown of the system on the basis of function. [MIL-STD-481A]

Functional baseline

The initial approved functional configuration identification. [MIL-STD-481A]

Functional characteristics

Quantitative performance, operating and logistic parameters and their respective tolerances. Functional characteristics include all performance parameters, such as range, speed, lethality, reliability, maintainability, and safety. [MIL-STD-481A]

Functional Configuration Audit

A formal audit to validate that the development of a configuration item has been completed satisfactorily and that the configuration item has achieved the performance and functional characteristics specified in the functional or allocated configuration identification. In addition, the completed operation and support documents shall be reviewed. [MIL-STD-1521B]

Functional Configuration Identification

The current approved technical documentation for a configuration item which prescribes (a) all necessary functional characteristics, (b) the tests required to demonstrate achievement of specified functional characteristics, (c) the necessary interface characteristics with associated CIs, (d) and CIs key functional characteristics and its key lower level CIs, if any, and (e) design constraints, such as, envelope dimensions, component standardization, use of inventory items, integrated logistics support policies. [MIL-STD-481A]

Hardware Configuration Item

A configuration item for hardware. [DOD-STD-2167A]

Independent Verification and Validation

Verification and validation performed by a contractor or government agency that is not responsible for developing the product or performing the activity being evaluated. IV&V is an activity that is conducted separately from the software development activities governed by this standard. [DOD-STD-2167A]

Informal test

Any test which does not meet all the requirements of a formal test. [DOD-HDBK-287]

Integrated Logistic Support

A composite of the elements necessary to assure the effective and economical support of a system or equipment at all levels of maintenance for its programmed life cycle. The elements include all resources necessary to maintain and operate an equipment or weapons system, and are categorized as follows: (a) planned maintenance, (b) logistic support personnel, (c) technical logistic data and information, (d) support equipment, (e) technical repair parts, (f) facilities, and (g) contract maintenance. [MIL-STD-481A]

Interface control

Interface control is made up of the delineation of the procedures and documentation, both administrative and technical, contractually necessary for identification of functional and physical characteristics between two or more configuration items which are provided by different contractors/government agencies, and the resolution of the problems thereto. [DOD-HDBK-287]

Interface Control Working Group

For programs which encompass a system/configuration item design cycle, an ICWG normally is established to control interface activity between contractors or agencies, including resolution of interface problems and documentation of interface agreements. [MIL-STD-483A]

Item

Any level of hardware assembly below a system; i.e., subsystem, equipment, component, subassembly or part.

Modification

The process of changing software. [DOD-HDBK-287]

Modular

Pertaining to software that is organized into limited aggregates of data and contiguous code that perform identifiable functions. [DOD-HDBK-287]

Nondeliverable software

Software that is not required to be delivered by the contract. [DOD-STD-2168]

Nondevelopmental software

Deliverable software that is not developed under the contract but is provided by the contractor, the government, or a third party. NDS may be referred to as reusable software, government furnished software, or commercially available software, depending on its source. [DOD-STD-2167A]

Nonrecurring costs

One-time costs which will be incurred if an engineering change is ordered and which are independent of the quantity of items changed, such as, cost of redesign, special tooling or qualification. [MIL-STD-481A]

Notice of revision

A form used to propose revisions to a drawing or list, and, after approval, to notify users that the drawing or list has been, or will be, revised accordingly. [MIL-STD-481A]

Physical Configuration Audit

A technical examination of a designated configuration item to verify that the configuration item "As Built" conforms to the technical documentation which defines the configuration item. [MIL-STD-1521B]

Preliminary Design Review

This review shall be conducted for each configuration item or aggregate of configuration items to (1) evaluate the progress, technical adequacy, and risk resolution (on a technical, cost, and schedule basis) of the selected design approach, (2) determine its compatibility with performance and engineering specialty requirements of the Hardware Configuration Item (HWCI) development specification, (3) evaluate the degree of definition and assess the technical risk associated with the selected manufacturing methods/processes, and (4) establish the existence and compatibility of the physical and functional interfaces among the configuration item and other items of equipment, facilities, computer software, and personnel. For CSCIs, this review will focus on: (1) the evaluation of the progress, consistency, and technical adequacy of the selected top-level design and test approach, (2) compatibility between software requirements and preliminary design, and (3) on the preliminary version of the operation and support documents. [MIL-STD-1521B]

Privately developed item

An item completely developed at private expense and offered to the government as a production article, with government control of the article's configuration normally limited to its form, fit, and function. [MIL-STD-481A]

Procuring Contracting Officer

The individual authorized to enter into and administer government contracts and make determinations and findings with respect thereto. [MIL-STD-481A]

Product baseline

The initial approved or conditionally approved product configuration identification. [MIL-STD-481A]

Product configuration identification

The current approved or conditionally approved technical documentation which defines the configuration of a CI during the production, operation, maintenance, and logistic support phases of its life cycle, and which prescribes (a) all necessary physical or form, fit and function characteristics of a CI, (b) the selected functional characteristics designated for production acceptance testing, and (c) the production acceptance tests. [MIL-STD-481A]

Production Readiness Review

This review is intended to determine the status of completion of the specific actions which must be satisfactorily accomplished prior to executing a production go-ahead decision. The review is accomplished in an incremental fashion during the Full-Scale Development phase, usually two initial reviews and one final review to assess the risk in exercising the production go-ahead decision. In its earlier stages the PRR concerns itself with gross level manufacturing concerns such as the need for identifying high risk/low yield manufacturing processes or materials or the requirement for manufacturing development effort to satisfy design requirements. The reviews become more refined as the design matures, dealing with such concerns as production planning, facilities allocation, incorporation of producibility-oriented changes, identification and fabrication of tools/test equipment, long lead item acquisition etc. Timing of the incremental PRRs is a function of program posture and is not specifically locked in to other reviews. [MIL-STD-1521B]

Program peculiar

Configuration items, processes and materials include all configuration items, processes and materials conceived, developed, reduced to practice or first documented for the development, procurement, production, assembly, installation, testing or support of the system/equipment/software/end product (including their components and supporting configuration items) developed or initially procured under a specific program. [MIL-STD-490A]

Prototype

A model suitable for evaluation of design, performance, and product potential or an instance of a software version that does not exhibit all the properties of the final system; usually lacking in terms of functional or performance attributes. [DOD-HDBK-287]

Recurring costs

Costs which are incurred for each item changed or for each service or document ordered. [MIL-STD-481A]

Release

A configuration management action whereby a particular version of software is made available for a specific purpose (e.g., released for test). [DOD-STD-2167A]

Retrofit

Incorporation of an engineering change (at any level) in accepted or in-service items. [MIL-STD-481A]

Reusable software

Software developed in response to the requirements for one application that can be used, in whole or in part, to satisfy the requirements of another application. [DOD-STD-2167A]

Software Development File

A repository for a collection of material pertinent to the development or support of software. Contents typically include (either directly or by reference) design considerations and constraints, design documentation and data, schedule and status information, test requirements, test cases, test procedures, and test results. [DOD-STD-2167A]

Software Development Library

A controlled collection of software, documentation, and associated tools and procedures used to facilitate the orderly development and subsequent support of software. The SDL includes the Developmental Configuration as part of its contents. A software development library provides storage of and controlled access to software and documentation in human-readable form, machine-readable form, or both. The library may also contain management data pertinent to the software development project. [DOD-STD-2167A]

Software engineering environment

The set of automated tools, firmware devices, and hardware necessary to perform the software engineering effort. The automated tools may include but are not limited to compilers, assemblers, linkers, loaders, operating system, debuggers, simulators, emulators, test tools, documentation tools, and data base management system(s). [DOD-STD-2167A]

Software inventory number

An assigned number which uniquely identifies each CSCI of the software development project. [DOD-HDBK-287]

Software plans

A collective term used to describe the contractor's plans, procedures, and standards for software management, software engineering, software qualification, software product evaluation, and software configuration management. [DOD-STD-2168]

Software quality

The ability of a software product to satisfy its specified requirements. [DOD-STD-2168]

Software Specification Review

A review of the finalized Computer Software Configuration Item (CSCI) requirements and operational concept. The SSR is conducted when CSCI requirements have been sufficiently defined to evaluate the contractor's responsiveness to and interpretation of the system, segment, or prime item level requirements. A successful SSR is predicated upon the contracting agency's determination that the Software Requirements Specification, Interface Requirements Specification(s), and Operational Concept Document form a satisfactory basis for proceeding into preliminary software design. [MIL-STD-1521B]

Software support

The sum of all activities that take place to ensure that implemented and fielded software continues to fully support the operational mission of the software. [DOD-STD-2167A]

Software test environment

A set of automated tools, firmware devices, and hardware necessary to test software. The automated tools may include but are not limited to test tools such as simulation software, code analyzers, etc. and may also include those tools used in the software engineering environment. [DOD-STD-2167A]

Spares and repair parts

Spares are components or assemblies used for maintenance replacement purposes in major end items of equipment. Repair parts are those "bits and pieces," e.g., individual parts or nonreparable assemblies, required for the repair of spares or major end items. [MIL-STD-481A]

Specification

A document intended primarily for use in procurement, which clearly and accurately describes the essential technical requirements for items, materials, or services, including the procedures by which it will be determined that the requirements have been met. [DODD 4120.3]

Specification Change Notice

A document used to propose, transmit and record changes to a specification. In proposed form, prior to approval, the SCN supplies proposed changes in the text of each page affected. [MIL-STD-481A]

Subcontractor

A subcontractor is an individual, partnership, corporation, or association, who (which) contracts with a contractor to design, develop, design and manufacture, manufacture items, which are or were designed specifically for use in a military application. [DOD-HDBK-287]

Support equipment

Support equipment is that equipment required to make an item, system, or facility operational in its intended environment. This includes (a) all equipment required to maintain and operate the item, system or facility including aerospace ground equipment, and ground support equipment and (b) computer programs related thereto.

System

A composite of subsystems, assemblies (or sets), skills, and techniques capable of performing and/or supporting an operational (or non-operational) role. A complete system includes related facilities, items, material, services, and personnel required for its operation to the degree that it can be considered a self-sufficient item in its intended operational (or non-operational) and/or support environment. [MIL-STD-481A]

System Allocation Document

A document which identifies the aggregate of configuration items by software inventory number and the system configuration at each location. [DOD-HDBK-287]

System Design Review

This review shall be conducted to evaluate the optimization, correlation, completeness, and risks associated with the allocated technical requirements. Also included is a summary review of the system engineering process which produced the allocated technical requirements and of the engineering planning for the next phase of effort. Basic manufacturing considerations will be reviewed and planning for production engineering in subsequent phases will be addressed. This review will be conducted when the system definition effort has proceeded to the point where system characteristics are defined and the configuration items are identified. [MIL-STD-1521B]

System engineering process

A logical sequence of activities and decisions transforming an operational need into a description of system performance parameters and a preferred system configuration. [MIL-STD-499A]

System Requirements Review

The objective of this review is to ascertain the adequacy of the contractor's efforts in defining system requirements. It will be conducted when a significant portion of the functional requirements has been established. [MIL-STD-1521B]

System specification

A system level requirements specification. A system specification may be a System/Segment Specification (SSS), Prime Item Development Specification (PIDS), or Critical Item Development Specification (CIDS). [DOD-STD-2167A]

Tailoring

The process by which individual requirements of standards, DIDS, and related documents are evaluated to determine their suitability for a specific acquisition, and the modification of those requirements to ensure that each achieves an optimal balance between operational needs and cost. [DOD-HDBK-287]

Technical Performance Measurement

The continuing prediction and demonstration of the degree of anticipated or actual achievement of selected technical objectives. It includes an analysis of any differences among the "achievement to date," "current estimate," and the specification requirement. "Achievement to Date" is the value of a technical parameter estimated or measured in a particular test and/or analysis. "Current Estimate" is the value of a technical parameter predicted to be achieved at the end of the contract within existing resources. [MIL-STD-499A]

Technical program planning and control

The management of those design, development, test, and evaluation tasks required to progress from an operational need to the deployment and operation of the system by the user. [MIL-STD-499A]

Test Readiness Review

A review conducted for each CSCI to determine whether the software test procedures are complete and to assure that the contractor is prepared for formal CSCI testing. Software test procedures are evaluated for compliance with software test plans and descriptions, and for adequacy in accomplishing test requirements. At TRR, the contracting agency also reviews the results of informal software testing and any updates to the operation and support documents. A successful TRR is predicated on the contracting agency's determination that the software test procedures and informal test results form a satisfactory basis for proceeding into formal CSCI testing. [MIL-STD-1521B]

Top-down

Pertaining to an approach that starts with the highest level of a hierarchy and proceeds through progressively lower levels. For example, top-down design, top-down coding, top-down testing. [DOD-HDBK-287]

Training equipment

All types of maintenance and operator's training hardware, devices, visual/audio training aids and related software which (a) are used to train maintenance and operator personnel by depicting, simulating or portraying the operational or maintenance characteristics of an item, system or facility, and (b) must, by their nature, be kept consistent in design, construction and configuration with such items in order to provide required training capability. [MIL-STD-481A]

Upgrade

To improve the performance and capability of a software product or other attribute. [DOD-HDBK-287]

Updating changes

Updating changes (unique to the Air Force) are configuration changes to previously delivered systems, equipment and munitions, including related Contractor Furnished Equipment (CFE), and delivered spares for which the change requirement is identified prior to the established AFSC/AFLC program management transfer, regardless of the method of generation. This includes change requirements identified during production, testing and operation. (See AFR 57-4). [MIL-STD-483A]

Unit

The smallest logical entity specified in the detailed design which completely describes a single function in sufficient detail to allow implementing the code to be produced and tested independently of other units. Units are the actual physical entities implemented in code. [DOD-HDBK-287]

Validation

The process of evaluating software to determine compliance with specified requirements. [DOD-STD-2167A]

Vendor

A vendor is a manufacturer or supplier of a commercial item. [DOD-HDBK-287]

Verification

The process of evaluating the products of a given software development activity to determine the correctness and consistency with respect to the products and standards provided as input to that activity. [DOD-STD-2167A]

Version

An identified and documented body of software. Modifications to a version of software (resulting in a new version) require configuration management actions by either the contractor, the contracting agency, or both. [DOD-HDBK-287]

Waiver

A written authorization to accept an item which during production or after having been submitted for inspection, is found to depart from specified requirements, but nevertheless is considered suitable for use "as is" or after rework by an approved method. [MIL-STD-481A]

Work Breakdown Structure

A product-oriented family tree, composed of hardware, software, services and other work tasks, which results from project engineering effort during the development and production of a defense materiel item, and which completely defines the project/program. A WBS displays and defines the product(s) to be developed or produced and relates the elements of work to be accomplished to each other and to the end product. [MIL-STD-481A]

F References

[1] Boehm, B.W., and P.N. Papaccio. "Understanding and controlling software costs," *IEEE Transactions on Software Engineering*, vol. 14, (October), 1988.

[2] DeMarco, T. *Controlling Software Projects – Management, Measurement, and Estimation*, New York; NY: Yourdon Press, 1986.

[3] DSMC. *Systems Engineering Management Guide*, Second Edition, Fort Belvoir, VA: Defense System Management College , 1986.

[4] EIA. *DOD computing activities and programs: Ten year market forecast issues, 1985-1995*, Electronics Industries Association, (October), 1985.

[5] Jones, T.C. (July 1983) *Demographic and technical trends in the computing industry*, Software Productivity Research, Inc.

[6] Martin, E.W. "Strategy for a DoD software initiative," *Computer*, vol. 16 (March) , 1983.

[7] Nash, S.H. and S.T. Redwine, *A Map of the World of Software Related Standards, Guidelines, and Recommended Practices*: IEEE, 1980.

[8] Putnam, L.H. *Software Cost Estimating and Life-Cycle Control: Getting the Software Numbers*, Los Alamitos, CA: IEEE Computer Society Press, 1980.

[9]   Roetzheim, W.H. *Proposal Writing for the Data Processing Consultant*, Englewood Cliffs, NJ: Prentice-Hall, Inc., 1986.

[10]   Roetzheim, W.H. *Structured Computer Project Management*, Englewood Cliffs, NJ: Prentice-Hall, Inc., 1988.

[11]   Roetzheim, W.H. *Computerized Project Evaluation*, PC Accounting, Winter/Spring 1989, CA: 1989.

[12]   Roetzheim, W.H. *Structured Design Using HIPO-II*, Englewood Cliffs, NJ: Prentice-Hall, Inc., 1990

[13]   Russon, L., and S. Streifer, "A Systems Engineering Approach to Support Design of the Navy's SL-7/T-AKR Fast Logistics Support Ship Conversions," *Marine Technology*, July, 1985.

[14]   Weiss, Edmond *How to Write a Usable User Manual*, Englewood Cliffs, NJ: Prentice-Hall, Inc., 1986.

Index

473